Among the Ruins

Among the Ruins

The Story of David

Silke Chambers

LUMINARE PRESS

WWW.LUMINAREPRESS.COM

Luminare Press
442 Charnelton St.
Eugene, OR 97401
www.luminarepress.com

LCCN: 2020923806
ISBN: 978-1-64388-506-3

"I am like a desert owl,
like an owl among the ruins"
Psalm 102:6

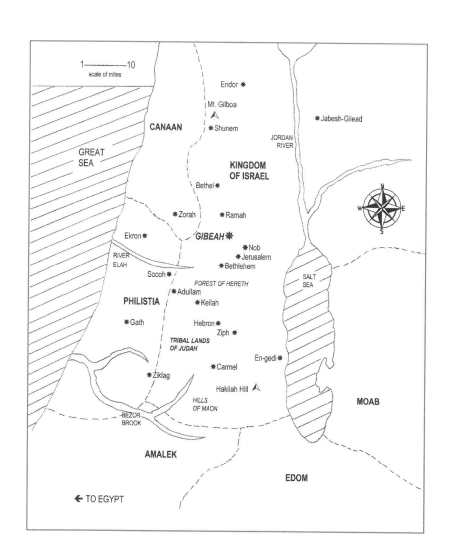

Table of Contents

PART ONE

PART TWO

PART THREE

PART ONE

1

A Fight With a Lion

It was the frantic bleating of sheep that alerted David.

The lioness stole across the hillside, stalking a lone lamb that wandered away from the rest of the flock. Their strident calls went unheeded by the late spring lamb, and he continued to nibble blades of grass absently, his short legs stumbling over stones and clumps of earth.

David was stretched out on the hillside after a meal of flatbread and cheese, dozing in the sunshine. The sheep, becoming aware of the danger, roused themselves one by one from their midafternoon drowsiness and took up the warning call directed at their youngest member.

Finally hearing the desperate bleating, David sat up and whirled around, instantly alert. He targeted the lion across the hillside through narrowed eyes.

Easing himself to the ground behind a dense shrub, he crept toward the lion until he was about twenty paces closer. His thoughts were filled with the responsibility he had to protect the flock—they were his family's livelihood. The milk and fleece were used by the clan to make cheese and woolen fabric, or traded with other settlements to provide for their needs. They couldn't afford to lose even one sheep.

He would not let his family down.

David's heart pounded into the dry earth as he lie there, sizing up the predator. He observed the muscular shoulders, taut with ready energy, the piercing eyes, completely focused on the lamb. Where were Nate and Rad, his brothers who were watching the flock on the other side of the hill? Would they hear the distressed calls of the sheep and come to help him?

The little lamb lifted his head and finally become aware of the danger. He let out tiny, fearful bleats, frozen in place. The lion edged closer. David knew he couldn't wait—he had to act.

Rising to his full height of nearly five feet, he kept his eyes fixed on the tawny cat as he reached into his pouch and pulled out a stone, fitting it expertly into the pocket of the sling. His movements attracted the attention of the lion and she swung her head toward him.

David gazed into the cold eyes and heard the throaty growl.

In that instant he became the lion's prey. Slung low, she advanced quickly.

He gasped and his heart jumped. He took a step back and swung the sling overhead, flinging the stone in an arc toward the lion. She sprang sideways and landed heavily on all four feet, dodging the stone. Recovering instantly, she bounded toward him.

He trotted backward and whirled the sling once again, hurling the stone with all his might as she picked up speed.

The stone smacked her square in the face, and she crashed to the ground, sending up a shower of dust and grit. She pawed at her head and roared in pain and rage. Blood stained the dirt where she lie.

Grasping the dagger he wore on his belt, he rushed to the felled predator and plunged it into her chest. She howled and turned to sink her teeth into his arm. He stumbled back as her teeth clenched a mouthful of air.

He righted himself hastily as she came back for another try at him, and jammed his pouch full of stones into her open mouth. He fell to his knees and stabbed her in the chest again. This time his blade hit home, and he was answered with a rush of blood, fresh from the heart. She died in seconds.

He collapsed next to the dead animal, spent from his fight with her.

As he lay on the warm earth, he was aware of his brothers, Nate and Rad, coming from where they had been guarding their flock on the other side of the hill. They approached him lying against the dead lion—amidst blood that could be his.

He heard Nate say, "Oh my God, he's dead!"

David tried to open his eyes and prove that he was indeed not dead. He could feel his brothers handling him, lifting his head. He heard them calling his name. Finally, the cool water he felt pouring into his mouth caused him to choke and cough into coherence. He opened his eyes and glanced from one to the other faces of his brothers, intense with concern.

"Hey! He's alive," Rad cheered, and pulled David into a hug.

Nate sat back on his haunches and said, "What you go and do that for? You should have called us."

"There…there wasn't time," David said struggling to sit upright. He took another drink of water. "She almost had the lamb in her mouth. She was this close." He held his hands out a foot apart. "I couldn't wait."

He finished explaining what happened in fits and starts, still breathless from the rush of adrenalin and physical exertion.

Once David recovered enough, he and his brothers called the sheep from where they had gathered together in a worried cluster, and led them to the stone sheepfold for the night. Leaving the flock in the care of hired workers, they began their trek home. They knew that scavenging birds and animals that appeared at nightfall would make away with the lion's remains.

When the three brothers arrived at the settlement, they relayed what happened on the hillside to their father, Jesse.

David looked up to his father, who was beaming at him.

He said to David, "You must truly have the Spirit of God upon you, to win a fight with a lion at such a young age."

Jesse turned to Nate and said, "David will sit next to me at dinner tonight." Placing his hand on David's slender shoulders, his father guided him to the food tent, followed by Nate and Rad.

David enjoyed this rare moment of honor in his family. Having five older brothers, he found few chances to prove himself. He kept pace with his father, head held high, wearing a triumphant smile.

2

The Lord Is My Shepherd

The next day David traveled the few miles to the royal city of Gibeah to fulfill his obligation as the King's personal musician.

"Come here, son," King Saul said. He was seated on his throne, forehead in hand, looking down at the leopard-skin robe he wore. Petulantly, he flicked a speck of lint from his lap.

David's sandal-shod feet scuffed the tiled floor as he tread through the sun-lit courtyard towards the King. He moved along the narrow reflecting pool and approached the throne of carved ebony wood at the far end.

Bowing, he said, "Yes, your Highness. What do you wish me to play today?"

King Saul looked up and raked his fingers through his thick hair. "I need you to play that song I like. You know the one, eh? That slow one with the low notes. I'm feeling nervous today."

David unpacked his lyre.

"It's those Philistines again."

In their quest for domination, the Philistines had once again invaded Canaan, a region between Israel and the Great Sea. Many small, unwalled settlements were simply overrun by the savage Philistines from the south. The Canaanites didn't have an organized military and depended on King Saul, who sought to expel the enemy from the region. It would serve to expand his own Kingdom of Israel as well.

King Saul closed his eyes and leaned back into the thick upholstery. His servant, standing behind him, made an impatient gesture, urging David to get started.

He quickly took up his lyre and sat on a cushion at the King's feet. He was glad for the soft surface to sit upon, as his whole body still ached from the fight with the lion yesterday, and his knee was tender where he fell on it. As he strummed the melody, King Saul's face relaxed into a smile.

David hummed as he played. The afternoon breeze stirred hanging chimes into tinkling along. Remote sounds of fountains in the outer garden murmured soothingly. Within moments, King Saul slouched, motionless and slack-jawed, in his seat. His breaths came slow and raspy.

While playing, David noted the spear leaning on the back of the throne. It had a specially made shaft of ivory, and the King always had it with him. He observed the King's appearance, and studied the deeply lined face, full beard, and shoulder-length black hair. A wide stripe of white hair that hung back from the King's forehead had originally puzzled him. At home his oldest brothers, who were in the King's army, told him it was the result of a battle wound. The hair growing from the scar would always be white.

An hour passed and shadows lengthened in the palace courtyard. The distant sound of a gong rang three times, announcing dinner for the royal family. The King's servant roused him gently.

This signaled the end to David's day, serving in the palace, and time for him to go home and help his brothers who were tending the flocks. He placed his lyre carefully in the felt bag his mother stitched for him.

"David!" King Saul said, rising from his seat.

"Yes, your Highness?"

The King winked and patted his head. "Same time tomorrow, eh?"

Clutching the lyre he said, "Yes, Your Highness. Same time."

David exited the palace and trotted homeward. The feel of stones beneath his feet and warm breezes kicking up dust-devils were familiar to him. The three mile trip back to the grouping of tents he called home offered time for reflection.

It had been a windfall to become King Saul's personal musician. David's father had acquired the lyre from a caravan coming through their settlement a few years ago and traded a basket of wool for it. David picked up the lyre and began strumming it that day, soon becoming proficient. Music was in his blood.

He had been recommended by one of the palace servants, a friend of the family, to try out for the job of the King's musician. The day his father sent him on this mission was a milestone in his life.

As he journeyed to the palace for the first time, he could see it shining brilliantly from a great distance, the sun reflecting off the giant sandstone blocks of which it was made. He passed through a tall arch that made up the entrance to the royal grounds, and noted numerous military stables to his right, and a walled garden to his left, lush palms thrusting their branches into the sky and over the wall. On the main portion of the palace he saw the three rows of windows, each shaded with a bright blue awning, as well as a central tower rising twice as tall. Archers stood at the ready on the flat roof, their armor blinding in the sunlight. Fifty more paces and he reached the front portico, it's roof supported by great columns. He ascended the few steps and approached the door, itself taller than any building he had ever seen. It opened heavily on huge brass hinges. He moved through a small reception room behind four guards and was ushered into the King's courtyard.

He had chosen to perform a familiar melody, one he often played to the sheep at home. The King immediately voiced his pleasure with the simple, pleasant sound of the lyre in his hands, and hired him on the spot.

After getting the position, David ran the whole way home to tell his family he had been chosen. Being the King's personal musician was a source of pride and satisfaction. Something none of his brothers could do. It was his alone.

He found himself humming new tunes often during the day, especially when tending sheep, and enjoyed putting words together, using the psalms he wrote as lyrics to familiar tunes when playing for the King.

Halfway on his trip home, he took a break. He sat on a large rock and rubbed his sore knee. The bruise had him thinking about his fight with the lion again, and about how he had to defend the tiny lamb. The flock of sheep depended on him for protection, and he had not let them down.

It's like our relationship with God.

David searched in his bag for the bit of charcoal and scrap of papyrus he usually had. Finding these items, he composed a psalm.

The Lord is my Shepherd, I have everything I need.
He lets me rest in green meadows; He leads me beside
peaceful streams.
He renews my strength.
He guides me along the right paths, bringing honor to
His name.
Even when I walk through the dark valley of death, I
will not be afraid,
for You are close beside me.
Your rod and your staff protect and comfort me.
You prepare a feast for me in the presence of my enemies.
You welcome me as a guest, anointing my head with oil.
My cup overflows with blessings.

He paused a moment, as he sometimes had trouble with the ending. What could top "my cup overflows with blessings"? Maybe something more far-reaching, more enduring. After a moment, he put these words together:

Surely goodness and unfailing love will pursue me all
the days of my life,
and I will live in the house of the Lord forever.

Psalm 23

As he re-read what he wrote, he smiled. This was worth saving. He would add this to his growing collection of writings, which he kept in a small wooden box by his bed.

Gathering his things, he stood, placed the bag over his shoulder, and jogged the rest of the way home, his wavy, russet hair tossed in the wind. Sinewy legs hardened by climbing the hillside daily, and tanned by the sun, pumped rhythmically as he ran.

He first went to his father's tent and announced his arrival. Jesse was lounging on a thick fleece, taking a break out of the heat of the sun. He suffered from achy joints and often had to rest his legs during the day.

"Back from the palace already, David?"

"Yes, Father. Supper time at the palace is time for me to leave. And I'm starving! Does Mother have the food ready?"

"The women have it set up in the other tent. Raddai ate already." Jesse struggled to sit. "Help me up."

David grasped beneath his father's arm and heaved upward, assisting him to a standing position.

"Thank you, son." He lumbered to the tent opening, David following. "I need you to go with him to help round up the flocks. It's Raddai's turn to stay with the sheep tonight. Nathan and Ozerem have been out there all day and can come back with you." David's father always used the formal versions of his and his brothers' names. Among themselves, the boys used each others' nicknames.

David had a quick meal of flatbread and lentil stew before accompanying his brother to the hillside. The two chatted on their trek. Rad, at age fifteen, was closest to David in age, being only two years older than him. They always had something to talk about. Today, he told David about a hawk that dove at him earlier that day, when he brought water to his brothers.

"What did you do?" David asked.

"I threw a rock at it." To demonstrate, Rad bent down and picked up a stone in his left hand and hurled it high into the sky, his right arm held out for balance. He quickly hid his right hand within the folds of his robe again.

David noticed Rad's reflex to hide his deformed right hand and felt a familiar pang in his heart.

Rad continued, "It came at me again, but after I threw a few more rocks it finally gave up."

Rad was silent and looking at David, expecting some response from him.

David swallowed. He had been listening to Rad's story, but the sudden glimpse of his brother's injured hand brought the incident with the wolf back to him once again.

He glanced sidelong at Rad and, focusing on his narrative, said, "She…she probably has a nest of young ones to feed. We better watch the lambs, or it may try for one of them. Maybe you should build up the fire extra big tonight to keep her away."

"Hawks don't hunt at night. The lambs will be safe," Rad said. "Tomorrow, I'll make sure they are pastured nearer the valley. The brush is more plentiful there. And there are several trees. It will offer better cover for the lambs."

David smiled at his brother. "Good idea." He admired how Rad usually had sensible solutions to daily challenges.

When they met up with Nate and Ozzy they helped round up the flock into the sheepfold and closed the gate. Nate built a quick fire for his brother—he was an expert at that. Then he and Ozzy and David returned home, leaving Rad and another shepherd to remain with the sheep for the night.

David's twin brothers, Nate and Ozzy, were near copies of each other. Both had wavy dark hair, like their mother, and tended toward being a bit hefty—a testament of enjoying too much wine and sweet dates and honey. Nate, however, was the more handsome of the two, with that characteristic cleft in his chin and piercing hazel eyes. Ozzy's face was softer, more rounded. The two ate dinner in the food tent, and afterward sat around on rugs joshing with David.

"Did you catch a look at Mical today, Dave?" Nate asked with a sly wink. He knew David had a crush on King Saul's youngest daughter.

David dipped his head and finished swallowing the bit of fig cake he was chewing. "No. She stays with her sister in one of the other rooms. I barely get to see her."

Ozzy gnawed a crust of flatbread. Between swallows he said, "Well…Maybe you can sneak into her room. You know…surprise her. You might catch her changing clothes for dinner." He guffawed at his suggestive wisecrack.

David grabbed a hunk of cheese and hurled it at his brother, hitting him in the arm and spilling his cup of wine. He snatched up the earthenware cup and drew back his arm to aim at Ozzy.

Ozzy rose from the rug, towering over him. "Hey, I was just joking," he said. "What's your problem?" He reached down, seized the cup from David, and prepared to throw it at him. David covered his head with his arms and remained low to the ground.

"Stop that!" Nate said, grappling with Ozzy. They wrestled for a moment, spilling more wine and a bowl of lentil stew. Finally, the twins sat down hard on the rug, their skirmish in a draw.

David glanced at Ozzy and caught him smirking. He heard him say under his breath, "Don't know what you expect a princess to see in you anyway, *shepherd boy.*" It stung.

David tossed aside the last of the fig cake and stomped out. Bitter at being the butt of his brother's jokes once again, he sat slump-shouldered on the stone bench by the tent next door. He kicked a stone and heard it strike something in the invisible darkness. He heard his brothers continue their joking until, eventually, a sharp reproof by their father silenced their tongues.

3

The Prophet's Visit

As David sat in the shadows he could feel his face begin to cool off in the chilly night air. He took a cleansing breath, filling his lungs and then exhaling deeply. Looking about, he recognized muted shapes of camels and donkeys that were tethered nearby. Familiar sounds of the clan settling down to sleep helped him relax. All was as it should be.

"Will you put that light out?" a gruff voice said, from within the tent nearest David.

"In a minute," another, gentler voice answered. Soon the tent was darkened. The two voices murmured to one another for a few moments, then, silence.

The faint bleating of sheep corralled in distant pastures wafted to him in the night. He imagined his brother, Rad, resting by the fire in the sheepfold, probably with an orphan lamb in his lap.

Looking up at the countless stars dotting the sable sky, he made an effort to put aside his argument with his brothers. He tried to think of something else. And, as at other times, when his temper was short and he felt misunderstood by his brothers, his thoughts drifted to the grand secret he held, and why he must try to be more patient, try to control his temper, and try to rise above.

It was because he would be the next king of Israel.

David's thoughts drifted to that day, two years ago, when it all happened. It was end of the rainy season and he had just turned eleven years old. The prophet, Samuel, had journeyed to their settlement near Bethlehem from the village of Ramah. He and his companions were invited by David's father to share supper with the clan, in keeping with the tradition of providing a meal and lodging to travelers.

David had been sent out to tend the sheep so his brothers could visit with their noteworthy guest. He had pictured his parents and five brothers seated with the prophet, his mother and the other women having surely prepared that roast lamb they always made at special occasions, with the delicious sauces to soak into fresh loaves of flatbread. He would have to be satisfied with cold leftovers.

He gritted his teeth at being excluded from the important event. It's always like that—he was left out of everything.

All the other brothers had important roles in the family. It was bad enough that his oldest brothers, Eliab and Abinidab, were already part of the King's army. The middle three brothers were either being brought up to also join the army, or to take over the family business of raising sheep and goats. David was often sent to do menial tasks so his brothers had time to learn how to use weapons, sheer sheep, or go on trading expeditions.

It was with these thoughts that he sat on the hillside that day. He closed his eyes and longed to be at the important dinner with the prophet. He wished he had brought his lyre along—at least then he would have something else to do besides watching fleece grow on sheep.

He got up and strode around the flock, kicking stones and watching them roll down the hill. When he turned around, he stumbled back a step, startled. Ozzy and Nate were there, looming before him, silent for a moment.

"Father wants you," Nate said. He stood with arms crossed, his head thrown back.

"Hmph," Ozzy said, smirking.

David looked up at both brothers in turn. "Why? What did I do?"

"They just want you to come," Nate said. "The prophet said he came to find the new king."

"New king? Did King Saul die?"

"Not that I know. But supposedly the new king is one of us, a son of Jesse."

"One of us?" David said, his eyes rounded.

"Yeah. Can you believe it? But the prophet didn't approve of the rest of us," Nate said, his voice bitter. He took a seat on a large rock among the brush.

Ozzy sat down too. "Probably won't like you, either. Skinny rat."

"Shut up, Ozzy. Anyway, Dave, you'll have to go and see for yourself. All I know is supper is being held up for you."

Nate and Ozzy began tossing back the jug of wine they brought with them. David stood near them, indecisive.

"You'd better go," Nate said firmly.

As David hurried along his heart pounded rapidly and his mouth felt like it was filled with sand. One of them was to be the next king of Israel. Surely it wouldn't be *him*. He was youngest, and small for his age. Why would his father send for him?

Skipping down the hillside, he viewed the circular arrangement of the nine large tents that made up his family's settlement, nestled in the valley, surrounded by sundrenched hills. Someone was bearing water in a large jar from the well at the outer perimeter. In the central clearing he saw his parents, brothers, and almost everyone else in a cluster. He wasn't able to see the prophet, who was probably in the middle of the group.

When he passed his mother's tent, he could smell the meat roasting over the fire just outside. He was met by Rad, who brought him to their father. The two oldest brothers, Eliab and Abinidab, were there as well. It was fortunate they happened to be on leave from the army the same week Samuel visited.

The unfamiliar character must be Samuel, the prophet. His white beard came to a point near his belt, which encircled a coarsely woven robe that hung loosely from his shoulders. A small clay vial was suspended around his neck by a cord. The vial held anointing oil, David knew. It was similar to the flask his father used during the yearly anointing of the ewes, when his family gathered to pray for a prosperous lambing.

Samuel beckoned to David, waving his lean arms. Jesse gave him a gentle nudge, and he stepped closer. The prophet looked toward the sky. He squinted his eyes in concentration and turned an ear upward, listening.

"Is this the one? This young lad?" Samuel said to someone no one could see. Then, turning to David, he grasped him by both shoulders and said, "Almighty God said you are the one. I am to anoint you the next king of Israel."

David looked up at the prophet, who was smiling broadly at him. He glanced back at his family, noting the astonished expressions of his brothers and the proud looks of his parents. His mother had her hands to her mouth. Tears glistened in her eyes.

Turning back to the prophet, he bowed his head and closed his eyes. The prophet lifted his hands from his shoulders and popped the tiny cork from the vial. David felt the viscous anointing oil flow onto his head, symbolizing the power and favor of God.

Peering through half-closed eyes, he observed the oil dripping from locks of his hair over his forehead as it descended in slow drops toward the earth, sending up tiny showers of dust and forming little pools in the dirt. He felt the slipperiness of the oil between his toes as he wriggled them. Gazing at his feet, David felt a surge of energy go through him. He straightened his back and looked up to the prophet as the feeling overwhelmed him. He filled his lungs with a deep breath of air. For a brief moment, he felt lifted off the ground.

The experience left him as suddenly as it came, leaving a tingling feeling in his hands for several moments after.

As David sat on the stone bench he stared into the night, remembering. He looked at his hands, open before him, and recalled how they felt that day, when he was anointed the future king of Israel. It was a secret ceremony, on an ordinary workday, among ordinary people. Sometimes he wondered if it was real. He also wondered why one of his oldest brothers, Eliab, or Abinidab, weren't chosen. They had more experience, more skill. What could he do? Play a lyre? Herd sheep?

He thought about what Samuel said to him after supper the day he was anointed. He took David aside and spoke to him privately, instructing him to keep his anointing secret.

He was to tell no one. He would be king of Israel in God's time and in God's plan.

Samuel also told him not to worry about being just a youth. God would use the growing-up years to prepare him for his calling. He left David with: *"Man looks on the outward appearance, but God looks on the heart."*

Did he have the heart of a king? As he sat on the stone bench his mind was a muddle of all the other things that preoccupied him—trying to make a dent in his family of five older brothers, pleasing King Saul as his personal musician, trying to catch a glimpse of Mical—he didn't know if he had what it takes to be king. *Good thing becoming king is a long time away.*

Tonight, once again his temper got the best of him. Will he ever learn to keep a cool head? Rising from his seat on the stone bench, David picked his way back to his brothers' tent. He was expected at the palace early in the morning and King Saul doesn't like to be kept waiting.

4

The Giant

A few years passed and David continued his service as the King's personal musician. He was at his post in the courtyard, waiting for King Saul to come and hear him play. He had been waiting for over an hour. Lounging on a cushion in the shadow of the throne, he strummed random notes on the lyre. Becoming bored and sleepy, he put his instrument aside and lay back, resting with arms behind his head. He looked up into the open stretch of sky.

It had been five years since he was anointed the next king of Israel, and even now, almost grown to be a man, he often questioned his qualifications to lead the nation. He comforted himself by remembering that God chose him when he was young, inexperienced, and foolish. He had to trust God to equip and empower him to do the job, as Samuel said, in *His* time.

Just being the King's personal musician was advantageous. He was able to observe the King in action, something that would help him when it was his turn to be king. King Saul's decisions and achievements, such as clearing the Philistines from Canaan and raising up a formidable cavalry, demonstrated a rule he would like to imitate.

He was sure with as much as King Saul approved of him, it would be easy to fall into his calling as the next king of Israel. Perhaps it would be his deathbed request, when the time came, for David to succeed him. He hoped it would be that simple.

As the sun grew high in the sky and shone into the courtyard, he rose to stretch his legs. Presently, he heard voices.

The speakers were on the other side of the row of tapestries that hung, ceiling to floor, along one side of the courtyard, separating the space from an ante-room used to hold those seeking favors of the King. It was easy to hear what they were saying.

"How goes it, Azariah? Did you hear about the soldier from Gath?"

"Gath? You mean that Philistine?"

"Yes. Their champion. I hear he's a giant. Over ten feet tall!"

Azariah scoffed. "No way. That's impossible. All those giants had been killed years ago."

"Well, there's at least one left," the other speaker said. "And he's been challenging our troops down in Socoh. When King Saul mobilized our army, instead of engaging in battle, the Philistines keep sending this champion to challenge our soldiers. He's taunting our men, saying if only one soldier would come and fight him, and win, the battle would be over."

David remained hidden against the tapestry as the conversation faded. The last words he heard were: "King Saul's been hoping one of our men would volunteer…"

That explained why, after all this time serving King Saul in the palace, he had not appeared today. He was with the army in Judah, trying to find someone who would step up and fight the champion of the Philistines—the giant.

Despite the fact that King Saul was not present that day, David was reluctant to leave the leisure and comfort of the palace. The cool breezes through the throne room were refreshing. Much cooler than among the tents at home. If he went home now, his father would surely find some work for him to do. He figured he could stay by the pool just a little while longer. He returned to his cushion and made himself comfortable.

In a moment, he heard a stirring from behind the tapestries and looked up to see the King's younger daughter, Mical, stroll into the courtyard. He caught his breath when she crossed the floor and stood near him, taking in how splendid she looked in her pale blue gown, held at her slender shoulders with jeweled clips. The fine, drapey fabric clung to her body, drawing attention to her youthful form. A young lady of about fifteen, she made David feel clumsy and exposed.

She looked pointedly at him and remarked, "Did you hear what they said?"

David's mouth went dry, and he tried to swallow. "You mean…you mean about the giant?"

She tossed her head. "My father is probably going crazy, trying to find someone who's brave enough to fight him."

"Or stupid enough. He's over ten feet tall!"

Mical sat down on the raised tiles surrounding the pool, legs outstretched. She leaned forward and drew a slender finger slowly through the water, creating ripples, and smiled at the goldfish swimming toward her, expecting a treat.

She spoke softly. "Some of our soldiers are big, too. Someone should try. At least it would bring honor to our nation."

Unfolding a napkin, she withdrew its contents, a flaky pastry. She broke it apart and dropped a few crumbs into the water, toward the gaping mouths of the goldfish. David watched her place a morsel of the pastry between her fresh pink lips. She paused and glanced sidelong to catch him staring at her. He looked away hurriedly.

After a moment, Mical stood up and stepped around the throne, passing David, still seated on a floor cushion. Her long gown brushed against his leg, sending a shiver through him.

"I'm sure…I'm sure His Highness will find someone to volunteer," he said. "It's just a matter of time."

"We may not have a lot of time left," she said over her shoulder. "The Philistines will attack anyway, if no one accepts their challenge" She disappeared through the doorway leading to the inner rooms, reserved for the royal family.

David stood up on legs unsteady as a newborn lamb's and moved to where Mical had been sitting by the pool. He sat on the raised edge and dipped a hand into the water, feeling foolish at the impotent remarks he made to the girl. Any self-confidence he felt fighting lions or playing the lyre so skillfully was lost in her presence. He longed for the chance to impress her. He sat thus for a time in irritated silence, frowning deeply.

After a few moments, David shook his head and roused himself from his frustrated thoughts. Looking around and noticing no one, he decided to leave the palace for the day. He trotted quickly along the stony path home.

The wheat fields outside of Gibeah were ready for harvest. Taking a short break, David reached out for a handful of wheat stalks. He rubbed the ripe grains in his hands and collected the wheat berries, popping them into his mouth. Glancing down, he observed a quail strutting from among the wheat. He stilled himself so he could watch her lead her brood of young ones in snatching up the few grains he had dropped, before disappearing among the wheat stalks again.

After one more handful of grain he took to the road again. The distance to his family's settlement outside of Bethlehem flew by.

He knew his brothers would be needing help with the sheep, and he couldn't wait to tell them what he overheard in the palace, about the giant from Gath who was threatening the Israelite army. He decided not to tell them about his encounter with Mical—it would only give them something about which to ridicule him.

As David approached home, he spied his father standing near an extra large tent. He called out to him.

Jesse had been supervising the biannual shearing with his sons and hired help. Woolly sheep with dirt-stained fleece were brought into one end of the large tent, and white sheep with short, choppy coats collected on the other side. When several shorn sheep were gathered, one of the workers led them to the pastures where Rad was shepherding that day. It was a busy time of year.

His father reached out to greet him. "David, I almost thought it was Eliab coming to see me. You're growing so tall, you're almost as big as your brothers."

David smiled, appreciating the compliment. Winded from his run, he said, "Thanks…Father. I have some news…from the palace."

"Come in the tent, son, and have a drink. Then you can tell me all about it."

Ozzy and Nate were in the shearing tent, chopping at a stubborn ram. Both young men were worn-out and sweaty from fighting uncooperative, nearly wild sheep all day. Many of the sheep were only handled during the twice-yearly shearing and were fretful about any encounter with people.

Nate was straddling the animal he was shearing, who had been placed on his back, kicking and bleating. Ozzy was trying to hold his four limbs out of the way.

"Darn it! Hold him still, Ozzy!"

The ram swung his head at Ozzy's ankles and caught him with a horn. "Ow!" Ozzy looked up and noticed David. "Hey, Dave. Come here and hold his head."

David lent a hand. Reaching under, he grasped the ram's horns and held on tight. Nate finished under the animal's neck and tossed the fleece onto a pile at the side of the tent. Finally done, the ram bounded away to join the rest of the sheep.

Jesse spoke up. "Take a break, boys. Let's hear what David has to say."

The four sat down on the wool-strewn ground and took turns drinking from the water jug. David told his family what he overheard about the giant from Gath, that he was challenging the Israelite army daily.

"Why doesn't one of our men fight him?" Jesse said.

"They say he's over ten feet tall and his armor weighs a ton. I just wish I was there. I wouldn't let that heathen Philistine beat our whole army. Give *me* a chance."

"Yeah, right! Why don't you just go and stab him with your little dagger. That should scare him." Ozzy said. He grabbed a stray twig from the ground and plunged it at David's arm. David jerked away and looked to his father for support. Nate and Ozzy had a good laugh. Jesse didn't notice. He was thinking.

"You know, son, you can go to the battlefield, if that's what you want."

"Really, Father?"

He faced David. "Not to fight, of course. But I think you should bring your brothers some provisions and possibly get some information from the front. Some more *accurate* information."

5

Judah and Tamar

David was restless that night. He was excited about the upcoming journey to the battlefront, and looked forward to being in the army camp, among the mighty Israeli warriors and cavalry horses. He pictured lines of regiments, well-clad in shiny armor, marching bravely to the front line. How great to be part of it! Sometimes this workaday life, watching sheep wandering about the hills, made him restless. He just wanted something to *happen*.

Maybe while he was at the battlefield the Israeli army would finally vanquish the Philistines and their giant. And then maybe his oldest brothers, Eliab and Abinidab, would let him celebrate with them. What a story he would be able to tell when he got back home.

David turned over in bed and, looking toward the tent opening, caught sight of his father standing there, checking on him and his brothers. He habitually made a last rounds of the property before turning in to his own tent. David would always recognize his father's large form, and felt safe whenever he saw him standing nearby.

He sat up and said, "Father, I can't sleep."

Jesse stepped into the tent and settled on the fleece

mattress next to his youngest son. "What's on your mind? Are you thinking about tomorrow's trip?" he said quietly.

David nodded, eyes bright.

Jesse picked at the fleece, pulling bits of wool and sending them drifting across the dirt floor in the nighttime breeze. "Yes…it's time you experienced life in the army camp. I'll send Jared to go with you. Your mother can do without him for a few days. He will keep you safe on the journey."

"Plus I'll have my dagger and my sling," David said.

Jesse smiled at David and nodded. "And don't ever think you're too young for anything. God had Samuel anoint you the next king of Israel when you were just eleven. I know I don't talk about it much, but it's something I think about often. It makes me proud of you. Proud of who you are that God thought you would be up to the task."

David was silent as the nagging worry came back to him. "But what if I do something wrong?" he said, at length. "What if I make a mistake and never get to become king?"

Jesse thought for a moment. "Let me tell you a story that may help ease your mind. This is a story about your great-great-great-great…um…grandfather. I'm not really sure how many generations back this goes. His name was Perez. And *his* father was Judah. It's about a mistake Judah made, and how God was able to turn it around to fulfill His plan."

He placed an arm around David and drew him toward himself. David leaned against his father's generous shoulder. He was a child again, listening to the familiar voice telling stories into the late hours.

"Long ago," Jesse said, "there was a rule that if a woman's husband dies without them having children, the woman would be permitted to marry her husband's brother. Her *first* son by that brother would be considered her *first husband's* child, and be heir to all his property, his name, and title. Now Judah and his wife had three sons, Er, Onan, and Shelah.

"The oldest son, Er, married first. He married a woman named Tamar. Er was killed in battle during the first year of their marriage. They had no children. So Judah let Tamar marry his second son, Onan, in order to raise up a successor to Er.

"Onan was wicked and selfish. He knew their first child together would be considered his brother, Er's child and heir. He refused to sleep with Tamar. So she was stuck. She couldn't marry anyone else, and her first husband, Er would remain without heirs. God doesn't take these things lightly, so he struck down Onan. Onan became ill with a disease and died. So, again, Tamar was a widow.

"Now Shelah, the third brother, was a young man, probably about your age. He would be of marrying age in a few years. Judah told his daughter-in-law to remain with him until Shelah was grown up. Then she could marry him, and raise up an heir to her first husband.

"So Tamar waited two years till Shelah grew up. Only problem was, Judah didn't keep his promise to Tamar. He let Shelah marry a girl from a neighboring village, instead of her.

"Tamar was stuck, again. But she was also clever, and had a plan. She knew Judah was going to another village to help with shearing—"

David broke in, "Shearing! They were doing that even back then?"

"Ha ha! Yep. Don't you know you come from a *long* line of sheep farmers? Where was I? Right—Judah was going to shear sheep. Tamar knew he would be away for a few weeks at least, and may be lonely for female company, if you know what I mean. So she traveled to the village and found where

Judah was staying. She disguised herself and covered her face with a veil. She offered to keep Judah company. He was lonely, so he agreed to get together with her.

"In the morning, when he left, Judah promised her a goat, as payment. He said he would bring it the next day. Tamar, being clever as she was, asked for a pledge from him, so she knew he wouldn't go back on his word about the goat. She asked for the cord and signet ring he wore around his neck—personal items that could only belong to him. And he gave them to her, figuring he would get them back the next day when he brought her the goat. Now, remember, this whole time Judah didn't recognize her.

"Problem was, Judah couldn't find her the next day. And of course that was because she returned home to their tents. She had fooled him. And before long, she discovered she was with child."

"I can definitely see a problem with her plan," David said. "I assume Tamar got pregnant that night with Judah. So what happens when he finds out? He doesn't know it was *her* that night in the village, right?"

Jesse smiled. "You forget, son, about the signet ring. Of course she was found out, and Judah was furious! He thought she was unfaithful, and became pregnant that way. He demanded to know who the father of the unborn child was, so he could punish them both.

"Tamar went to her tent and took something out of hiding. She brought to her father-in-law the signet ring on the cord. 'By the man who owns these things I am with child', she declared. Well, Judah was shocked. And very repentant. He apologized to her for not giving her his son Shelah in marriage. And he never slept with her again.

"A few months later Tamar gave birth to twin boys, Zerah and Perez. Perez was the firstborn, and your ancestor. So you see, even though Judah had plan A, plan B, and plan C, which all failed, *God* had Plan D. God always has another plan."

"*God always has another plan*," David repeated slowly to himself.

Jesse kissed him on top of his head. "Help me up, son."

David stood up and helped his father rise. He lay back down on his bed and allowed his father to cover him with a woven wool blanket.

"Always try to do God's will, David. But if you slip up, know that God will find a way to turn it around for good."

He watched his father shuffle out, closing the tent flap behind him, and thought about the story he told. David learned in his childhood that Judah, Tamar's father-in-law, was one of the twelve patriarchs. He was a son of Jacob, or 'Israel'. If even Judah made mistakes, David felt he at least had a chance.

He curled up beneath the blanket and easily fell asleep. He was peaceful at last in the knowledge that, despite any mistakes he might make, God would help him succeed. God would help him in his trip to the battlefront, and in his destiny as the future king of Israel.

6

On the Battlefront

David left Bethlehem for Socoh the next morning accompanied by Jared, another servant, and a caravan of four donkeys carrying provisions. Several sacks of roasted grain, loaves of bread, cheese, and two large wineskins were among the foodstuffs they were bringing to his oldest brothers on the battlefront. Some of the food was also meant as gifts for the captains and other commanding officers. It was a day's journey west, and they camped outside Socoh overnight.

They entered the Israelite camp early the next morning, just as the army was mobilizing to meet the Philistines at the valley of the river Elah.

Pausing in the shade of a nearby tent, David said to Jared, "Stay here with the supplies. I'm going to go with them."

He rushed away and caught sight of his brothers. *There's Abinidab.* "Hey, wait up!" he called out, and ran to him. They were joined by Eliab, the oldest brother.

Abinidab ruffled David's hair and said, "Hey, Davey, what brings you here?"

David glanced up at Eliab, who stood, silent, with arms crossed. He addressed Abinidab, "Father sent me with provisions. Food. And…and wine."

Abinidab thumped Eliab's shoulder. "Hear that? We eat good tonight."

"Hmph," Eliab said.

David looked up at both brothers, gnawing his lower lip. "Father...Father also wants to know about the giant. About... about the Philistine threatening our army."

Eliab, still frowning, raised an eyebrow at Abinidab. Abinidab shrugged a shoulder and said, "You see, Davey, it's like this—"

At that moment there was a blast from the ram's horn and a command for troops to assume their ranks. Eliab and Abinidab quickly armed themselves with swords and shields. Abinidab turned to give David a friendly smile before joining his regiment.

David slunk away and hid among the bushes and tall grasses that grew along the road. He observed the soldiers, grouped in regiments. Swordsmen carrying double-edged swords and circular shields, led the army. The leather armor they wore afforded greater movement, but at a price. Leather was more easily penetrated than metal. Following them came the archers, beautifully clad in scale armor and lightweight helmets. Cavalry took up the rear guard and also rode alongside the entire group, armed with spears or curved swords.

David waited until all the regiments marched by. He then scurried, crouched down, along the edge of the road. The brush provided ideal cover—he didn't want to be sent back to camp and miss all the action.

Nearing the valley of Elah, David sprinted to catch up to the rear guard of the Israeli army. His breaths came fast and his heart beat faster. He couldn't wait to see the Philistine army. And the giant. Was he as big and mighty as everyone said?

From his observation point behind the army David was able to see very little. The sounds of the enemy assembling across the valley reached him—troops of marching soldiers, the rhythmic clip of cavalry horses, the whirring sound of hundreds of chariot wheels. He heard a booming voice calling out to the Israelite army. *The giant!*

David scampered past the cavalry and regiments of foot soldiers, and found himself near the front line, off to the side, still hidden among scrub and tall grass. His line of sight continued to be obscured by soldiers and horses. He could, however, hear the words being roared across the valley: "Choose someone to fight for you. We will settle this in single combat. If you kill me, we will be your slaves. But if I kill your man, you will serve us. I defy the army of Israel!"

David quickly looked around at the Israelite army, at the swordsmen in the lead, armed with their sturdy shields and double-edged weapons, and archers supplied with many arrows. He glanced up at the cavalry soldiers, so impressive mounted on large horses also clad in armor. The horses seemed eager, pawing the ground with massive hooves. *Surely someone will volunteer. Someone will fight the giant today.*

As the giant finished speaking, the unthinkable happened. The Israelite army made a sudden about-face and, led by the cavalry, now at the forefront, began moving quickly in the opposite direction, back toward their camp.

Gripped with panic, David turned and began to dash through the brush to keep up with them. Then he thought differently. He slowed to a stop and looked around.

The giant. I must see the giant.

Keeping low, David crept on all fours back toward the edge of the valley separating the Israelite side from the Philistines. He inched along, the stony ground digging into his hands and knees, brambles catching at his clothing. The air was still dusty from the quick retreat of the Israelite army, making it hard to breathe. He stifled a sneeze. Jumpy, he flinched at a lizard darting among the stones in front of him. As he crawled along he could still hear booming laughter coming from the other side.

The dust began to settle and David could finally see in the distance. He shielded his eyes against the early morning sun coming from his right and, crouching down behind a handy clump of brush, was able to get a good look at the enemy army.

The first thing he noticed was numerous Philistine footsoldiers standing in formation along the opposite side of the valley. Flanking them were cavalry and chariots. There were so many chariots he couldn't see the end of them as he gazed from one side of the Philistine army to the other. It looked like thousands of soldiers and horses.

Focusing near the middle of the frontline, David easily picked out the form of the giant. He was standing, unmoving and powerful, gazing out over the valley. The rising sun reflected off his armor. He was surrounded on either side by the other Philistine soldiers, all impeccably equipped for battle. The soldiers stationed next to the giant provided a good reference to prove how large he actually was. He towered over his fellows, the best of them reaching about mid-chest to the giant.

David now knew why the Israelite army found the Philistine champion so intimidating. A bronze helmet, breastplate of scale armor, and bronze leggings and shoulder coverings made his armor impenetrable. Bulging arm and leg muscles were evidence that the giant was indeed a powerful warrior. In addition to a huge sword buckled around his waist, he carried a spear whose shaft was as thick as a weaver's rod. His curved shield was taller than the armor bearer who carried it.

It was no wonder none of the Israelite soldiers would agree to fight the giant in single combat. He looked like he could knock down even their best warrior with a single blow.

Kneeling at the edge of the valley, all alone, David felt exposed and vulnerable, and began to creep back carefully. He occasionally glanced behind him and noticed that, finally, the enemy army was withdrawing as well.

A warm breeze kicked up, stirring the dust and urging David on his way. He took his time returning to the Israelite camp, however. He was embarrassed by the Israelite army, who retreated in such a gutless manner. He had hoped to see some action, someone rising to the giant's challenge. At home he had heard legendary stories of valor and courage accomplished by the Israelite army. Today, he saw none of this.

Groups of soldiers were seated on the ground or on crude benches when David returned, conversing with one another in low voices as they ate breakfast. Absent was the usual joking and laughing whenever men get together.

David ambled among the tents and equipment of the army camp, looking for his brothers. A rangy soldier on horseback called out to him

"Hey, what are you doing? Where's your uniform?" he asked, reining in his horse.

David withered beneath his scrutiny. "I'm…I'm not a soldier. I just came to see my brothers. They're here somewhere…" He glanced around hoping to spot them.

"I'm General Abner. First in charge here." His manner was brusque. "Who are your brothers? They should know we don't allow family visits."

"Eliab and Abinidab. We are all sons of Jesse of Bethlehem."

"I know Eliab. Always bragging about something. Well, not even he volunteered to fight Goliath."

"Goliath?"

"Goliath. The giant. That Philistine has been threatening us for over a month."

David tossed a stray twig into a nearby campfire. "I saw him. He's big alright, but surely one of our men could beat him. It's not right, what he's saying about us." His voice grew louder. "He's nothing but a pagan Philistine. He should not be allowed to defy the great army of Israel."

The soldiers in the vicinity became quiet during David's passionate outburst. A few stepped closer toward him.

"Hey! You there," one of them said. "Why don't you volunteer, if it bothers you so much? There's a big reward."

David looked at him. "What is it?"

"No taxes for your whole family. And King Saul's daughter for a wife."

Mical! "Is that true? No taxes and—" David felt a blow to the back of his head. He turned to find Eliab glaring at him.

Eliab was the brother he barely knew. Sent off to serve in the King's army when David was a young child, he came home once or twice a year. Yet you couldn't deny the family resemblance—the wavy, russet hair and ruddy complexion was David's all over, in a more mature form. Eliab had the muscular build of a fighting man, and the temper to match.

"What are you doing, bothering the soldiers, asking questions about that Philistine? That's not for you to do, *little brother.*"

David felt his oldest brother's disapproval acutely. He rubbed the back of his head and felt his face become hot. He glared at Eliab. "Well, someone has to fight him. I don't see *you* volunteering!"

Eliab's eyes darkened. "Why don't you go back to your little sheep and play a song for them. You have no business on the battlefield."

David ducked another blow from his oldest brother and dashed away, teeth clenched and eyes clouded with hurt. Before long, Abinidab was walking with him, carrying a loaf of the flatbread he brought.

"Hey, Davey, leaving so soon?"

Glancing back, David saw Eliab laughing with the other soldiers around the campfire. "Yeah. Eliab wants me gone."

"Too bad. This food you brought is great, by the way. And our wine ran out three days ago. We really appreciate this."

His spirits buoyed, David said, "Thanks. Father will be glad to hear that. He wanted to make sure you and Eliab have enough to eat."

"Well…we do now," Abinidab said between bites. "And Eliab will enjoy what you brought, he just won't admit it."

"Oh. I almost forgot. Father wants a letter from you. He wants to know what's happening at the front. And please write about the giant. I don't think he believed me when I told him."

The two brothers entered a nearby tent and sat in the dim coolness, glad to get out of the bright morning sun.

"How did you find out about Goliath?" Abinidab asked.

"I heard about it at the palace. Everyone's talking about him. You know I'm still going there every day to play music for King Saul, right? Except he hasn't been there in a couple days."

"That's because he's here. That's his tent, over there." Abinidab pointed next door through their tent opening. It was obviously a royal accommodation, much larger than the soldiers' tents. David noticed a scarlet rug extending out of the entrance, and guards stationed at either side.

Abinidab gnawed off another bite of bread and offered the loaf to David. He tore off a piece and nibbled it absently. "I guess that means I won't have to show up at the palace for a while. Father will be glad. He's been busy with shearing all week. They really need the extra hand."

Abinadab brushed a stray lock of hair out of his eyes. His straight auburn hair was usually kept in a tidy bunch tied at the nape of his neck. After the retreat back to camp, it was coming undone.

"I remember those days, shearing sheep. Eliab and I used to have a contest to see how many fleeces each of us could cut. I usually won. One day I cut twenty-two fleeces. He only cut twenty."

David grinned. "I'll bet that made him mad. He always thinks that because he's oldest, he's better than the rest of us. I can't stand it." He lowered his eyes. "Try being youngest."

"You'll have your chance to shine, Davey," Abinidab said gently.

Despite also being much older than David, Abinidab was always protective of his youngest brother, and spent quality time with him during his infrequent visits home. David felt a tear stream down his dusty face in response to his brother's kindness.

"Remember what that prophet said? He said God chose *you*. Not Eliab or one of the rest of us. That means something. Just give it time."

David wiped his face with the back of his hand. He finished eating his morsel of bread and got up from the packed dirt floor. "I'd better go. Father will be waiting…"

Abinidab stood up and placed his arm around his brother's slender shoulders. "Stay. Don't let Eliab chase you away. We have to write a letter to Father anyway, right? You can go home tomorrow."

7

A Promise to the King

----◆----

David and the servants that accompanied him were put up in a spacious supply tent near the outer perimeter of the campsite. Stacks of wood and animal fodder were cleared to make room for them to sleep on the ground. The donkeys, hobbled outside the tent, were provided with a pile of hay and bucket of water.

In the evening, Jared built a campfire near the opening of the tent. David sat on a log before it, nibbling on a handful of raisins. He looked around in the approaching twilight. The hills that rose to the east were covered by broad-leaved evergreen shrubs and small, bent thorn trees. Occasional olive and fig trees also grew within the wooded areas they traversed on the journey to Socoh. A barely perceptible slope within the army campsite led the way to the river Elah, about a half mile north.

Seated near the fire, David's mood improved as he noticed everything that was going on. His attention darted from one campsite to the next. Soldiers were sparring good-naturedly, grooms looked after horses, and cooks were preparing supper. Jared retrieved enough stew for the three of them, along with some of the bread they brought.

He brewed a pot of mint tea, something the soldiers all drank. It was supposed to boost strength, and David found the flavor pleasing.

Activity all around was beginning to slow down as soldiers, servants, and other workers began turning in. David looked forward to the next day, and hoped to catch sight of the giant again. Maybe tomorrow someone will volunteer to fight. Maybe tomorrow someone will triumph over him.

He picked up his lyre and strummed it lazily, plucking out a simple tune, trying to calm his excited spirit enough to sleep. After a few moments, he was approached by someone dressed in a fine linen tunic, dark hair neatly arranged, and bowing in a subservient manner.

"David? Son of Jesse?"

"Yes…"

"I serve His Royal Highness, King Saul. He sends for you."

David rose from his place beside the fire, clutching the lyre to his chest. The King probably wanted a song before he went to bed, or maybe he was having one of his attacks of anxiety, and needed to hear a soothing melody. He accompanied the servant to King Saul's tent and remained bowed until acknowledged by the King.

"David, come on over. Surprised to see you here."

"I just came today. To bring provisions to my brothers, your Highness."

"Your brothers?"

"Abinidab and Eliab. Of Bethlehem."

King Saul glanced at his servant, who shrugged. "Well, never mind about that," he said. "Come, sit down next to me." He indicated a place at his feet. And to the servant, "Bring him a cup of wine, will you?"

David made himself comfortable.

"Brought your lyre along, did you? That's how I knew you were here. I heard you playing in the darkness."

"I've missed you at the palace, your Highness. But I understand you've been here because…." Trapped into a corner with his own words, he almost said, "that giant has your army scared to death." Recovering, he said, "…the army needs your guidance."

King Saul waved a hand dismissively. "Yes, yes. I'm sure your brothers told you about the giant, Goliath. It's really tiresome. Why don't those Philistines just settle for an all out battle? This intimidation stuff is for the birds. Our men are itching to fight. Give them something physical to do, like plunging a spear into one of those heathens, and they can't wait to do it. They're no good at these mind games that champion of theirs insists on playing." He slipped into an irritated silence and took a sip of wine from a golden goblet.

The wine service looked incongruous compared to the primitive furnishings of the other tents. The royal tent was not lacking in luxuries. An ebony daybed was covered in several wild animal skins. Colorful tapestries lined the inside of the tent and thick rugs surrounded the immense wooden chair upon which the King sat. All indicated a great deal of effort and labor to move the King to the battlefield.

King Saul picked at minute crumbs on his lap. "I'm waiting for someone to step up and fight the bastard. I really don't want to just *send* someone to certain death." To himself, he added, "Yet, even if one of my soldiers was killed for his effort, it would give us a good reason to attack those pagans."

David took a first sip of wine, then placed the cup down. He felt a wave of energy come over him. As the King continued grumbling, he gazed at his hands, open in front of him. They were tingling. He remembered the other time he felt this way. It was when he was anointed the next king of Israel by the prophet Samuel. It was power from God.

He rose to his feet and stood facing the King. "I'll do it. I'll fight the giant."

King Saul sat back in his seat. Eyebrows raised, he studied the youth who stood before him, earnest and willing, surveying his slender shoulders and arms, and his lean face conspicuously lacking facial hair. "Son, it's good of you to offer. This is actually the first offer anyone has made to fight him. But he would squash you in an instant, wouldn't he? You are barely more than a boy, and he has been a soldier in the army since he was a boy."

In that moment David knew he had to make a believable case for what he was volunteering to do. He recalled the quickness and strength he experienced, even as a youngster, when fighting predators in the pastures of his home. He knew he had special ability and protection from God. But to convince the King?

He took a step forward. "You don't understand, your Highness. God will help me. I have used a dagger and sling to kill lions and bears at home when they threaten my father's flocks. God helps me. He makes me strong and quick. When I was just a child, I stabbed a lion in the heart. Last year I grabbed a wolf by the jaw and clubbed it to death! I *know* I can do it. The God who has saved me from the teeth of lions and wolves will protect me from this heathen Philistine!"

His enthusiasm was contagious. "Well said, young David," King Saul said. He turned to the servant. "What do you think? Should we give him a chance?"

The servant shrugged.

"Hmph," King Saul said. He rested his chin in his hand and was thoughtful for a moment. David watched him through unblinking eyes.

Glancing behind him, King Saul said, "If you will have any chance against Goliath, you must take my armor. It's stored there in the back of my tent. General Abner will help you try it on. I'm not sure if it will fit you, but at least it will protect you. You'd better wear it."

General Abner was summoned. David stood by King Saul's side as he laid out the plan to the general.

The General pursed his lips and knitted his brow. "Sounds desperate, your Highness. I'm sure I could coax one of my men to take up the challenge tomorrow. They may just need a little more *persuasion*. We can threaten half-rations until someone agrees to fight the giant."

King Saul waved away the suggestion. He drew David closer to him, his arm around his shoulders. "This young man already volunteered. He says he can do it." He faced David. "Go to the back of the tent, son. You will see my armor there. Bring it here."

David did as he was told. The servant went to help him.

King Saul looked behind him, making sure David was out of ear-shot. He lowered his voice and said to General Abner, "Look, if he succeeds, our army will strike and finish the job. If the giant kills the boy, our army will attack anyway. It's win-win."

"Except for the boy, of course," General Abner whispered harshly.

King Saul hissed through clenched teeth, "Better than losing one of our soldiers. We may lose enough as it is. We can't wait any longer."

David and the servant returned carrying the armor. General Abner helped him put it on. When he placed the bronze helmet on David's head he stumbled a step back, top-heavy in the headgear. Quickly, General Abner fitted the breastplate of scale armor across his chest and trunk, cinching the leather straps. Again, he careened backward. He wasn't used to the heavy armor, and it severely restricted his ability to move.

"Forgive me, your Highness. This won't work."

"What's that?"

"This…armor. It's too heavy and I can barely move. I can't fight in this." He flapped his arms uselessly. He took off the armor and laid it at King Saul's feet. "I have my own weapons, my own way of fighting. With them and the power of the living God, I promise to defeat that Philistine, and bring victory to the Israelite army."

Later that night David stole away from the dying campfire he had returned to after his conversation with King Saul. He spent the night in prayer as he searched the perimeter of the camp for a source of water. In a dried creek bed he found five smooth round stones, each the size of his fist, perfect to fit into his sling. These he placed into his bag.

He caught sight of his sling, hanging partially out of the bag. He pulled it out and ran his fingers along the stitching in the leather. The rough texture of the straps provided good traction when whirling it over his head. The widened pocket in the middle was smooth from countless stones. It smelled of dirt and sweat. It's familiarity gave him fortitude—he recalled the successes he had with it, the times he used it to protect the flock and himself. This sling, a gift from his father, had been faithful to him on many occasions. He prayed it would help him be victorious tomorrow.

He carefully placed the sling back into his bag, returned to the supply tent, and slept fitfully until dawn.

8

Felling the Giant

--------◆--------

David's deepest sleep always seemed to be during the hour right before sunrise. Despite the restless night he spent, he was sleeping soundly when the ram's horn and the call to prepare for battle was sounded. He was dreaming about Mical. She appeared to him in the sapphire gown that took his breath away. She was handing him his sling and a stone…

Eyes still closed, he began to stir. He put out his hand, expecting to feel the familiar softness of the fleece he always slept on at home. Instead, his hand touched the cool, dry earth of the tent floor. He opened his eyes and stared into the face of one of the donkeys that accompanied him to Socoh. It had stolen into the tent and was stolidly chewing a mouthful of fodder, dropping bits of hay and saliva onto his face.

David groaned and brushed the debris away as he unwound himself from the blanket he slept in. Just then, the tent flap opened and the friendly face of his brother Abinidab was the first thing he saw. Eliab, eyes darkened, barged in past him. The donkey skittered out of the tent. David sat up, alarmed.

"What's this I hear about you wanting to fight Goliath? Are you out of your mind? Has all those days being in the hot sun finally fried your brain?"

Amazing. He cares.

Eliab continued his rant. "Don't you know we're responsible for you? If anything happens to you, Father will never forgive us. Probably write us out of our inheritance."

"Hold on." David said firmly. "My decision to fight the giant is…is between me and King Saul. It's none of your business."

Abinidab held his palm out to Eliab. "It's brave of you to offer, Davey. Really. But you don't have to do this. General Abner just told us someone was preparing to fight Goliath. He was certain we would be in battle with the Philistines today."

David blinked and shook his head. "That's *me. I'm* the one who volunteered. I talked to General Abner last night."

"And he's letting you do this?" Abinidab said.

"I can do it," David said, nodding confidently.

Eliab's eyes glowered. He stood up in the center of the tent. "You're crazy if you think you can do better than the warriors in the King's army."

David got onto his feet and leveled his eyes at him. He knew he was youngest, but was soon to be a man, and had to stop letting his brothers intimidate him.

He took a big swallow and said, "God will protect me. I know He will be with me on the battlefield and help me win the fight." Leaning forward, he pointed at his brother. "And you have nothing to say about it."

Eliab made a sudden movement, snatching at David's outstretched finger. David, quicker, withdrew it in time.

Eliab countered with a shove at his shoulder, nearly toppling him. David steadied himself and approached, fists raised.

At that moment General Abner appeared within the tent opening. Abinidab hurriedly stood at attention.

Eliab spun to see his commanding officer give him a disapproving look. The ram's horn was sounding for the second time.

"Your brothers will have to return to their regiments, David," General Abner said. He inclined his head. "I think you can prepare for battle by yourself?"

"Yes, sir," David said as his brothers edged toward the tent opening.

Glancing back, Eliab's parting words were: "Don't you dare bring disgrace on our family."

The General, alone with David, said quietly, his face grave, "Despite what his Majesty wishes, you can still back out of this, if you want. You're not officially part of his army."

David shook his head. "No. I made a promise to the King. And I don't want to back out. I can be ready in a few minutes."

"Very well," said General Abner with a firm nod. He turned and stepped out of the tent.

David reached for a loaf of flatbread, took a healthy bite, chewed and swallowed. He took a long drink of water and wiped his mouth on his sleeve. Rising from the ground, he straightened his clothes, grasped a walking stick, and reached down to pick up his shepherd's bag. This he slung over his shoulder. The weight of it reassured him. Five stones. Five chances to kill the enemy. There was serious potential within these stones.

Sounds of the army mobilizing—the steady cadence of horses' hooves, the rattling of weapons as soldiers armed themselves—emanated through the walls of the tent as he readied himself. In a few moments he exited into the early morning sunlight to find the entire army standing in formation, waiting for him. He took a step backward, momentarily uncertain.

General Abner approached on his horse. He leaned over and said, "Son, are you ready?"

David's heart was a whirlwind of emotions. His greatest motivation was to please King Saul, and bring glory to the Israelite army. His own ambition, however, was to show up his oldest brother. It would be incredible to outshine Eliab for once, and do something to impress the rest of his brothers. But it wasn't his triumph yet, and as it was God who roused the drive in him to do this, he knew to give God the glory once he prevailed. And he would prevail.

He looked up and said, "Yes, I'm ready. The living God of our forefathers will empower me." Gaining momentum, he said, "Let me in front. Together we will march to the valley of Elah where you will witness the destruction of the giant."

With steady steps, he strode to the front of the army, a shepherd's tunic his uniform, walking stick in one hand and sling in the other.

The army marched on, David in the lead. Ram's horns blasted the battle call. As they approached the valley of Elah, they could hear the Philistine army answering back. David's eyes caught the sunlight reflecting off their armor and shields.

Then he saw the giant.

Goliath, standing powerful on the other side of the valley, began making his proclamation once again: "Choose someone to fight for you. We will settle this in single combat. I defy the army of Israel!"

At those words, David stepped away from the protection of the army, glancing back just once. He moved down the gradual slope to the dried riverbed, treading over clumps of brittle grasses and cracks in the parched mud. The rising sun was beginning to warm the ground, causing small lizards to appear from the cracks. His nose stung from the dust that settled in the valley—dust stirred up by the thousands of Philistine soldiers and chariots. He heard the screech of a hawk and raised his eyes to see it dive at something in the distance. Focusing on the opposite ridge, he continued striding forward.

Feeling alone and vulnerable, David wished he had someone else with him—a soldier, his brother, even Jared. Someone. But there *was* someone with him—the God who brought him here, who helped him slay lions and wolves, and who had him secretly anointed king when he was just a child. The living God of his forefathers was with him. With God, he was the majority, and the Philistine army was to be pitied. With God at his side he could not fail.

As David neared, he saw Goliath notice him for the first time. He stepped forward and his words boomed across the valley. "Who are you sending to fight me? Am I a dog that you come at me with a stick? Come here little one, and I will give your flesh to the hawks and wild beasts to devour."

David continued up the slope, approaching the giant, and stopped about fifty paces away. Winded, he said, "You… you may come at me with a sword and spear, but I come to you in the name of the Lord Almighty—the God of the Israelite army, whom you have defied."

David keenly felt the expectation of the Israeli army reaching him from across the valley. He threw down his walking stick and stood directly facing the giant. "Today the Lord will conquer you and your army," he said, his voice growing louder. "Wild beasts will feed off the flesh of *your* fallen soldiers. This is God's battle, not ours. The Lord will give you to us!" His final words rang across the valley.

Goliath guffawed. "'God's battle'. Ha! You want a fight? You shall have one." He glanced back at his fellow soldiers and laughed once again. Turning to David, he casually raised a spear.

David pulled a stone out of his bag and fitted it into the sling. With narrowed eyes he quickly assessed Goliath for a weak spot, a strategy he often used when fighting wild beasts. Spotting the broad forehead exposed beneath the helmet, he focused on it.

Standing ready, knees bent and sling gripped in his hand, he felt a surge of strength go through his body, all the way to his fingertips.

Goliath advanced.

David raced toward him, swinging the sling over his head once, twice, three times. He shot the stone and watched it soar through the air.

Goliath stumbled back as the stone met its mark, sinking deeply into his forehead, crushing his skull. Like one of the great cedars of Lebanon, he was down, sending up a cloud of earth. The fallen giant and the two hundred pounds of armor he wore shook the battlefield.

The Philistine army was paralyzed for one incredible moment as the dust settled around their fallen champion. Dark blood emerged from the cavity in his head.

Adrenalin surging, David rushed to the fallen enemy. He grasped the sword Goliath wore at his side and pulled it from the sheath. A powerful downward blow severed the head of the giant from the body, and David held it up, triumphant. The Israeli army broke into a cry of jubilation.

All was chaos. The Philistines were already retreating as the Israelites thundered across the valley. Chariots, turned too tightly, upended, horses thrashing in their harnesses.

Foot soldiers trod over each other as they fled, desperate to outrun the Israeli army.

David cowered in the shelter of the giant's shield as his army raced by, chunks of dirt pelting it, thrown by horses' hooves. General Abner swept up to him on his black horse and reached down to take possession of Goliath's head. "Well done, young man! King Saul has been waiting for this." With those words he spurred his horse on to follow the army on the heels of the Philistines, holding the head aloft by a shock of black hair.

Anxious to get away from the headless body of huge Goliath, David struggled to his feet and stumbled away a few paces. The sword of the giant caught his attention, off to the side where he had flung it, and he reached for the oversized weapon. It would be the perfect trophy for slaying the giant. As he held the sword upright in both hands, he realized his fingers were still tingling. The weapon was vibrating. He looked heavenward and murmured a prayer of thanks for God's help in defeating the giant, for God's power in his life.

When he arrived at the deserted army camp, he sent the servants to collect the giant's helmet, which had been thrust off when he fell to the ground, and the rest of the armor. Later, he would pack the sword and armor on the donkeys to take home to his father.

But for now, David crawled into the tent, lay down next to an obliging donkey, and passed out.

That evening the soldiers celebrated with the food and supplies they plundered from the Philistine army camp. They had chased the enemy all the way back to the Philistine strongholds of Gath and Ekron.

Waking from slumber, David heard a familiar voice near the doorway of his tent.

"Yeah, that's my brother…we've always been real close."

David peered out of the tent to catch a glimpse of his oldest brother chatting with a group of soldiers as they strolled by. "I taught him everything he knows. You know it's because of me he is such a crack shot with that sling." Eliab's boast faded along with the group's footsteps. David didn't know whether to be angry or laugh off his blatant lie.

Later, General Abner visited David in the supply tent. He rose to meet him and noticed the general carried a sack, hanging heavy from his hand. He peered in to see it contained the head of Goliath, his dead eyes frozen in the expression of horror he had just before the stone crushed his skull.

General Abner handed the sack to David. "Here, son, take this. You should be the one to present it to King Saul. Your bravery won the battle for us. It's only right that you should get the credit you deserve." David grasped it tremulously.

When they entered King Saul's tent, he rose from his throne and approached David. David bowed and held the sack containing the head of their defeated enemy out in front of him with both hands. He was glad when the King's servant relieved him of it.

"Stand up straight, David," King Saul said. "Where is your homeland?"

"Bethlehem, in Judah."

"When you return to your father, you must tell him that I require for you to move into the palace. I want you near me at all times. You will be trained to lead my army into battle, to further victory. With your skill and the favor you have with God, we are sure to win many battles."

DAVID'S RETURN TO HIS HOME OUTSIDE BETHLEHEM caused a sensation. Jared raced on ahead to announce their arrival. David was still about a hundred paces away when he saw his father, large and eager, trudging toward him, his wool cloak flapping in the breeze.

When he caught up with David he instructed the other servant to take the donkeys home and tend to them. Alone with his son, Jesse simply said, "David," and turned his head side to side, a wide smile on his lips.

"You heard?"

"I heard. Jared told us." Jesse draped an arm across David's shoulders, shoulders that seemed broader today, somehow. "Is it true you dropped that Philistine giant with one stone?"

David beamed. "One stone."

The two entered the encampment to find the entire clan had gathered to cheer the return of the one who led the Isrealite army to victory over the enemy.

David enjoyed being hero for the day. He presented each piece of armor, weapons, and the sword of the giant to his family. Each item was more impressive than the last. Nate especially enjoyed wielding the huge, blood-stained sword. His small sons tromped around, together holding the breastplate in front of them, until their mother, Deborah, sat them down for supper.

A special meal was held in David's honor that night. He reclined on a rug next to his father and enjoyed the specially prepared meal of roast lamb with leeks, garlic-seasoned flatbread, and brown sauce. The giant's armor and weapons were displayed outside the tent for all the clan to admire.

After the meal, Nate's wife and sons retired to their sleeping quarters, giving him time to spend with David. The four brothers relaxed outside around a campfire, heating leftover scraps of lamb on sticks. Rad asked many questions about David's adventure.

"What made you volunteer to do it?" Rad said, threading his branch with a few bites of meat.

"It just felt right," David said. "Before I realized what I was doing, I told King Saul I could kill the giant. I knew God would enable me."

"I can't believe it! What did Eliab and Abinidab say?"

"They…they tried to talk me out of it. And then Eliab tried to take credit for it afterward, saying *he* taught me how to use a sling."

"Hm. Sounds like something he would say."

"You should have told him it was *me* who showed you the proper use of a sling," Nate said, tossing his head back. "Why would he say that?"

"You can chose your friends, but you can't pick your brothers," Ozzy said.

David chuckled. "I knew I would be able to beat Goliath, no matter *who* taught me how to use a sling. I can't explain it, but as I stood there facing him, I felt this surge of energy go through me. It seemed like the power of a hundred warriors were in me right then, helping me to aim, giving me extra strength to shoot the stone from the sling, and to use the giant's own sword to cut off his head."

David held his hands out before him, palms facing upward. "And afterward, standing there, holding the sword, I felt the same tingling in my hands that I felt when the prophet anointed me with oil. I knew God was with me that day. I knew God gave me the power to have victory over Goliath."

Shadows in the encampment lengthened as the brothers talked. The fire burned low and faces became a blur in the waning light. The camaraderie David felt with them that night warmed his heart, and he sensed even the older ones finally respected him.

One by one they grew silent, each lost in his own thoughts.

After a few long moments, Ozzy said, "Is there anything left to eat?"

Rad passed him his stick with a last bite of charred lamb on it. Ozzy snatched it up and gnawed at it.

Rad yawned. "I'm going to turn in."

David said, "Me too. I have to leave early tomorrow morning. King Saul wants me to move into the palace as soon as possible."

The brothers disbanded to get ready to sleep. Rad went with David, the two speaking to each other in low voices. Ozzy and Nate retired to the men's tent.

9

Aт тhe Palace

David woke the next day as birds were beginning their morning songs and the delicate pink light of dawn peeked over the horizon. He dashed out of the tent, eager to start his trip to Gibeah. The rest of the clan was just rising, or still savoring the last few minutes of sleep before they had to start the day's work.

His mother, of course, was already up, preparing breakfast. He rushed through his meal and packed together a spare cloak, his lyre in its bag, and his precious wooden box of writings. Jared carried the basket of food his mother had prepared and, after hasty goodbyes with the family, the two set off for Gibeah.

Moving to the royal city after living in a tent settlement all his life was something David looked forward to. Everything was new and exciting—smooth roadways, massive stone buildings, the palace garden filled with unusual foliage and animals. As a sign of favor for defeating Goliath, King Saul allowed him to live in the palace, rather than the barracks with the rest of the new recruits. A group of rooms opened to the outer walkway around the back of the palace, reserved for General Abner and King Saul's sons, who were all officers in the army.

David was allotted one of these rooms, furnished with a chair, a comfortable bed, and his own washing stand. He was also provided with a new suit of clothes, armor, and a whole supply of weaponry—bow and arrows, sword, and shield.

David's military education began soon after he got settled, and he was expected at the training grounds daily. The young soldiers practiced archery, sword fighting, hand-to-hand combat, and strengthening and agility exercises. He became acquainted with a few of the new recruits, and sought them out for company during off hours. He also got to know King Saul's son, Captain Jonathan.

Jonathan made sure David was part of his own regiment. About ten years his senior, he was aware King Saul planned to groom him into one of his main men—Israel's secret weapon against the Philistines—and spent extra time with him in training exercises.

THE RAINY SEASON AND BARLEY HARVEST PASSED. THE long days of sun and no rain were filled with drills, endless archery practice, and tasteless army stew. The monotony of it left David feeling bored and uptight. How many more times can you shoot an arrow at a reed circle?

The companionship of his fellow recruits wasn't the same as being with his family at home. He began to miss the edgy banter with his brothers, his father's stories, and the delicious meals his mother prepared. He even missed taking care of sheep on lazy summer days. Did his family back home ever think about him? Loneliness hung on him like an oversized cloak.

One day following archery practice he was surprised by a visit from Jared. It had been nearly a year since the servant traveled with him to Gibeah and helped him move into the palace. David trotted to the edge of the practice field to meet him. "How goes it, Jared? Do you have news from home? How are my father and mother?" His eyes were wide with expectation.

"They are all well," Jared replied. He indicated the camel kneeling on the ground next to him. "I brought you some provisions. There's cheese, and date and fig cakes. And look—your mother sent a wool blanket and fresh tunic." Jared unfolded the cloth bundle to show David.

David glanced at the camel laden with baskets and packages. "Is there a letter? Any word from my father? My brothers?"

Jared hedged. "I'm sorry…I don't think anyone packed a letter. I was just told to bring you supplies."

"Hm. I haven't heard from my father in months, and when he finally does think of me, it's just to send food. Just *things*. I want to hear *news*. From *home*." He sat down next to the camel, plucked a few blades of the fibrous grass that grew there, and held it out for her. She reached for it with soft, mobile lips, closed her eyes, and chewed contentedly.

David continued his outburst. "I should have known beating Goliath would only last so long. I don't know why I thought it would earn me some respect in my family." His voice quieted. "I'll always be just the youngest son."

Jared shifted his position, seated on the ground, and kept silent, glancing at David occasionally. David continued feeding the camel handfuls of grass, glad someone appreciated him.

At length, Jared gazed at the horizon, at the sun beginning its descent in the west. He said, "I'm sorry…I have to be getting back to your father before dark. Can I leave these things somewhere?"

David stood up and tossed his quiver of arrows over his shoulder. "Oh, just bring it to the palace. I'm staying in one of the outer rooms on the first floor. Tell the attendant it's for me and he will show you where to put it."

"Some of these supplies are for Eliab and Abinidab. Do you want me to leave them with you too?"

David scoffed. "Why? I never see them. The older soldiers don't associate with us. They've forgotten about me too."

Jared picked up the lead rope and urged the camel to rise. He turned in the direction of the palace and walked a few paces with David.

"When you get to the palace, someone should be able to tell you where to find my brothers." He ambled back to his regiment at the archery stations and was joined by Jonathan, who had been waiting for him.

"Ready for some more target practice?" Jonathan said.

"Hm. Sure," David murmured. He adjusted his quiver on his shoulder. "I just had a visit with someone from home. But he's going back now. I'm ready."

"Everything okay?"

David sighed. "Same as before. I get a bundle of clothes and some food from my father. He never visits, or even sends a letter. He just sends it with a servant. It's not fair."

Jonathan placed a hand on his shoulder as they walked together. "You have to understand—General Abner made a rule against soldiers having visits by family members. To keep them from becoming distracted. When you go on leave next year, you can visit your family and catch up."

David kept silent.

Jonathan said, "Now that you are a warrior, young David, it's up to you to make your own destiny. You cannot depend on your father, or your family anymore. You are your own man."

David felt his face flush at Jonathan's gentle admonishment. His heart's desire was to impress his mentor.

"I know that," he said, trying to sound sure of himself. "I'm just concerned, you know, about their *welfare*. My father is aged and his health has been poor. I want to make sure they are taking good care of him at home." David glanced sidelong at Jonathan, hoping his excuse sounded believable.

Jonathan grinned to himself. "Of course. You're a good son."

The two continued tromping across the training field, past soldiers shooting arrows at targets made of reeds woven into tight rounds, set up on pikes. They stopped near a stand of trees at the edge of the field.

"You're becoming skilled at the regular targets. I watched you shoot the center with most of your arrows earlier today." Jonathan turned to the tree behind him. In it were hung several smaller reed circles on ropes. He reached out and grasped one. "It's time you learn to hit moving targets." He released the reed circle and let it swing free.

David secured the leather guard onto his left forearm and chose an arrow from his quiver. The arrows, specially made for the sons of King Saul, had arrowheads of flint, a harder material than bone or metal. Eagle feathers were used as the tails. Eagles were the bravest and swiftest of all birds, and using the feathers on arrows guaranteed success in warfare. Jonathan had given him ten of his own arrows.

He stood sideways, feet shoulder-width apart, and faced the swinging target. He positioned the arrow and, at full draw, could feel the potential energy within the tightly drawn bowstring. Releasing it, he watched the arrow fly between tree branches and hit the edge of the reed circle.

Jonathan retrieved the arrow and brought it back. "When you are ready to aim, close your eyes. Picture the target as a Philistine soldier bearing down on you. Aim for his throat."

David did as instructed. He closed his eyes and imagined himself on the battlefield, valiant and brave, showing up his fellow recruits—and his brothers—proving his worth to them. He held his position for a moment, keeping the arrow back on the bowstring. Opening his eyes, he quickly focused on the moving target and released the arrow. It struck center.

He beamed at his success, and saw that Jonathan was smiling, too.

The two spent the rest of the evening practicing. David's mood lightened as Jonathan instructed him on how to improve his stance and how best to aim the arrow to avoid hitting branches. It was fulfilling, learning a new skill, one that would help him in battle. Having Jonathan spend extra time with him helped ease David's loneliness for his family. He felt a connection to his commanding officer, who was fast becoming a good friend.

10

Mical

·····➤·····

Two years passed since David's triumph against Goliath. As promised, King Saul exempted his entire clan in Bethlehem from paying taxes. He also promised David his oldest daughter, Merab, to wed, when he came of age.

Before moving into the palace, David was vaguely aware of who Merab was, and felt he had seen her once or twice during his role as the King's musician. The thing that nagged at him now was, his supposed betrothal to Merab had never been made public. He felt kept on a string those first years in Gibeah, at the mercy of King Saul to proclaim the betrothal whenever it suited him.

His objection to this was tempered, however, by his continued attraction to the younger daughter, Mical.

Living in the palace, David had many opportunities to see Mical. He would catch her lounging with friends in the palace walled gardens, dipping an unshod foot into the lily pond on a hot day. At other times she would be with her mother on the portico, having a lesson in needlework or mosaics. Occasionally he caught her by herself. These encounters were usually unsatisfying.

One day during the heat of the dry season, after finishing training exercises, David headed to the walled garden to cool off. His skin was sweaty and sunburnt from being in the practice field all day. The tight leather armor rubbed under his arms and around his neck and made him feel itchy all over; it was a relief to remove it. He thought splashing himself with cool water sounded like a good idea.

He left his leather breastplate and leggings leaning against the garden entrance and strode toward the fountain pouring through the garden wall into a shallow pool. He held his head beneath the splashing water, allowing it to soak his hair and drain across his shoulders. Sitting on the low stone wall surrounding the pool, he removed his tunic.

Just as he reached down to splash himself, he heard giggling, and glanced up to see Mical seated on a bench behind a group of shrubs. He quickly ducked behind the stone wall and donned his tunic again. When he looked back up at her, she was still laughing.

"Don't worry," she said, "I'm used to seeing animals of all kinds in these gardens. None of them are clothed, either."

"What are you doing here?" David said.

She tossed her head. Today, she wore her hair coiled in an elegant style, surrounded by a jeweled tiara. Her willowy neck glistened with perspiration in the warm summer evening and her gown draped over her knees, revealing feet shod with barely-there sandals. She crossed her ankles and said, "I live here, remember? What are *you* doing here?"

He stood up next to the fountain and smoothed his tunic down to his knees. Trying to appear casual and unconcerned, he strolled around the pool and kicked a pebble across the path. He found a place to sit on the stone wall surrounding the water, facing Mical.

Stretching his legs, he placed his hands behind him on the damp stones and leaned back into his shoulders. He sniffed arrogantly and said, "Well…hitting center on *all* the targets today was exhausting. Just though I'd—" before slipping backwards into the cool water, splashing Mical as he went down.

———✦———

DAVID'S HARD WORK AND THE EXTRA TRAINING BY JONAthan pain off so well that, at the age of twenty-one, General Abner appointed him captain of his own regiment. They were triumphant in many battles, instilling order in south Judah, keeping the Edomites at bay.

King Saul's pleasure with him was obvious. He acted openly proud of his prodigy and was known to say that he himself was to be credited with being an astute judge of character. He knew David would be a great success.

David's men served their commanding officer with heartiness and enthusiasm. A charismatic leader, none worked harder at perfecting warfare skills than he. It was an example his troops constantly tried to live up to.

As a result of his successes in battle, David grew full of self-confidence. He became more muscular, and wore his ruddy beard in a short style that showed off his chiseled jaw line and strong chin. Deep, muddy-brown eyes beneath thick russet eyebrows looked at Mical with longing. Each time he saw her he fell more in love with her. The way she gazed at him these last few months, eyes bright with admiration, he could sense that she was finally beginning to feel the same way.

He looked forward to coming back to Gibeah following military campaigns, and longed to see her. Visiting her at the palace, he told exciting stories of his army's conquests in battle, and brought her gifts—once a small glazed earthenware camel, another time a cuff bracelet of hammered gold. After one such victory, he brought back a lovely scarf of fine linen.

He was still living in the officers' quarters on the first floor, and was used to taking the liberty of visiting other areas of the palace, since he had been living there for over five years, and was supposedly betrothed to King Saul's daughter, Merab. The further interior you went, the more intimate were the accommodations, with the inner-most suites reserved for the queen and her children.

It was into one of these inner rooms that David found Mical, lounging on a day-bed thick with colorful upholstery. She sprang up to greet him as he entered the room. He held his arms out to her.

Merab was seated in a rush chair across the room, and shot him a questioning look as he greeted Mical. He had not expected to see her and took a step back toward the doorway.

He knew she was aware of King Saul's plan for them to marry eventually. The two had occasion to see one another at formal events and infrequently at family dinners, Merab sidling up to him, making sure she had the place next to him at the table. She acted openly possessive of him, triumphant over her younger, more attractive sister, who usually had the edge. Other than that, David never spent any time with her personally. And King Saul *still* hadn't made public their betrothal, which suited him just fine. Maybe he would forget about it.

The fact was, David just didn't feel attracted to her. Merab was nice-looking in her own right. A more faded version of her younger sister, she had the restrained demeanor of her mother and rarely ventured from her side. He preferred Mical's more robust beauty and dramatic personality.

"Merab," David said, bowing over one arm.

"Hello, David," Merab said. She set aside her needlework and stood up. Mical stepped away from her position near David.

He thought quickly. Smiling winningly at Merab, he said, "I brought you something. Here—it's a new scarf," and thrust the package into Merab's hand. She untied the string around the folded scarf and draped it over her head. It was pale blue and green and matched her grey eyes beautifully.

Merab whirled around. "It's lovely! Thank you," she said, smiling intimately at David. Mical shirked in the corner of the room, lips pressed together, obviously miffed.

David cleared his throat. "It suits you well." He then indicated Mical. "I hope, Merab, that you don't mind if I take your sister out for a minute—I have something for her, too. I just forgot to bring it with me."

"Of course," she said, dismissing her with a wave of her fingertips. "She may go."

David beckoned to Mical. "After you," he said, and shot a smile at Merab before turning to leave. Mical left the room ahead of him, eyebrows drawn together.

Once they left the room, David grasped Mical by the hand and led her rapidly through the corridors of the palace. They exited to a bright blue sky, sun high in the heavens, and made their way to the walled garden—it was the only place they could be alone—and found a secluded spot behind a stand of palm trees.

Only then did David feel the freedom to reach out to her.

Confused, she resisted his embrace and backed away. "What was that all about?"

"I'm sorry. I meant that scarf to be a gift for *you*, not your sister. Except I didn't expect to see her there with you."

"You seemed glad to see her. Glad to give her a gift."

"It's not like that." He reached out his hands again and said, his voice earnest, "My heart belongs to you. I hope you know that by now."

Mical moved in closer, now ready for his embrace. "And mine to you. I don't need a gift. It makes me happy just to have you back safe from battle. Let Merab have that old scarf. I have *you*."

David's strong hands closed in on Mical, feeling the delicate shoulder blades beneath the sheer fabric of her gown, this one the color of sunset. She leaned in against him and he could feel her heart beat against his chest.

This was the first time the two had been alone together in such an private setting, and he felt a strong desire to have her. He gazed down into her eyes, golden as the desert sand, and lowered his head. His eyes closed and lips parted.

Just as Mical stood on tiptoe to receive his kiss, a breeze blew through the palms, stirring scented flowers in the garden, causing them to release their fragrance and Mical to sneeze. She backed away from him and sneezed three more times.

Giggling, she said, "I'm so sorry. These flowers always make me sneeze." She reached into her handbag for a scrap of fabric to dab at her nose. David watched her, his heart keen with disappointment at the lost opportunity.

The moment gone, the two sat in the shade of the palms and chatted for a few minutes. David relayed a few stories about the Israeli army's recent conquest. Mical had one or two nuggets of palace gossip to tell. Eventually, their conversation came back to Merab.

"I don't know what to do when your father brings it up again. About me marrying your sister. I really don't want to marry her." He gnawed his lower lip.

Mical smiled a sly smile. "We can hope she falls in love with someone else."

"And, why do I have the feeling that you have someone else in mind?"

"Ha ha! We have a distant cousin named Adriel. He comes to visit every few weeks. I see him making eyes at her across the dinner table. She pretends not to see, but sometimes she smiles back at him."

"You have a scheme?"

She took his hand into her own and looked at him, eyes twinkling. "I'll think of something."

"And if your father approaches me, I'll try to put him off. It shouldn't be hard. There's always something I can do with my regiment. We'll find a way."

11

Meeting In the Garden

David's dreaded audience with King Saul came sooner than expected. One day the following week, after drills, he was summoned to meet the King in the garden. He returned his gear to his room, and hurried to the meeting place, his heart in his throat. They strolled the paths for few moments, two guards following at a discreet distance. David's attempts at small talk fell flat, and he listened to the King's self-important remarks with half an ear.

Brilliant emerald and sapphire peacocks roamed the confines of the garden and King Saul fed cracked wheat to his favorite, a large male peacock that dominated the others and rounded up all the peahens for himself. The bird was at this time displaying his gorgeous plumage. David bent to pick up a stray feather that fell from his tail—he thought Mical might like it.

Presently, King Saul faced him and placed a hand on his shoulder. "David, son, there is a reason I requested you to see me."

"What do you wish, your Highness?"

"I know I promised my daughter to you when you killed that heathen, Goliath. I am ready to make good on my promise. Merab, my oldest, is ready to settle down. She just turned twenty-two and it's about time she married. Good news, eh? What do you think?" He looked at David with raised eyebrows.

David was silent for a moment, thinking. He didn't want Merab, he wanted Mical. But he didn't want to anger King Saul by rejecting what he probably thought was a very generous offer. And obviously Mical hadn't the time to put her plan into action yet.

"Your Highness, really, you don't have to do this," he said, bowing his head. "Who am I, that I should be the son-in-law of the great King Saul? I come from a no-name family. Find a more worthy man to marry your oldest daughter." He hoped his self-effacing demeanor would appeal to the vain, self-centered King, and release him from this obligation.

"It's true—you come from a commonplace lineage. And all you have I have given to you, eh? But at the same time, a promise is a promise. Now, don't worry about a thing. I just have a small favor to ask of you." He placed an arm around David's shoulders. "It was kind of a lucky stroke for you to kill that giant those few years ago. Really just beginners' luck, eh? What I need you to do is to prove yourself in battle against the Philistines once more. Conquer them and Merab is yours!"

"But—"

The King held up a hand. "Oh, I know how much you appreciate this. Don't waste time protesting. I have decided. Your betrothal shall be announced tonight."

King Saul strode back to the palace, accompanied by the guards. David remained in the garden. He sat on a stone bench and set the peacock feather beside him. He felt defeated, and wished he had presented his case better. He should have told the King he didn't want to marry Merab. He should have been more straightforward and admit his love for Mical. He sat with shoulders hunched, disappointed in himself.

At that moment, Mical came near.

"Were you here the whole time?" he asked.

She nodded.

"Your father…your father doesn't understand. And I don't know how to tell him I don't want to marry your sister without having him get upset, maybe send me away. Then I wouldn't see you again." He looked down and scuffed his sandal on the gravel path.

"You'll find a way." She sat next to him and took his hand in hers. "So…seems he wants you to win another battle."

"Mm-hm."

She laughed bitterly. "That's so like him. Tricking you into winning against those heathens when you already won that battle six years ago."

"It's the price I have to pay. At least it will buy us time and give you a chance to work on your sister," he said. "And then we can be together again."

Mical faced David, eyes calculating. "Well, I've been doing some thinking. Our cousin, Adriel, is coming next month. He and his family are planning to stay for a long visit. I'll find a way to get him alone with my sister. Since you have to go back to war, it will give them time to get acquainted."

She was quiet for a moment, then said, her voice breaking, "Just promise you will come back. Don't let those Philistines take you away from me."

He gave her hand a squeeze. "Not a chance."

The two remained silent in the burbling sound of a fountain behind them. King Saul had the fountains installed at great expense when he built the palace gardens, many years ago. Small canals leading from underground springs diverted water to the gardens, creating a lush paradise full of exotic plants, animals, and water treatments that seemed absurdly out of place in the arid conditions that surrounded the royal city. It was a tribute to King Saul's larger than life persona.

Hearing rapid chattering, David looked up to see a family of monkeys dive into a basket of fruit that was affixed high up a nearby tree trunk. The monkeys were gifts from officials in Egypt, tokens of their friendship with King Saul. They had their own personal servant, who placed fresh fruit in the basket three times a day.

He pointed out the cute scene to Mical using the peacock feather. She giggled, snatched the feather from him, and held it to her face playfully. Today, her hair was caught up in combs made of seashells, ringlets of curls loose about her face, framing it. Her gown stirred in the breeze, revealing the mature shapeliness of her twenty-year old body. He gazed at her and couldn't help himself. He wanted—*needed*—her to be his wife.

She got up and began trotting away, glancing at him over her shoulder, still from behind the feather. He chased her, laughing, around the garden until he caught her. The two found a place to sit in a more secluded area of the garden and he encircled her body with his strong, tanned arms.

"Mical," he said. "You know…you know I long to marry you one day. Don't you?"

She looked down and toyed with the feather in her hand. "I know. I've known for a long time."

He placed a finger under her chin and tilted her head upward to meet his eyes. "Do you want to marry me?"

She smiled at the grave look in David's face and threw her arms around his neck. "Oh, David! Of course I do!" She released him and said, "We just have to get you out of marrying my sister."

Later that evening, David sought advice from his former mentor and, now, good friend, Jonathan. After years of training and many recent victories he viewed himself on a more equal plane with Jonathan. There were times, however, when he needed his friend's solid counsel.

He searched in a place he was sure to find him—the training field, and stood together under a full-leaved fig tree to watch the young men practice hands on fighting techniques.

"These new recruits," Jonathan said. "I find myself becoming more impatient with them the older I get. How do you tolerate their mistakes?"

"I don't know…." David said, unable to really concentrate on Jonathan's train of thought. After a moment of silence he said, "So…I came here because I wanted to talk to you about something."

Jonathan turned to David and nodded.

"I've been walking out with your sister, Mical. I guess I should tell you…I'm in love with her. I think about her day and night. She's in my dreams. I…I want to marry her."

Jonathan grinned. "She is a hard-headed girl. Selfish. Stubborn. But you should be able to handle her."

David laughed gently. "I think she handles me sometimes. I can't bear being without her." He paused. "Problem is…the King wants me to marry Merab."

"Merab? I didn't think she would ever marry. She won't leave Mother's side."

David looked down and kicked a stone near his foot. "The King told me this morning he expects us to wed after this next war with the Philistines. After we win."

"So. Lose," he said, peering sideways at David.

Was he serious? "Lose?"

Jonathan gave a nod.

David shook his head. "I can't do that. I can't lose on purpose. It would be a betrayal to my troops. Their lives wasted." He thought for a moment. "No…there's got to be another way."

Jonathan leaned against the tree and looked toward the setting sun. His regiment was falling in, marching back to the barracks. He faced David. "Follow your heart. It will lead you on the right path."

David knitted his brow. He had hoped for a more substantial piece of advice. Something he could *do*. 'Follow your heart'. What kind of advice was that?

He thanked Jonathan for his time, bid him goodnight, and walked back to his room at the palace. His heart. Someone else gave him a piece of advice once about the Heart. It was Samuel, the prophet.

Man looks on the outward appearance, but God looks on the heart, Samuel said on the day he anointed David the next king of Israel.

Was his marriage to Merab, or Mical, part of his destiny? Did it fall in line with him becoming king? If God looks on the heart, He would know that his heart belonged to Mical. Even if he married Merab, his heart would always desire Mical.

'Follow your heart'. Good advice, after all. He would follow his heart, the heart within him that God sees. The heart that would lead him to Mical.

DAVID'S CAMPAIGN AGAINST THE PHILISTINES WAS SUC-cessful. It was a prolonged conquest, taking several months of organizing, traveling, and completion. Battles with Philistine armies from the Five Cities generated losses on both sides. In the end, the western-most boundary of Judah, bordering Philistia, was secured. David requisitioned space in some of the walled cities in west Judah to house army troops. He wanted the Israeli militia to be a present force to the neighboring enemy.

David and Mical had planned that when he returned, victorious, he would demand her as his wife. After finally ridding Israel of the enemy, David felt he would have the right to make that request of King Saul. With that scheme in mind, he threw his whole heart into the war.

Mical promised to do her part, and plotted a way to get her sister and Adriel together. She also pined openly for him while he was gone, hoping that when her father knew she was in love with David, he wouldn't object to them marrying.

AFTER A YEAR, DAVID RETURNED FROM WAR, TRIUM-phant. Seated on his white Arabian steed he led columns of soldiers through the city of Gibeah amidst wild celebration. As regiments marched in formation, women danced aside them, playing instruments and singing:

"King Saul has killed his thousands, and David his ten-thousands."

Nearing the palace, David caught sight of the King's family—her royal Highness, the Queen, several younger children, and the two daughters, Merab and Mical. They were all seated on the front portico beneath the royal canopy in order to enjoy the parade of the triumphant army.

He looked down from his horse to see Mical smiling broadly at him. Next to her was Merab, looking wilted and miserable in the heat, leaning on the arm of a man he did not recognize. This must be the distant cousin, Adriel. Merab glanced up to David and, meeting his eyes, looked away quickly. She tightened her grip around Adriel's arm.

Later, David learned that Merab had indeed been given to Adriel for his wife while he was away fighting the Philistines. Despite his anger at the flippant way King Saul went back on his promise (he now realized the King was not one to be trusted to keep his word), he was relieved that he wouldn't be forced to marry the dull Merab.

David and Mical met on the portico the evening of his return. They stepped down and walked, arms linked, into the garden, enjoying the brilliant sunset and returning breeze.

"You don't think your father will try to prevent me from marrying you, do you?" David said.

"He knows how much I love you. He seems pleased," Mical said. She gripped his arm and gazed up at him as they walked. "You should talk to him soon. Ask him tomorrow."

He grinned. "Tomorrow?"

"*Yes*. While he's still in a good mood from our victory. He wants to be seen as being fair with you; after all, you did defeat the Philistines. If people hear that he isn't fair with you after that, they'll all be against him. And that's the thing he fears most. He's afraid someone will try to overthrow his rule." She whirled to face him head-on. "Oh David! You must speak to him soon."

"Okay," David said, laughing at Mical's take-command tone. "I'll ask him tomorrow. I'll *demand* it." He reached out and took her in his arms. He caught the scent in her hair—lavender mingled with vanilla. Aroused, he inhaled deeply, filling his nostrils with the fragrance.

He exhaled and said, "Believe me, you were all I thought of while I was gone. The way you looked in that dress you wore last summer..." He tilted his head to peek at the shadow in the center of her low-cut neckline.

She peered up at him, a bemused smile on her lips. Fingers entwined around the back of his cloak, she pulled him closer and lifted her chin.

He leaned in and touched his lips to her neck, feeling the warm pulse quicken. He kissed the angle of her jaw, found her mouth and, lips parted, greedily slid them over hers, tasting the sweetness within.

He came up breathless, wanting more, but staggered a step back on weakened legs.

She moved toward him and clutched his robe, drawing him close, and leaned her head against his broad chest. He enclosed her with his arms.

The two stood in the fading sunset, holding onto each other and the hope that soon they would be together as husband and wife.

12

The Challenge

King Saul spent that evening with his concubine. She was a young lady of the Moabites—part of the spoils of war—and lived comfortably in the palace apartments reserved for mistresses and concubines of the King. They talked quietly in bed and relaxed against overstuffed pillows covered in fine linen. The concubine nuzzled his neck.

"Hmmm…Did you enjoy the parade today, love?" King Saul said.

She sat up and smiled. "I did."

"What was that song they were singing as David rode in, eh? I heard bits of it from under the awning when the army marched by. Something about King Saul killing thousands…?"

"Yes…I think it went, 'King Saul has killed his thousands and David his ten-thousands.'"

A dark mood struck Saul as soon as he heard this. His jaw tightened. *What? David owes all he is to me! How dare he accept such praise!* He flipped off the covers and stormed out of the room.

THE NEXT DAY DAVID VISITED KING SAUL IN THE PALACE courtyard. He was feeling bold and successful and decided it was time to ask for Mical's hand in marriage. To sweeten the deal and to remind the King of his latest conquest, he brought a few treasures to present to him—prizes of their victory over the Philistines.

He strode into the courtyard and found the King pacing around the reflecting pool, spear gripped tightly in his hand, his face dark as his mood. The servant in attendance was keeping up with difficulty.

Alarmed, David quickly hid behind one of the great tapestries hanging on one side of the room.

King Saul bellowed, "What's this I hear about David killing ten thousands and I only thousands? I am Commander-in-chief. I have conquered hundreds of thousands!"

The servant was saying soothing phrases, trying to calm his master. David caught his eye from his hiding place.

Furtively, the servant approached and pleaded with him. "Only you can calm him…Play your lyre for him like you used to."

"I can't do that," David whispered. "I've never seen him this worked-up before. I don't think I can calm him down." *And now is not a good time to ask for Mical's hand in marriage.*

The sudden silence of the room was more startling than the previous raucous carryings-on by King Saul. David turned to see the King glowering at him from in front of the tapestry.

He took a step forward and bowed low, placing the gold and brass trinkets he brought on the floor. "Your Highness, I bring these—"

An unexpected kick by King Saul sent the items clamoring across the floor. David prostrated himself, genuinely afraid, and held this position until he heard footsteps. When he looked up and gazed along the courtyard, past the reflecting pool, he saw King Saul had returned to his place on the throne. He was leaning, forehead in hand, emotionally spent.

Cautiously, David approached. He picked up his lyre, forgotten among a pile of large cushions lying against the courtyard wall. He sat cross-legged on the floor, cradling the instrument. He tuned it. Tenuously, he strummed a soothing melody, glimpsing at the King intermittently as he played, trying to gauge his mood.

He seemed to be softening. His eyes were closed and he had a near smile on his lips. David relaxed and continued to play. He looked down and plucked out a cheerful tune the King liked.

While concentrating on the lyre strings, he spotted something speed toward him out of the corner of his eye.

The spear!—it pierced through his cloak and into the floor where the King had hurled it, just missing his leg.

Eyes dilated, David glanced up at King Saul standing in front of the throne, his deeply lined face twisted in a sneer. He made a sudden move.

David tossed down the lyre and fled, tearing his cloak on the point of the spear.

From that day on, he felt the change in King Saul's personality. From what he heard the King say just now in the throne room, it was clear he was jealous of his success. He decided to make himself scarce until the King's bad temper passed.

David avoided Mical the rest of the week—he didn't want to face her having *not* talked to her father about getting married. He immersed himself in military training to keep out of King Saul's way. As demanding as the physical part of war games was, it wasn't nearly as emotionally draining as keeping up with the King's changing disposition.

From his room on the first floor of the palace, David often heard the King having heated discussions with his army personnel. Sometimes these meetings ended with him throwing things, or riding away at a gallop, bellowing at them over his shoulder, only to return placated, even in high spirits, and wondering at the sour mood among his staff. They never knew what to expect of him.

Here, on the training field, soldiers worked together to better themselves at sword fighting, archery, and hand-to-hand combat. Among his comrades-in-arms David knew where he stood. They had each others' backs.

Instructing a group of soldiers later in the week, David looked up to find King Saul and General Abner approaching on horseback. Everyone bowed low.

King Saul dismounted and commanded them at ease. He pulled David aside in a friendly manner he distrusted. "David, your men are doing well out here, eh? Ready for another great victory at battle, are they?"

David glanced across the training field at the archers. "They are always ready to fight."

"Good, good," the King said, eyeing General Abner, next to him. "I know just the chance we can give them."

Something in the way King Saul said it made David wary. He gnawed his lip and tried to keep his distance, hanging back a little as they walked.

"I've decided to give you another chance at being my son-in-law. I know you and Mical have a little thing going. I see the way she looks at you. And the way you look at her."

David caught his breath.

King Saul continued. "I don't blame you. She's a beauty! Much more attractive than her older sister, eh? Anyway, here's what I need you to do." With General Abner at his side, King Saul explained to David that for the price of merely one hundred dead Philistines Mical would be his.

"Son-in-law to the King!" General Abner said. "What an honor. You should accept this offer. You and your men could accomplish this in no time."

David wasn't thinking that he wouldn't be able to do what was being asked of him. He was thinking that it would be a senseless massacre to kill one hundred of the Philistines that he had already conquered. It would just incite them.

He also wondered what King Saul's ulterior motive was. Generosity? Favor? No. This opportunity was also a chance for him to be slain at the hand of the Philistines, a much more likely intention.

David looked up to see King Saul and General Abner staring at him in expectation. He tried an old argument.

"I guess I just don't feel worthy. I am just the poor son of a shepherd. Who am I to be son-in-law to the King…?" His voice faded into the lame protest. He hoped his excuse would buy him time, and that he could convince the King, at a later date, to accept a less dangerous and less bloody dowry for his daughter.

"Nonsense!" King Saul boomed. He clapped David on the back forcefully. "I would be very disappointed if you refused my offer." He lowered his voice to a near-whisper and hissed, "I won't *let* you refuse."

David shook his head and blinked a few times at the King's threat. When he looked back at the King a broad smile had replaced the menacing expression.

"Tell your men of your new mission," he said briskly. "I'll give my daughter the good news myself."

The King mounted his horse, and rode off with General Abner to leave the speechless David feeling very small in the training field.

As he watched them ride away, he thought about King Saul's words: "your new mission". He didn't even know what it was. It wasn't like he could just ride into a Philistine city and pick off a hundred soldiers for no reason.

A moment later, Jonathan rode up. David greeted his friend with a tight-lipped smile.

"How goes it?" Jonathan asked, dismounting. He walked with David, reins in hand, his horse trailing behind.

"Your father was here," David said. "Seems he's agreed to let me marry Mical—"

"Great!"

"—for the price of one hundred dead Philistines."

Jonathan kept silent.

David stopped and turned to his friend. "Problem is, we were just in battle with them, and won. The borders are secure. There's no reason to fight them again."

"There may be," Jonathan said. "I heard the Philistines attacked the city of Zorah in Canaan. They need our help."

13

Two Hundred Sandals

⬩———⬩

A week later, David and Jonathan set out with five hundred foot soldiers and a hundred cavalry to save the city of Zorah from the Philistines. They reached their destination fifteen miles northwest of the royal city of Gibeah in the late morning hours, and camped about a mile from the city walls, hidden among the foothills of the Judean mountains.

The Philistines had laid siege to Zorah, one of few walled cities in the region, and were encamped around it. They had stopped up the natural springs that provided water to the city, and set a guard at the gates, preventing any inhabitants from leaving. It was a waiting game.

David sat on his horse on a high ridge, observing the city below.

"Jonathan," he said. "I don't see any way through the Philistine camp to the city." Numerous campsites surrounded it, with rows of tents, tethered mules, and supply wagons. At this time a throng of foot soldiers marched in columns around the city walls making a racket even David could hear, almost half a mile away. The shouting, clanging armor, trumpets, and ram's horns rang across the region. The commotion must be unnerving to the city dwellers.

"The Philistines are new to siege warfare. They like to attack, be on the offensive," Jonathan said. "But Zorah is a well-fortified city with thick stone walls. If the Philistines weren't trying to enlarge their territories by moving northward they probably wouldn't have bothered with it."

"That's just like them—expansionists. We close off Judah to them and they set their sights on Canaan." They moved on, keeping the horses at a slow walk in a wide perimeter around Zorah. "So they will wait until the city surrenders?" David asked.

"Or starves."

On the way back to their camp, David said, "I'm thinking there may be a way to approach the Philistine camp undetected. I don't see anyone guarding the supplies or tents—the soldiers are all marching around the city. We'll send Josh to check out the situation when it gets dark."

Jonathan nodded. "He's a good choice."

They arrived back at camp in time for the evening meal—David always enjoyed eating with the soldiers. He preferred sitting by a campfire, drinking boiled tea, and eating simple army stew to the overdone meals at the palace. It gave him the feeling of friendship and togetherness he longed for growing up. Always in competition with his brothers, he regretted not getting closer to them, savoring their company. He looked upon his fellow soldiers as 'brothers' and enjoyed the position of respect he had with them.

After supper David sent a few men led by Josh, King Saul's lead spy, to the Philistine military camp.

David and Jonathan were in conference when Josh returned. The two stepped outside the tent to greet him.

Josh removed his dark hood and shook out his curly black hair. He sat on a large rock beside the dying campfire. "We reached the encampment at sunset. Stayed hidden behind the tents. They were just turning in. We heard talking through the tent walls." Josh reached into his pouch and pulled out a fig. He split it open and brought it to his mouth.

"Well? What were they saying?" David asked, waving a hand impatiently.

Chewing on the fig, he said, "I'm sorry…we found these ripe figs on the way back…. So good!" He swallowed and said, "The Philistine army marches around Zorah every morning and evening. The soldiers in the tent were talking about it. Getting tired of marching. Just want to attack and get it over with."

David walked a few paces away from the campfire, chin in hand. He returned and said, "Who guards the encampment when they march?"

"No one."

"Are you sure?"

"Why would they?" Josh looked from Jonathan to David. "Siege warfare is exhausting, boring, and people become complacent, off their guard. They focus on the target, hoping they give up soon."

"He's right," Jonathan said. "It's why we don't do it. I hear some armies get tired of waiting and begin to dig tunnels, or ramps to the top of the walls, if they can't tear down the gates."

"We have to be sure," David said.

"I am sure," Josh said, pulling another fig from his pouch. "There was no guard."

David pressed his lips together and watched the glowing embers in the fire pit. Looking up at Jonathan, he said, "This will work in our favor. Tomorrow evening, we will be there to welcome the Philistines back to camp after their march."

The three finalized the plans for the next day and turned in to their separate tents. David crawled, fully clothed, between two sheepskins, the only luxury he allowed himself on the battlefield. The smell of fleece and lanolin comforted him and usually ensured a deep sleep. Tonight it brought him back to the childhood tents of his family's sheep farm— to carefree days in the sun, taking care of the flocks, and just embarking on his relationship with King Saul.

Those early days, playing the lyre at the King's feet, David felt belonging, purpose, and a special favor with him. The King treated him like a son, a confidant, and had allowed him to be privy to intimate discussions with advisors while strumming out background melodies. His well-chosen tunes were often helpful in calming the King's attacks of anxiety.

It all changed when he slew the giant.

Training in Gibeah, David had aspired to become another General Abner, another Captain Jonathan. He knew his military prowess would help him attain that goal. And ultimately, he hoped, his commission by God to be the next king of Israel.

But King Saul's increasing jealousy of his success was becoming a problem. His dark moods put the whole Israeli militia on edge. Many officers were willing to do anything to keep his temper at bay, even forego their own wishes to have favor with the King.

David wasn't ready to make that concession. This whole charade, being here in Zorah, was one more bow to the King's unreasonable demands. Sure, the city needed help. But now? At this time? The siege could have been waited out longer. Perhaps Zorah had a plan. Perhaps the Philistines would have ultimately given up.

This requirement to kill one hundred people at the King's pleasure was just further proof of his unstable personality and desire to keep David under his control. And it was all in the guise of giving him what he wanted: Mical as his wife. Even *that* was being controlled by King Saul. What if after killing the Philistines the King decided he wanted another dowry? What's to say he wouldn't change his mind, make yet another request?

When I return to Gibeah, I have to put an end to these mind games.

David tossed several times between the sheepskins. He finally fell into a deep sleep an hour before dawn.

During their morning meal together, David had a discussion with Josh about the lay of the land and landmarks around Zorah. He charged Jonathan with leading a group of swordsmen to hide within a gorge about twenty paces from the enemy camp. Josh was to give the signal when it was safe to advance. David would have the cavalry within hearing distance, hidden among surrounding hillocks and groves of fig trees, ready to charge. It would be a two-point strike.

"It should be quick," David said, draining his cup of tea. "We just have to kill one hundred of them."

"One hundred?" asked Josh.

David sighed. "Yes. The bride-price for Mical, King Saul's daughter. His specific request." He pictured Mical, pleading with him to ask the King for her hand, and felt his heart skip at how much he wanted her.

"So that's why—"

Jonathan broke in. "We will also be doing the people of Zorah a great service."

"Yes," David said. "Of course."

"And, David," Jonathan said turning to his friend. "It should be two hundred."

"What?"

"We should kill two hundred Philistines. I know my father. He will expect it."

"All right. Two hundred. Two hundred dead Philistines." David stood up and stretched his back. He addressed Josh. "Since you will be setting out first, eat an early supper, and have whoever is accompanying you do the same. We will follow shortly after."

Josh gave David a brisk nod.

"And Josh…collect the right sandal of each Philistine killed, so I can present them to the King."

As the sun began setting over the coastal plain and the Great Sea, many miles west, Josh and his fellow spy donned dark cloaks over their armor and trekked to Zorah. They knew they were close when they heard the uproar of the soldiers at their evening march around the city, and stole into the enemy camp, finding it empty except for a few animal tenders feeding the mules and horses.

Waiting until even those workers were out of sight, Josh gave the signal from behind a tent—three owl calls. In a few moments, he heard the rustling sound of Jonathan and his men stealing into the campsite, remaining hidden in the shadows of the tents and wagons.

It wasn't long before the clamor around the city stopped and the Philistines came trudging back.

It was time. They were unwary and tired.

Jonathan and his men rushed the enemy soldiers, striking before they could unsheathe their weapons.

Josh tossed off his cloak and joined them, drawing his sword with his left hand and driving it into the first Philistine he encountered, seated at a cooking fire. He toppled off the bench, a look of surprise on his dying face. Josh grimaced, pulled off the man's right sandal, and tossed it aside.

Looking up just in time, he blocked a blow from another Philistine. He caught the soldier's arm with a downward thrust and ran his sword through his neck, dodging a gush of blood as he withdrew it. The Philistine dropped where he stood.

As a spy, Josh had little experience with real combat, and this encounter had him shaken. He crept behind a supply wagon and paused for a moment, taking several deep breaths and waiting till his hands stopped trembling. He did his part for Zorah, but knew he had another task. Approaching a fellow soldier bent over a dying Philistine, he tapped him on the shoulder.

Evading his comrade's weapon, Josh said, "Hold on! It's me."

"Sorry!" he said, lowering his sword.

"It's okay. Here, help me get the sandals."

They crawled among the dead and dying and removed the right sandals, tossing them aside, while still dodging sword-thrusts. They came upon two of their own men, cut down during the battle, unmoving and bleeding from extensive neck and chest wounds. Josh felt bile rise in his throat and turned away.

During the melee, from the east came David and the cavalry, riding into the Philistine camp to help finish the job. Swords clanged and glanced off metal armor. Sparks flew in the night air. Blood stained the legs of horses darting through the camp.

As the fighting continued, David rode up to Josh and skidded his horse to a stop. "How many? Do we have enough?"

Josh indicated the sack of sandals. "One eighty. We need twenty more."

David frowned. *Twenty more lives.* He rode off at a gallop around the fighting. In the darkness he could make out his cavalry and foot soldiers slaying several more Philistines. He saw Josh frantically pulling off sandals and tossing them into the bag.

When he circled back, Josh shouted at him in the darkness, "One more!"

David glanced to his side to catch a Philistine running toward him, spear outstretched. Spurring his horse, he steered him into a tight turn. He held out his sword, and whacked the spear out of the Philistine's hands. Leaning into the stirrup, he plunged his sword into his neck.

"Josh!" He called and pointed his sword at the dying Philistine. "Here's your last one."

Josh ripped off the sandal and shoved it into the sack.

David sounded the call for retreat. He wasn't going to kill any more Philistines than needed. And he felt he gave the city of Zorah a definite edge over their enemy.

The Israeli army and cavalry retreated the mile to their encampment. The soldiers that had been left behind had all tents and equipment packed. They traveled hurriedly through the night back to Gibeah.

David let Jonathan take the lead on the return trip. He loosened his reins and allowed his horse freedom to travel at its own pace, head down, to the side of the columns of soldiers.

As David rode through the night, he planned what he would say to King Saul. He knew this would be a turning point in their relationship, and feared it wouldn't be well received.

14

A Royal Wedding

Two days after the return from Zorah, David was ready to talk to King Saul. He waited outside the double doors of the courtyard, holding onto a large woven sack.

He didn't care what mood the King was in. He wasn't concerned about his temper or the ever-present spear. All he knew was that he just returned from killing two hundred Philistines, the bride-price for Mical, and he had the two hundred sandals to prove it. The King wasn't going to break another promise. He would see to that.

He watched through the narrow space between the double doors as King Saul, accompanied by his servant, strolled into the courtyard from the private back room. The King leaned his ivory-shafted spear against the throne and sat down. The servant took his place behind the throne and rubbed his shoulders.

"Go left. Left! Down a little…. Now go right. More right. More! That's it…." He leaned forward as the servant rubbed a knot out of a muscle.

David passed through the doorway and approached the throne from across the courtyard. He remained bowed, ten paces away, until acknowledged by the King.

King Saul sat up and summoned David with a wave of the hand. "Why don't you come here? Tell me of your latest conquest, eh? Jonathan filled me in on some of it last night."

The celebratory supper the previous night was intimate. Family only. David had been seated next to Merab's husband, Adriel, and endured discussion about barley and wheat prices this season. Adriel was employed by King Saul as keeper of the accounts. Merab left the table early—being with child gave her a handy excuse whenever she wanted to be alone.

Mical shot David amused looks across the table whenever Adriel quoted him yet another figure. David wished he could leave the disagreeable family event and be alone with his betrothed.

Jonathan sat at King Saul's right, as usual, and gave him a lengthy account of their time at Zorah. David was grateful that Jonathan kept the King's attention, preventing any direct contact with him. He had to prepare himself. During supper, through the six courses of the meal, and enduring the repetitious monologue by Adriel, David's mind was on how he would confront King Saul the next day. Later, back in his room, he spent some time before going to sleep rehearsing what he would say to the King tomorrow. He prayed it would go his way.

The time was now. David looked up at King Saul on the throne, beckoning to him. He lugged the sack in front of him and dropped it on the tile floor where it fell open, spilling several sandals.

King Saul wrinkled his nose. The sandals smelled like sweat and blood. A few flies drifted out of the sack and flew upward.

"Count them," David said. "There's two hundred. Two hundred dead Philistines for your daughter, Mical."

"*Two* hundred?" King Saul raised his eyebrows. He turned to the servant. "Well? You heard him. Count them."

David rolled his eyes, unable to believe the King would actually require proof that there were really two hundred sandals. The servant counted them, picking them out of the sack with thumb and forefinger, pincer style, and making a pile off to the side. David reached down and began handing them to him to expediate the job.

"…one-ninety-nine…two hundred," said the servant, looking at the King.

David stood up straight and lifted his chin in triumph.

King Saul glanced at the pile of sandals and made a dismissive gesture to the servant. He bagged the sandals and took them outside.

The King shifted in his throne and leaned back into the cushions. "Well, David. Looks like you met my challenge. I knew you would come through. Now you can be my son-in-law, eh? Let's plan your wedding, oh, I don't know…maybe next year."

David was incensed. He expected this, and was prepared. "No," he said. His voice rang through the courtyard. "No delays. We wed next month."

He advanced several paces. The King sat up, alarmed, and grappled for his spear. David didn't flinch. He remained standing in front of the throne, challenge in his eyes.

King Saul held his spear upright and slowly lowered it onto David's shoulder. David held his position.

Abruptly, King Saul lifted the spear. He chuckled. "Young David. What a warrior I have made of you. Of course you may wed next month. That was my intention all along, wasn't it? Just wanted to make sure *you* really wanted it."

Alone with the King, David stepped up to the throne, closing the small gap between them. He lowered his voice and said, "You are my King, and the anointed one of Israel. But you will not come between me and my heart's desire."

He spun on his heel and strode out of the courtyard.

When he stepped out of the palace he was accosted by Mical, running to him and clasping her hands around his neck. David picked her up and whirled her around, laughing. "We wed next month!"

———————

The royal wedding was the event of the year. David's new mantle of white lambswool was accented with a black and white striped shawl, worn across his shoulders. He wore a white turban decorated with gold and silver ornaments. The straps of his new sandals wrapped around his muscular calves.

Mical was arrayed in a brilliant floor-length linen gown with close fitting sleeves and bodice. She had a headscarf of the same drapey material, topped with a gold tiara. The whole ensemble was edged in gold embroidery. Mical, Merab, and their mother had worked on it day and night all that week.

Guests were treated to a wedding banquet worthy of King Saul's legendary riches. Exotic dishes made with goose, beef, lamb, and fish were accented with vegetables and lentils. Sweet dates, figs, and other fruits and nuts were served with honey. Wine was available in large urns at every table. Members of King Saul's family, army officers and their wives, and officials from cities all over Judah made up the guests. Everyone ate and drank their fill.

David left the head table to mingle with some of the guests. He searched to see if anyone from his own clan had come. He already knew Eliab and Abinidab were on maneuvers with General Abner, but was pleased to see Rad seated with several older, well-dressed guests. He made his way to a vacant place at the table.

"David. Brother," said Rad, standing to greet him, "I hardly recognized you!" He fingered David's shawl. "This is nice."

"Ha, ha! Nor I, you," David said, "How much older you look." Rad sported a thick growth of beard and was dressed in a finely woven cloak, which reached past his knees. His sandals were shiny with a coating of lanolin. It was obvious he did what he could to look his best for the occasion.

Rad sat down at the table again. With an air of confidence, he introduced David to those seated with him— officials from the city of Bethlehem. He took a sip of wine. "Father would have come, but word of your wedding reached us only five days ago."

"I hope he is pleased to hear of my marriage."

"He bragged about it to anyone who would listen! Especially at the meeting of the elders of Bethlehem. He is one of them now."

"An Elder?"

"Yes. He's making some changes that will benefit sheep farmers and other tent-dwellers around the city. We now have a cooperative for shearing. All clans send two men to the other farms during a designated week. In that way every farm has enough workers to get the job done in half the time. Plus we don't have to pay them, as we are all helping each other."

"Is that why Nate and Ozzy…?"

"Yes," Rad said. "They were expected at the farm of our neighbor, Joab, for shearing this week. Next week it will be our turn. It's a good system."

David leaned back in his chair. "It *is* a good system. I'm glad Father is part of it. Please tell them how much I wished they had been here."

"I will." He reached into the center of the table, to a platter laden with nuts and dried fruit and made a pile of these delicacies on the table before himself. He popped a few almonds into his mouth.

"Looks like you're getting enough to eat," David said with a smile. "I had better attend to my wife."

Rad swallowed. "*Your wife*. How nice that sounds." Keeping his right hand hidden in the folds of his robe, he grasped David's forearm in his left hand. "It's so good to see you. I'm glad I came."

David returned the gesture. "I hope to visit home with Mical soon. Maybe after shearing, so Father will have more time." He stood and gazed at his brother, so grown up now, sitting with city officials, comfortable in their presence. "I am very pleased you were able to come to my wedding feast." He stepped away to join Mical at the head table.

Jonathan, seated to David's left, rose to his feet and gave a toast. "Here's to David, champion of King Saul's army." He grinned down at the couple and raised a cup of wine. "He has finally surrendered to my little sister, Mical."

Guests at all tables raised cups to join in the toast. "To David and Mical."

The newlyweds remained foolishly absorbed in each other throughout the rest of the feast. David was anxious to have his wife all to himself. Mical, trying to have a few private minutes with her new husband, was constantly interrupted by friends, cousins, and the wives of her older brothers, coming up to the head table to offer congratulations.

"What a handsome husband," said one.

"So, you've snagged the famous captain of the King's army," said another.

"Keep the cooking fire going at all times," advised a cousin.

"Where did you get these delicious pastries?" asked a friend, nibbling at a flaky pastry dripping with honey. "My sister will want these at her wedding next year."

In the end, the newlyweds gave up any attempt at having an intimate conversation, and resolved to be good hosts, knowing eventually it would all be over and they would have each other to themselves.

David gazed over the sea of celebrating guests. The Queen, Merab, and Adriel sat at the royal family's table. Merab's newborn daughter fretted unconsolably during the feast and she was ineffective in calming her. Finally her mother took the baby and hushed her to sleep. David was amused to observe Merab, his one-time betrothed, fussing at Adriel about something. She finally turned her back to him, arms crossed. *Dodged an arrow, I did.*

He eyed King Saul, seated in his ornate raised chair, looking preoccupied, fidgeting with an empty wine goblet in his hand. Without meaning to, he caught the King's gaze, at once piercing and hostile. He quickly focused on his own wine cup, in front of him. When he looked back at the royal table, the King had gone.

The next day, the couple moved into a house of their own near the city wall. King Saul offered them their own apartment in the palace, similar to the private suite of rooms given to Merab and Adriel. David, however, was anxious to be out from beneath his scrutiny and insisted they live apart from the rest of the royal family. Their home offered more privacy, and they weren't subject to the King's rants on a daily basis.

David enjoyed setting up housekeeping with his bride. Their new home was a spacious structure with a newly renovated courtyard. A less lavish version of the royal garden, it was easily maintained and planted with indigenous herbage. They enjoyed relaxing in this pleasant space and took most of their meals there, as well as using it to entertain the occasional guest. Around the courtyard were the first floor rooms—space for servants and storage, and a place to eat during inclement weather.

Above these rooms was the couple's private loft. There they spent the better part of the week following their wedding, discovering each other, lying with each other on soft sheepskin, forgetting to eat, greeting the mornings in each others' arms.

———

DURING AN EVENING STROLL IN THE COURTYARD KING Saul became a topic of conversation. Mical rested her head against David's arm. "I saw my father today."

"And how is his Highness?" David said.

She giggled and looked up to his face. "Fine. Actually in a good mood."

"That could only mean one thing," he said with a sly grin. "He's thought of another way to get back at me for stealing you away. I really don't think he expected me to be successful in his challenge."

"I'm glad you were. I prayed every day you would come back to me safely. Oh, David. I was so worried…"

She paused and leaned with her back against the courtyard wall, gazing at him. Her eyes glistened and a tear dripped down her face. David released her hand and brushed his thumb against her cheek, wiping away the tear.

He pulled her into an embrace and rested his chin on top of her head. "Coming back to you is always my top priority," he said. "I will never let you down."

15

The Secret

David's friendship with King Saul's son, Jonathan, continued to flourish. And now his good friend was also his brother-in-law. The newlyweds received a gift from Jonathan—a ewe lamb.

"To remind you of your homeland, and to keep my sister company while you are away winning battles," Jonathan said.

David, who had had enough of sheep to last the rest of his life wasn't amused by the practical joke. His wife, however, was delighted by the nimble, delicate creature and insisted it accompany her wherever she went.

David often saw Jonathan on the training fields. One day his friend approached after drills. Both mounted, they rode side by side.

"How goes it, brother?" David said.

Jonathan gave him a penetrating look. "I'm glad we have a chance to talk privately."

David raised his eyebrows and gave a nod. Jonathan stopped his horse near a cluster of thorn trees and David did likewise.

A long moment of silence stretched between them. The horses rested, heads down, occasionally flicking an ear at a fly. The sun was setting behind them, bathing the sky in shades of pink and orange. David held his peace, waiting for his friend to speak.

Finally, Jonathan said, "It's my about my father. He's been in one of his moods again."

David sighed. "Oh, that. I'm used to that."

Jonathan looked sharply at him. "No. Listen, David. I had to take him seriously. This time he talked about killing you."

David wheeled his horse around to face Jonathan. "Why? What have I done? All I do is win battles for him and bring him the spoils. Why does he hate me?" His tone was angry, but he really felt wounded at the King's animosity toward him. "Can't you talk to him…?"

"I *have*. I reminded him of how you killed Goliath the Philistine, when you were just a boy. It was the beginning of our edge over the Philistines. I told him that you risked your life for him then, and you continue to serve him now, winning battles with the help of the living God."

Jonathan urged his horse on. They rode slowly along the edge of the practice field. "I begged him not to hurt you, an innocent man, one who has been on his side from the beginning, and who obviously has favor with God."

"What did he say?"

"He broke down and said he promised he would not harm you. He said he would call off the one he hired against you."

"He hired someone to kill me?"

Jonathan nodded slowly.

"So what's the problem? He's threatened me before. Remember, I told you about the time he threw his spear at me? It was after our victory against the Philistines. I've learned how to avoid him." Offhandedly he added, "I'm not worried about it. He's just blowing smoke."

David looked into the distance and gnawed his lower lip. Despite the bravado, his face was drawn with apprehension.

Jonathan, mouth set, observed David. "I just don't trust him. Don't forget he married Merab to someone else after he promised her to you."

"A blessing in disguise. But I know I can't take him at his word. I'll be careful."

"That's all I ask. I don't want to lose my brother-in-law before you produce at least one child for me to tease!" Jonathan spurred his horse and rode off at a gallop.

"Hey! Not fair!" David called out, urging his horse into a run. The two enjoyed a lighthearted moment, chasing each other. One of few during the arduous business of training for war.

David walked his horse cool after the run with Jonathan. He stabled it and headed home, head down, deep in thought. He entered the walled courtyard of his home and observed Mical, and the servant, Lydia, bringing food to the table.

"Lydia. Leave us," he said.

Lydia scurried to an inner room. Mical glanced at David with questioning eyes.

He paced across the courtyard, turned back, and said, "I hear your father, the King, has threatened to kill me. Did you know about this?"

"I…I don't—"

"Well—you need to talk to him, Mical. Tell him to leave me alone. Tell him all I want to do is continue to serve him loyally as one of his officers. Like Jonathan. Like Abner. He has to stop threatening me."

"I can't tell him that," Mical said. She looked sidelong at him as she filled cups on the table with wine.

"Or *won't* tell him."

She turned to him. "Really? Why would he listen to me, anyway? I think I've had three real conversations with him my entire life. He doesn't listen to me, or…or anyone."

David dropped into a chair. He picked up a cup of wine and rotated it in his hand. Quietly, he said, "I think he's jealous of me."

She sat down across from him. "Jealous of you? Why would he be jealous of you?"

"Oh…it started with that song the women sang during the victory parade a year ago."

"Hm. I remember that. '…David has killed his ten thousands.' My father hates anyone being thought of as better than him."

King Saul's jealousy was a product of David's success—no master has an easy time seeing his apprentice overshadow him. But David wondered if there was more to it. Did the King have a premonition about his future and the future of his dynasty? Did he view David as a contender for the throne?

Maybe it was time he told Mical about becoming the next king of Israel. As his wife, she should know, for she would be part of it, and it may help her better understand his own ambition, and the danger he faced at the hand of King Saul.

David was silent for a moment, indecisive. Should he tell her? Should he reveal his secret, his destiny, his mission? Since he had been anointed the next king of Israel at age eleven, his father and the rest of his family kept the information confidential. No one outside of the family knew. Not even Jonathan. Or her.

He had a strong feeling that this was the time. He longed for someone to talk to about it, and wanted to take her into his confidence. Then she would be united with him in his goal, as God intended for married couples.

"That's not the only reason," he said, focusing on the pattern of the wine cup in his hand. "There's something I need to tell you. Something that might explain your father's bitterness toward me." He took a sip of wine. "I'm…I'm going to be the next king of Israel."

There. He said it.

He was still looking down at the table when he heard Mical's reaction. She was laughing.

"Oh! Oh…David," she said, her eyes merry. "You had me there. You—king? Good one." She dipped her wedge of flatbread in the sauce and nibbled at it, still smiling.

He felt his heart sink. He looked at her, his face earnest. "No…really. It's true. I was anointed the next king of Israel as a child, by the prophet Samuel. He came to our tents. He said the next king was to be a son of Jesse. I'm the youngest son, and he anointed *me*."

Mical looked up from her meal, a bite of flatbread halfway to her mouth. "What? Are you serious? Not one of my brothers?"

He shook his head.

"Why? How? How do you know?"

"It was so long ago that the prophet came. He said God would prepare me to be the next king of Israel as I grew up, and that it would happen in *God's* time, and according to *His* plan."

She remained silent.

"You…you believe me, don't you?"

"Y-yes. Of course."

She poured herself more wine and took a few nibbles of food, lingering over her meal. He watched her closely.

She put her cup down and looked at him. "But why are you just telling me this now?"

David sighed. "You don't understand. Sometimes I go weeks without thinking about it. And when I'm with you… getting to know you…you're all I thought about."

Mical chewed slowly as she digested this information. "And my father is jealous because he knows this?"

He shook his head. "No…No. At least, I never told him. I've had to keep it a secret. Just my family knows. And now, you."

"Jonathan?"

"I haven't told him yet. I don't know if I will."

She leaned forward. "Well, I'm not going to tell my father. Don't worry about that. He'd probably throw his spear at me."

David smiled gently. "I won't let him harm you."

He reached for Mical's hand across the table, and took a moment to admire the soft skin, the shiny fingernails. He looked up and gazed into her eyes. "Becoming the next king of Israel has been my destiny for many years. It's something I've learned to live with. Sometimes it's a burden, and I don't really feel prepared for the task."

"It probably won't happen for a long time."

"Right. And when I feel unsure of myself, I remember what the prophet said to me the day he anointed me: '*Man looks on the outward appearance, but God looks on the heart*'. I know that God saw something in me that will make a good king. He will help me fulfill my calling in His time."

They finished their meal and Mical summoned Lydia to clear up as she and David went to bed in the upstairs loft.

As he lay next to his wife, he felt as if a heavy weight was lifted from him. He was glad he confided in her. It was a relief that someone else knew his secret. And as his wife, it was important she was privy to his destiny. She would be part of it.

He lay, thus, listening to her regular breathing. He turned to her and wrapped his arms around her, nuzzling her hair, his eyes closing. The next thing he knew was bird-song and the bright light of morning coming through the bedroom window.

16

Plotting and Scheming

Mical saw David out the door in the morning on his way to work. She handed him a basket of food for his mid-day meal, then turned to a project she had been working on with Lydia.

"I don't know, Lydia. I thought these tapestries would work to cover the window, but now I think they are too heavy."

Lydia lifted the thickly folded cloth, weighing it in her hands. "Yes, this is heavy. And too dark. You would like curtains to let in a little light, no? How about the striped linen you got for your wedding?"

She retrieved the thinner fabric from the storage room. It was a soft white with narrow grey stripes. Mical had been planning to use it as a new tunic for David. As she unfolded it and held it up a beam of sunlight shone pleasingly through it.

"This will work. Good idea, Lydia. Let's try it out over the window near the door." The women cut a square from the fabric and stitched all four edges. They hung it on a taut rope strung above the courtyard window on pegs. Standing back to admire the new curtain, Mical clapped her hands. "I can't wait to show David when he comes home."

After the project, the two had their afternoon meal together. "I'm glad they let you come with me when I got married," Mical said to Lydia. "Since David only allowed me one servant, it's a good thing it's you."

"I'm glad to help. I had so much free time on my hands when I was just your maidservant in the palace. It's good to feel useful and needed, no?"

Mical laughed. "Oh…you are that. Definitely needed."

Lydia cleared the table and busied herself with some other work in the house. Mical remained in the courtyard and reclined on a soft woven rug, her head on a pillow. Her pet ewe lamb, kept in the courtyard, joined her on the rug, cuddling up to her and placing its head in her lap. She worked her fingers into the fleece on the lamb's head and gave it a scratch. As Mical rested she had time to think.

She recalled the strange and unexpected conversation she had with her husband last night. The future king of Israel? She still couldn't believe it. And yet she knew it was true. David was always honest with her. He wouldn't have made this up. And why? No…it had to be true.

That being the case, Mical smiled as she imagined herself queen. That would mean she could move back to the palace. Sometime. In the future. But all the same, it was something to look forward to. This spare existence her husband insisted they live was at first a novel experience. But now she missed the luxuries and convenience of palace life. It would be nice to get back to it.

Just as she was picturing herself in her old suite of rooms, she saw a shadow on the new curtain draped across the courtyard window. She stood up and edged to the window, creeping closely against the wall. She lifted the corner of the curtain and peered out, alarmed to see a pair of turbaned men seated beneath a thorn tree across the street. They were just sitting there, in the shade, watching her house, curved swords at their sides. A third joined them, crossing the street away from her house.

Mical fled into the inner rooms, startled by what she saw.

When David came home from work that evening, Mical immediately pulled him through the courtyard doorway and into an inner room.

"What are you doing?"

"Shhhh," she hissed. She opened the door a crack and peered out, surveying the courtyard, before turning back to David. "Did you see those three men outside when you came home?"

"Outside?"

"They were sitting under the thorn tree across from our house."

"Let me have a look." David quietly re-entered the courtyard and crept toward the window. He looked out through a slit of space between the curtain and the window frame and saw the three men under the tree. They appeared idle, seated together in a conspiratorial group. Probably waiting for a chance to jump some poor soul who ventured near in the dark of the coming night.

He drew back and checked the courtyard door to make sure it was locked, then returned to his wife. "Was that curtain always there?"

"No," she whispered. "Lydia and I made it today. But that doesn't matter." She was sitting on a stool before a washing stand. David leaned against the doorway. "This afternoon I sent her out to wander near those men and see if she could hear what they were saying. She took the lamb out for a walk and when she came near them, she overheard them talking about you." She looked up at him. "They were bragging about their plan to jump you when you left for work tomorrow morning."

David paced the length of the room. "Jonathan warned me something like this may happen. It's your father. Remember yesterday when I told you he was threatening me? He must have hired those jackals to attack me. I should have known he wouldn't call it off."

He turned to face her. "We have to think of a plan."

Mical was plotting already. "I know. We'll go to upstairs to bed like usual. We can't act like we suspect anything. You'll have to escape after nightfall. It's the new moon—dark enough so no one will see you." She stood up and grasped his arm. "Oh, David! If you don't get away tonight, you may be dead in the morning!"

After an uneasy supper, they ascended the ladder to their loft bedroom. They spoke in hushed tones, making plans, promising to wait for each other. They prayed together:

> *Deliver me from my enemies, O God;*
> *be my fortress against those who are attacking me.*
> *Deliver me from evildoers*
> *and save me from those who are after my blood.*
> *You are my strength, I watch for you;*
> *you, God are my fortress,*
> *my God on whom I can rely.*

Psalm 59

They dared not sleep, but remained watchful until all activity in the city ceased. Finally, in the small hours of the night,

David strapped on his sword and stole out of the upstairs window. He paused and held his wife for a brief moment, breathing in the scent of lavender in her hair and clinging to her slight frame.

Releasing her, he asked, "Sure you will be okay?"

"Of course. I can look after myself." She pressed her lips together and smiled sadly.

He thought a moment. "If your father comes, tell him it was my idea to leave. Tell him…tell him I threatened you if you wouldn't help me. I don't want him blaming you for my escape."

He kissed his wife a final time. She braced a rope against the window frame and, just before lowering him into the back alley, said, "Wait! Where will you be?"

"With Samuel," David whispered harshly as he disappeared into the darkness. She returned to bed to await the dawn.

Lying awake in bed, Mical's thoughts raced. *What if those men come in the house early in the morning. If they don't find David here, they'll run him down, probably catch him! I have to buy some time…*

Glancing around, her eyes lit on the life sized plaster statue in the corner of the loft, a wedding gift from Merab and Adriel. She rose from bed and slid the statue under the covers, where David slept. Locating a cushion covered with shaggy brown goat's skin, she arranged it on his pillow, and it became a passable substitute for the back of his head, in the early morning light, at least.

She crept down the ladder and into the courtyard. Trying to appear casual and unconcerned, she strewed a few wisps of hay on the ground for the lamb and picked up a piece of embroidery to work on. The first rays of morning sunlight illuminated her work space at the table.

Before long, there was loud rapping at the door and three armed men barged into the courtyard.

The lamb bleated and Mical shot up out of her chair. "What do you think you're doing? Why are you coming into my house at this hour?"

One of the men approached, a sneer on his face. "Hey, little lady, don't get all worked up. We're just looking for your husband, the captain. Isn't he going to work today?"

"Well," Mical huffed, "If you must know, he's sick. He's still in bed. And don't…don't you disturb him. Or you will answer to the King." Involuntarily, Mical glanced toward the upstairs loft.

"Come on!" said the ruffian, pushing his way past Mical. The three men ascended the ladder, swords drawn.

The pounding in Mical's chest created a rushing sensation in her ears. She crouched down against the courtyard wall, clutching the lamb against her. Would they discover her ruse?

After a moment, the men came back down the ladder. Without a word they exited the courtyard and made their way down the street in the early morning light.

Mical waited. She had a headache and longed to go back to bed. She hoped it was over, but dared not let her guard down. When she checked upstairs, after the men left, she found everything undisturbed. Would they be back?

She attended to a few household chores to keep her mind from racing, and prepared herself a light breakfast. She shooed away the sparrows that descended to the table, searching for crumbs. David enjoyed enticing them into the courtyard and feeding them millet and bread crumbs, but she thought they were dirty, and waved a linen napkin at them till they took wing. Finally, unable to eat much, she picked up her needlework again and sat near the window where she could watch the street.

An hour passed before a knock at the door revealed King Saul at her threshold. She leapt up to greet him. "Father, why did—?"

He pushed past her and mounted the ladder, followed by the three armed men from early that morning. Mical hurried up behind them just in time to see her father throw back the covers of the bed, a dagger raised in his hand.

"What's this?" He spied the statue hidden beneath the covers and turned to face his daughter. "Where is he?" he said, eyes darkened.

He began crowding his daughter into a corner of the loft. Spotting the dagger still in his hand, she knew she had to think fast.

Backing away, Mical said, "Oh, Father! David…David threatened me. He said he would kill me if I didn't help him escape. I had no choice!"

MEANWHILE, DAVID RAN THROUGH THE NIGHT WITH A heavy heart, wondering if God had forgotten about him. He was heading north, toward Ramah, to see Samuel. It had been over ten years since Samuel anointed him the next king of Israel. Full of self-doubt, David had to see the man who commissioned him for his life's work.

17

"It All Began with Donkeys."

David appeared, travel-worn and breathless, at the prophet Samuel's doorstep shortly after sunrise. He had run the entire twelve miles to Ramah, and, regrettably, had woken a few other households in the village before finally locating Samuel's house.

Samuel welcomed him to his home with open arms and open heart, and led him into the main room. A fire burned in a pit in the center of the space. The air within was dense, as the only exit the smoke had was two small windows high up on the wall.

The prophet lived a spartan existence. Niches in the thick dried mud walls housed food staples and cooking vessels. A rolled-up sleeping mat leaned in a corner; next to it was a basket of fuel for the fire. Thick woven rugs around the fire beckoned to David.

"Sit down. Sit down," Samuel urged, waving his arms at the haze in the house "It's not so smoky near the floor."

"Thank you, my friend," David said.

"You're just in time for breakfast." Samuel offered a basket of food to him.

David reached in and withdrew a few dates and a wedge

of flatbread. Samuel poured tea for them both and took a seat on the rug across from him. They ate in silence.

"It took me a moment to recognize you," Samuel said, at length. "You have grown so tall, so old. How long has it been? About ten years since I first met you near Bethlehem?"

David drained his cup of tea and sat back on the rug, finally sated. "Eleven years."

"Ha ha! You were such a little mouse back then."

"I've been living in the palace for six years, now, since I killed the giant, Goliath."

Samuel chuckled. "I heard about that. Quite a feat. I hope that proved to you how much God's favor is upon you. I know at that young age you had doubts."

David gazed into the smoldering embers before him. "I did…I still do, sometimes."

Samuel stirred the fire with a branch, sending sparks upward. "Remember what I told you when I anointed you at your father's tents? *Man looks on the outward appearance, but God looks on the heart*'. God knows you have what it takes to be King."

"I remember…but it's been so long ago. I just wonder when—*if* it will ever happen."

"Why?"

"Well, in the first place, King Saul *hates* me. He's trying to kill me. I don't understand it, but that's why I'm here, to get away from him. One day he acts like he's my friend. Next day he's moody and jealous, yelling at me and threatening me with that spear." David paused. Quieter, he said, "He gave me Mical in marriage."

"That dark-haired beauty?"

"Yes." David's lips pressed together in a sad smile. "And last night she helped me escape through the upstairs window. There were men across from my house waiting to attack me. King Saul sent them."

Samuel gave a surprised look.

David nodded. "Yes, King Saul. My wife overheard them planning to jump me this morning. That's why I had to leave last night."

He fell silent. He was thinking about their night together, hiding, frightened. Was it was only hours ago that he took comfort in the sweet smell of her skin, her warmth? What was she doing now? Was she safe?

He got up abruptly. "I have to go."

With effort, Samuel rose from the rug and intercepted David at the doorway. "Wait a minute. What are you doing?"

"It's Mical. I have to make sure she's okay." He pushed his way past Samuel and out to the street.

Samuel caught up with him several paces from his home. He reached out and clutched his cloak. Wheezing, he said, "Don't…don't go back just yet. You said the King is going to kill you."

David turned and stood quiet before Samuel. He let out a deep sigh, dropping his shoulders and gazing at the ground.

Samuel leaned forward and looked up into his eyes. "What makes you think he would welcome you back with open arms now? You don't want to make your wife a widow. You're just newly married!" He tugged on David's sleeve. "Come back. You want her to be safe? Seems the best idea right now is to stay away." David allowed Samuel to lead him back to his house.

"I just wish I understood why King Saul treats me like I'm his enemy," he said as he and the prophet got comfortable by the fire again. "All the battles I've won, and my loyalty, don't mean anything to him." He peered at Samuel.

"Was he always like this?"

"What, moody and unpredictable?" Samuel said. "No. Not always. You don't realize it, but the Spirit of God fell upon you—when you were anointed king—because it left him. He used to be the same as you. Ambitious. Passionate. Godly. Then he made some stupid decisions, and pride got in the way."

"When was that?"

Samuel laid a finger against his chin. "Well…one time King Saul was on the battlefield and got tired of waiting for me to offer the sacrifice, so he did it himself. A job only a qualified priest should do.

"Also, he would ask me for God's directions before he went to war with anyone. But then he wouldn't do what God required of him. Like the time he went to war with King Agag of the Amalekites and failed to annihilate the entire population of people and animals. They were an idol-worshipping lot who had some very depraved ideas of what could be done in the name of their religion. God wanted the entire evil influence wiped out.

"But King Saul spared some of the women. And the best animals, too, claiming they were for me to use as sacrifices to God.

"I told him 'to obey is better than sacrifice'. But he wanted to do his own thing. And as a result, the Amalekites are a still a scourge in our side to this day."

Samuel got up, retrieved a few camel chips from a basket in the corner, and tossed them into the fire pit. He then reclined on the rug again. "I find a fire to be soothing to my achy limbs and aesthetically pleasing. Most around here use one only for cooking twice a day. I try to keep mine smoldering all the time."

The prophet looked into the glowing fire, at the occasional blue flame that licked up stray bits of straw.

He began his story. "It all began with donkeys."

"Donkeys?"

He laughed. "Yes, *donkeys*. Saul was a young man at the time. He was living in the land of Benjamin. His father sent him to search for some donkeys that had run off from their farm. That's how he came to Ramah. Looking for donkeys. He heard that I was living there, that I was a seer."

"A 'seer'?"

"Yes. It's an old-fashioned word for 'prophet'. You know, because prophets can 'see' into the future. So I was called a 'seer'. Saul thought I might be able to tell him where his donkeys went. By now, it had been a couple days since he left home. He figured his father had ceased caring about the donkeys, and started worrying about what happened to him. So Saul was quite anxious to find them and return home.

"At about this time, I received a message from God that a man from the tribe of Benjamin will come searching for me, and that I am to anoint him king. You see, up till that point, Israel had no kings. Judges ruled the land. I was actually the last Judge. But ever since the Ark of the Lord had been stolen by the Philistines, the people wanted a ruler to lead them in victory against their enemies."

David broke in. "Hold on, when was this, when the Ark was captured? I seem to remember it vaguely, in history lessons I endured as a child. Sadly, I didn't pay attention as well as I should have, so I'm a little unclear as to the details."

Samuel sat up on his rug and warmed his arthritic hands near the hot embers. "Well, that's going back a ways. Back to when I was a little boy. You probably know that I served the priest Eli in the Temple since I was about two years old. Back then we worshipped in a stone building, which also housed the Ark. The curtain walls and structures of the original Tabernacle had been dismantled and placed in storage.

"My mother was barren, and she prayed to God for a son. She promised God that she would give that child to Him to serve in the Temple if He answered her prayer. That's how I came to live with the priest Eli since I was a little child. I was the baby that opened her womb. I ended up with five sisters and brothers, so God really blessed my mother when she kept her promise. They visited me yearly in the Temple, but I never returned home.

"As a young man, I realized that Eli's sons were corrupt and were stealing from the treasury. There were also rumors that they were sleeping with women outside the Temple walls. It grieved Eli, so he trained *me* to succeed him as Judge of the land.

"At this time, also, Israel was at war with the Philistines. When we were finally defeated, someone came to Eli's house and told him. They told him that his sons were killed in battle and the Ark of God was stolen from the Temple by the enemy. Eli was so shocked by the news that he fell over backwards and broke his neck! He had been Israel's leader and spiritual advisor for forty years, and now he was dead and Israel defeated."

David absorbed this amazing account for a moment. "What happened to the Ark?"

Chuckling, Samuel said, "That's an interesting story in itself. No one wanted it. Everywhere it went, it brought bad luck and sickness. You see, the Philistines didn't understand its significance. They didn't realize that God's very presence dwelt between the wings of the gold angel statues on the lid of the Ark. They didn't know about the stone tablets of the ten commandments or the pot of manna stored within. The Ark had power, amazing power. Not because of the objects, but because of Who inhabited it. That's why it's always kept in the most secluded part of the temple. The Philistines just thought of it as a favorite relic of those they defeated, and took it out of spite.

"At first it was taken to the Philistine city, Ashdod, and placed in the temple of the false god Dagon. In the morning, they found that the huge stone idol of Dagon had fallen down before the Ark. The people raised it back up. The next morning, it had fallen again and broken to pieces. Then the people of Ashdod began to develop tumors and boils. The plague affected everyone. The council of the Five Philistine Cities met and decided to move the Ark to Ekron. Then to Gath. Everywhere it went, people developed tumors and many died. They were scared to death of it."

David said, "Gath. Hmm. That's where Goliath was from. What irony."

"It is. Seems we've come full circle with our enemies, doesn't it?" Samuel stroked his long white beard. "The funny thing is how we got the Ark back. The rulers of the Five Cities called upon their priests to advise them how to get rid of it. It was decided they would place the Ark on a cart along with some gold offerings. Two milk cows were yoked to the cart and allowed to leave town, on their own. If they traveled down the road to Beth Shemesh, towards Israel, then the Philistine council agreed that the plague had indeed been brought upon them by the God of the Hebrews. If the cows wandered any old way, they felt it was all a coincidence."

"Where did the cows go?" David asked.

"Why, they went straight down the road to Beth Shemesh, lowing loudly all the way! As if someone was driving them there. Of course you know someone was—God, Himself. There was great celebration along the road as the Ark of God returned to Israel.

"Now that brings us to why the Israelite people wanted a King. Since Eli was dead, I was the Judge, and operated in that capacity for many years. I took to visiting all towns in Israel and Judah on a yearly basis. Then I would return home, to Ramah, and hear cases here, too. It was a good system."

"What changed?"

"Well, like I said, ever since that war with the Philistines, there was talk about having a king. I think the people felt they would be more protected with a kingdom, instead of trusting in God for their protection. I got the go-ahead from God to find them their first king. I warned them, however. I told them if this happened, their sons would be drafted into his army. They would be heavily taxed and have to turn over part of their property for use by the King and his officials. They would lose much of their freedom. Stupid—they still wanted a king."

"Is that when you met Saul?"

Samuel nodded. "Yes. That takes us back to the donkeys. Saul approached me that morning. I recognized him immediately from what my housekeeper had told me—she was a great gossip and somehow always knew what was going on in town. She said he stood head and shoulders above all others, and that he was extremely handsome, with flowing black hair and an impressive beard.

"Before Saul could speak, I told him that the donkeys had already returned home. I also told him that he was the basis of Israel's hope—the first anointed ruler of Israel. He knew, like everyone else, about the talk of finding a king.

"He was astonished, and protested, saying, 'I am only from the most insignificant family of the tribe of Benjamin, the smallest tribe in Israel.' I told him it wasn't up to him, or me, but that *God* had picked him. I hosted a fancy dinner party for him with many other important guests. You must remember, I didn't always live such a meager existence. When I was the Judge, I lived large. Being a mere prophet doesn't pay as well. But back then I was both.

"The next day, Saul prepared to leave, still somewhat in a daze from all that happened. I detained him. I poured the anointing oil on his head and told him he was to be the king of the great nation of Israel. Our *first* king. He returned back to his hometown a changed man, full of God's Spirit. But as I instructed him, he told no one what had happened."

David peered at Samuel. "I don't understand. How did he start being King? When did he take the throne?"

Samuel sat with eyes closed, resting his arms on folded legs, tired from the extensive narrative he had just delivered. Feeble in his old age, he sat, thus, for a few minutes.

David got up, lay a blanket across the prophet's back, and gently rubbed his bony shoulders. He then fetched two earthenware cups he spied on a shelf and filled them both with water from a nearby jug. He offered one to Samuel, before seating himself again on the rug.

Samuel took a sip of water. "Thank you, son…I'll tell you. I'll tell you how Saul began to rule. Eventually, I called a meeting of representatives from all the tribes of Israel. I announced that since they continued to press me to appoint a king, we would do it God's way—by casting lots. You know the old saying, 'Man may cast lots, but God determines the outcome.' We had to do it this way because no one but myself and Saul knew he had already been secretly anointed king. This way all would believe it was God's will, which it truly was, and not just my own choice.

"So we cast lots for the tribe which the new king was to come out of. I knew what would happen, of course. The tribe of Benjamin won. Then we cast lots for the clan within that tribe. Saul's clan was chosen. At this time, we assembled all men from his family. They all traveled here in great anticipation to have one of their own appointed king. The lots were cast. They settled on Saul, of course. I was not surprised. But I *was* surprised when we were not able to find him! 'Lord', I said, 'Where is he?'"

"Where did you find him?"

"Ha, ha! Among their baggage. He was *hiding*. We finally found him behind a camel loaded down with tents and blankets and coaxed him out. This beautiful young man, head and shoulders taller than all else, was hiding, he was so uncertain about his new calling. He was then brought before the company and hailed King. That's how it began."

David smiled. "I find it difficult to picture him hiding."

"I think he had doubts, too, David. Like you."

"Yes, I do. Especially when he is trying to kill me." He let out a heavy sigh.

Samuel lay down on the rug. He was tired and fading fast. In a sleepy voice he said, "But don't you understand, David? Don't you know why he's trying to kill you?"

"No, that's what I've been saying...."

"Because...because even though he doesn't know it, he *feels* it. That *you* will be the next king of Israel. His hatred toward you comes because he knows his dynasty is at an end. So you see, young David, it's all in God's plan...God is in control."

As Samuel slept, David thought about what he said. He *will* be king. King Saul feels it, and fears the end of his reign. It made sense now. David determined that he would start living his life in preparation for when he would rule. He promised himself that he would always look to God for guidance, and leave behind the faithlessness of his youth. He prayed:

> *Search me, oh God, and know my heart.*
> *Test me, and know my anxious thoughts.*
> *See if there is any offensive way in me.*
> *And lead me in Your plan for my life.*

Psalm 139

In this purposeful state of mind, David lay down on the rug by the fire, and slept, not knowing that his pledge to himself would soon be challenged.

18

Return To Gibeah

───────◆───────

Strengthened in body and spirit, David lived with Samuel in Ramah until the next new moon, hoping it was enough time for King Saul to cool down.

It was different, living with Samuel. Feeling conspicuous in his flashy robe, David sold it at the marketplace to help provide for Samuel's daily needs—food, firewood, wine. He wore his tunic and a cast-off cloak Samuel gave him. He also got used to eating simpler meals, enjoying lentil and barley stew, and flatbread spread with honey. He and Samuel rose with the sun and went to sleep at sunset.

Samuel invited David to travel with him to sacrifice at the Tabernacle, now set up in Nob. Still in hiding, he declined. He kept busy at the house, cooking simple meals, or sitting outside, weaving rushes into the mats Samuel sold at the marketplace, or sprinkling crumbs for pigeons to snatch up.

As weeks went by, however, he longed to see his wife and ensure her safety. It was maddening, not knowing, and he soon began preparing to make the journey back to Gibeah. Surely the King will be over his bad mood by now. It should be safe to return.

That afternoon, Samuel came home visibly shaken.

Out of breath, he wheezed, "David…son…you must leave at once." He began shoving him toward the door.

"Hold on, why am I leaving?" David said.

"King Saul…King Saul's army is in Ramah…They came this morning. I heard about it at the marketplace. I heard they came looking for *you*." He pressed a parcel of food into David's hands. "You know the first place they will look is here. That's why you have to leave. *Now*."

David was silent. *How did King Saul know?* His heartbeat quickened. He would have to be on the run again.

He crept to the doorway and peered out. Exhaling deeply, he observed no one there. Yet.

His eyes darted around the room until he located his sword hanging on a peg. He lifted it down and fastened it around his tunic, beneath the cloak. He glimpsed the vial of anointing oil hanging there on its peg, and touched it gently, taking a second to pause and remember…When he turned back to the prophet he said, "How can I thank you for your kindness? You have not only sustained me physically, you have boosted my morale spiritually. I am now ready to lead the country of Israel as the next king."

Samuel reached his hands up to David's shoulders and looked into his eyes. "Don't forget what I told—"

Just then, the rhythmic sound of marching soldiers reached them through the windows. Pushing David toward the door, Samuel said, "You must leave now. They're coming!"

Once again, David was saved just in time by someone who cared for him. He crept out of the front door, and dashed around to the back of the house. He lost himself in the busy streets of Ramah, glad for the simple garments he wore that helped him blend in.

He decided to return to Gibeah. He must find Jonathan. Jonathan would know King Saul's next move.

A late season thunderstorm hindered David's progress south for a few hours. He sought refuge from the rain in a rocky cleft in the hillside. Waiting, he thought up another psalm:

> *I love you, Lord; you are my strength.*
> *The Lord is my rock and my fortress.*
> *I will call on the Lord, who is worthy of praise,*
> *For He saves me from my enemies.*
>
> *God opened the heavens and came down;*
> *Dark storm clouds were beneath His feet.*
> *Mounted on a mighty angel, He flew,*
> *Soaring on the wings of the wind.*
>
> *The Lord thundered from heaven;*
> *The Most High gave a mighty shout.*
> *He shot his arrows and scattered His enemies;*
> *His lightning flashed and they were greatly confused.*

Psalm 18

Once the rainstorm ceased, David returned to Gibeah as unobtrusively as possible. Instead of going home to Mical— she always makes such a fuss—he sought out Jonathan, the only man he could trust.

Skulking through the alleyways of the royal city, he thought maybe it was time to take Jonathan into his confidence. Maybe he should tell him his secret about becoming the next king of Israel. But how would he take it? He knew Jonathan was in line for the throne. It might anger his friend, make him feel he would never get the chance to rule. Telling

Jonathan would expose the fact King Saul's dynasty will end because of him. And Jonathan may turn on him, causing him to lose his only friend and ally.

Still conflicted, he crept aside the palace garden wall and watched for Jonathan within the shadows. At length, he saw him stride across the portico, heading toward the stables. David stepped up and met him there.

"Get away. I have nothing for you." Jonathan said, taking him for a beggar.

Removing the coarsely woven cloth covering his head, David revealed himself. He held his arms out wide. "Nice way to greet your brother-in-law!"

"David?"

David shot him a broad smile. "The one and only."

"My brother! Where have you been?"

David glanced behind himself, then back to Jonathan. Drawing him into the shadow of one of the great pillars, he lowered his voice and said, "In hiding. You remember that night you told me your father hired someone to kill me? Well, it was true. He didn't call it off."

"I found that out later, much to my shame."

"What? No, you're not to blame. You warned me, and with Mical's help I escaped that night. I've been living with the prophet, Samuel, in Ramah."

"That explains the new dress code," Jonathan said with a smile.

David laughed gently. "I've just been learning to live more simply."

"Tell me you've been to see Mical already. She's been sick with worry."

"No. I needed to see you first. I had to leave Ramah because the King sent soldiers to look for me there." He grasped his friend by the arm. "Help me, Jonathan. I can't run from King Saul forever. There must be a way to appease him…"

"My father isn't still seeking to kill you. His purpose in going to Ramah was probably just to bring you back home. If he meant to harm you, I think he would have told me. He keeps me informed of all his movements."

"Are you joking? He wouldn't tell you that. Don't you see? He knows we are friends." His voice caught. "I feel as if I am only a step away from death and here you are trying to make me believe everything is okay."

Jonathan murmured soothing phrases and placed a supporting arm around his shoulder. "I will do whatever you need me to do. Now, come with me." They stepped off the portico and walked toward the stables. "I was on my way to get my horse. We can talk more privately there."

Once there, David took a deep breath and let it out slowly, through pursed lips. "On my journey back here I gave this a lot of thought. Here's what we should do—tonight, when you and your father are at the New Moon feast, I'll be at home with Mical. If he notices me missing at the table, and asks you about it, tell him I had returned, but had to leave again to go to Bethlehem for our annual family reunion. Tell him I asked your permission. If he's okay with that, then I'll know I'm safe. But if he gets angry, I'm sure it will be because he had further plans to do me harm, and wanted to use the activity of the feast as a distraction to capture me."

"Good thinking. With you gone, he'll feel it's another lost opportunity."

David looked at his friend earnestly. "Please don't turn me in, if we do this. Don't tell him where I really am."

"Of course not. But where will you be?"

"With Mical, like I said. Then tomorrow night I'll hide behind that big mound of boulders in the old training field. You know it's hardly used anymore, so it's all overgrown, and no one will see me. Notify me there of what happened."

Jonathan gave instructions to a groom to ready his bay stallion for training that day. As the groom saddled the horse, they stepped outside. "Listen," he said. "After the New Moon feast I *will* come to the training field to talk to you. However, my father may have someone watching me, especially with you missing. He may not believe the story about you going to your home town. He's so paranoid—he might think I am harboring you. I have to be careful. I don't want it discovered I've been communicating with you."

He paused, thinking for a few minutes. "I know. I'll give you a sign. The morning after the feast, I'll go out to the field to practice archery. Since it's something I do every day no one should be suspicious. If I shoot the arrows beyond your hiding place, you will know that I am alone and I'll be able to tell you what happened at the feast. If I shoot them on this side of the rocks, that is, between me and you, It's because I'm being watched, and will have to meet up with you some other time. So listen carefully."

David nodded.

Jonathan gazed up into the distance, past the great archway leading out of the palace grounds. "I hope I will be able to give you good news. My father's hatred toward you will be his undoing. And I won't stand by while he destroys you." He turned to David and grasped his forearm. "I would be losing my best friend."

The groom appeared leading Jonathan's horse. Jonathan took the reins and walked the horse away from the stable,

David keeping pace beside him, his face once again hidden behind the head covering.

"There's something else I have to tell you," David said.

"Okay?"

"It's…I…Do you have just a few minutes? Can we sit down somewhere?"

Jonathan draped the reins over a low branch of a thorn tree and they sat on the ground beneath it.

David pulled up a few blades of grass and twirled them around his fingers, silent for a moment. "I've wanted to tell you this for a long time, but didn't know how," he said. "You know I'm always honest with you. I value our friendship, and respect you as the King's son. What I'm trying to say is…"

Jonathan nodded, keeping silent.

"I'm going to be the next king of Israel." He held his breath, waiting for his friend's response.

"Hm. I am aware of that," Jonathan said with a smile.

David's heart skipped a beat. He let out a sigh. "Mical. She told you."

"She did. But don't be angry with her. She was worried about those ruffians who wanted to attack you—they were still hanging around, maybe hoping you would come back—so I stayed with her a few nights until they left. We talked… and she confided in me."

David's eyes narrowed. "Who else did she tell?"

"No one. She knows how important it is. And she doesn't want our father to know." Jonathan's voice got quiet. "She's afraid for your life."

"Me too." David was still for a few moments, looking into the distance. He observed a troop of soldiers coming back from drills to stable their horses. It was time to go back into hiding.

Before rising from the grass, he looked at Jonathan with raised eyebrows and said, "Are you okay with it?"

"What, me?" Jonathan said, getting onto his feet. He thumped David on his back. "I don't want to be king. I'd rather be leading the army. That's my calling. And if being king is yours, I shall support you with my whole heart."

David watched him mount his horse. His throat tightened and his eyes grew moist. What a gift. What a gift it was to have such a loyal friend. He hoped someday to have the chance to repay his generous spirit.

"I have to see Mical," David said, "I'll be at our meeting place tomorrow night."

He walked briskly toward his house, keeping in the darkness of the backs of buildings on the way. He was anxious, eager even, to see his wife. To hold her. To spend the night in her company. How excited she would be to see him. And yet…she broke his confidence. How could she betray him so casually? He hoped she didn't tell anyone else, and hurried home to make sure.

As David stepped through the door of his courtyard, he upset an ivory vase on a pedestal positioned just inside the entry. Mical, startled, sprang from an upholstered bench, spilling her needlework basket. She gawked at him, taking in the overgrown beard that nearly hid his face, and his hair, tangled and dirty, falling across the shoulders of his shabby cloak.

"Mical, it's *me*," he said, picking up the vase and setting it back in its place. He noticed a few changes had taken place during his absence. His wife had decorated the courtyard to more closely match the palace she grew up in. The opulence of wall-hung tapestries, marble statues crowding in each corner, and a table laid with golden serving-ware seemed overdone.

"I know it's *you*. Why did you stay away for so long?" She bent down to pick up her needlework things. Placing the basket on the table, she remained turned away from him, her back stiffened at his offence.

"What? I was *hoping* it would give your father time to cool off. But it seems he's still after me." He reached out and touched her hand.

She jerked away, and spun back toward him, eyes sharp with hurt. "Well, he's been asking me every day if you've returned, or if I know where you went. Do you know how stupid I feel, that I don't even know where my own husband is?"

"Where do you think I was?"

"I don't know. Maybe you have a mistress somewhere. Maybe you were with her." She crossed her arms. "You don't know what people say."

"What people say? You of anyone should know about what people say. What about what *you* said? What about that?"

She peered at him, eyes questioning.

"About me becoming king of Israel…"

She shook her head.

"…to *Jonathan*."

"Oh…that."

"How could you? Don't you know how important it was to me that you kept what I said between us? I wanted to tell your brother when *I* thought it was time. That wasn't up to you." He looked at her pointedly. "Who else did you tell?"

"Who else? No one. I'm not stupid. I certainly understand how to keep quiet. And of course I don't want my father to know. Think I like the idea of being a widow?" She took a step toward him, her resistance foundering. Voice softer, she said, "I just told my brother because…because…I missed you. It was hard, you not being here. I just needed someone to talk to."

Someone to talk to. He could believe that. She liked to talk. And she talked about everything. At least it was only Jonathan she told, and not anyone else.

She sniffled and swiped a tear from her cheek. He reached out and enfolded her in his arms. "I'm sorry, my lamb. I'm sorry I wasn't here for you. I only stayed away so long to avoid your father." He held her for a few moments, relishing the way she felt, soft and warm.

"So…where were you?" she said into his shoulder.

"You don't remember? I told you when I left. With Samuel. In Ramah."

"Oh, David, I don't know where that is. I was so worried," she said, taking a step back and looking up at him. "You could have been anywhere. The neighbors…they said all kinds of things. Mean things. And my mother, and Merab too."

He sighed. "I was there the whole time. Learning to live a less complicated lifestyle. And learning how better to trust God with my destiny. *Our* destiny. I would never be with another woman. I thought about you every day I was gone. I only want to be with you."

They stepped into the inner room, behind the courtyard. After a light supper they retired to the privacy of the upstairs loft.

In time, in the quiet twilight of that evening together, Mical relaxed and behaved as the woman David fell in love with—cheerful and positive. As he washed up, she told him the local gossip and the latest goings-on at the palace. She told him how much she missed him and had prayed for his return.

She told him how King Saul, when he finally calmed down a few days later, allowed her to explain why she helped him escape that night—having learned there were men looking to attack him. Then she pleaded with her father to stop trying to hurt him.

"So you *did* talk to your father for me," he said with a gentle smile.

"Mm-hm."

He gazed at his wife as they lie on the fleece mattress, and she looking longingly into his deep brown eyes. Now that his hair and beard were combed, and the dust and sweat of the day washed off, he was much more appealing. He held her close and felt the familiar curves under her light linen garment. His mouth found hers and they lost themselves in each other.

They spent the next day upstairs. Mical gave Lydia the day off and she and David lounged in bed together, talking in hushed tones. He told her of the plan he and Jonathan had. "If I have to leave again, your brother will come and tell you."

"I hope I don't see him. I hope *you* return to me instead," she said. "Oh, David, why does it have to be like this? You have done nothing to deserve my father's anger. Why is this happening?"

David stroked her chestnut hair and tried to remain optimistic, despite his own misgivings. At length, he said, "My lamb, as Samuel the prophet says, it's all in God's plan. We have to trust Him. He is in control. He's appointed me to an important mission and He will help me accomplish it."

Mical sat up and grinned. "Yes. And I can't wait! Then you will be king and I will be queen. We can move back into the palace and enjoy our riches."

David's smile faltered. Is this what she thought it was all about? "Yes…But my main purpose is being a godly leader and ruler to our people. I'm not really worried about riches. I've learned to enjoy living with less."

"Well, you may be used to it," she said, "but I like having a lot of gowns and different kinds of food to eat. And servants. You don't know how hard it is doing all the work myself."

"I know, I liked all that too. And we shall have it again. I'm just saying a lavish lifestyle shouldn't be our main goal. We both have to answer to God and do the work He has called us to do."

19

Jonathan's Sign

————◆————

While David was spending time with Mical, Jonathan attended the New Moon Feast. He hoped to determine his father's true intentions about his best friend.

He took his usual place at the feast table, to the right of his father, who was at the head. David's seat, on Jonathan's other side, was conspicuously empty.

King Saul and his guests feasted on roast peacock and lamb. Salmon was brought at much expense from the Great Sea and served stuffed with quinoa mixed with an assortment of spices. Cold cucumber salad drizzled with vinegar was also served. As usual, wine was available at every table.

King Saul did not mention David's absence that first night. He was enjoying the entertainment at the feast. Scantily clad maidens danced to the music of flute, harp, and cymbals. They skipped around the table and caressed the King's face and shoulders as they passed by.

A mock battle took place during the feast in an adjoining room. Troops of actors dressed as Israelite and Philistine soldiers rushed each other. Of course the Israeli army was completely victorious over the Philistines, who all ended up dying very dramatic deaths. After the scene, all actors rose and bowed to great applause from the guests at the feast.

On the second night of the feast, after the first course, King Saul gazed over the length of the long table. He addressed Jonathan, indicating the empty seat next to him. "I don't see David at the table," he said. "I know he's back from his visit with Samuel. My spy—I mean—I heard from my wine taster before dinner."

Jonathan swallowed a generous gulp of wine and wiped his mouth with a napkin. "He *was* back. But when I saw him yesterday, he said his father wanted him to come to a reunion with family from all over Judah. He asked my permission to go to Bethlehem. I know he hasn't been home in a few years, so I said it was okay." He hoped his rehearsed speech had a ring of truth.

King Saul clenched his jaw. He slammed his fist on the table, causing several cups of wine to spill and all conversation at the table to stop. The guests stared at the confrontation unfolding before them.

He stood to the full height of his impressive stature and glared down at his son. "You dare allow that jackal, that *rival* of mine, to escape to his home town? Don't you know he's planning to take the throne from us? Why do you think he's so successful with his troops? He's secretly forming his own army to start a revolution. As long as he is alive, our dynasty will always be in danger." Spittle sprayed from King Saul's mouth as his voice became more strident. "You are shaming our royal house by not turning him over to me. It's time to choose a side."

Jonathan tried a calm approach. "Father, he has no desire to overthrow your rule. He has been loyal and…"

The King snatched up the spear he always had handy. Jonathan knew by the look in his father's face, the way his eyes became black as deep wells, that he was in danger. He'd seen it before, on the battlefield. When his father rode down the enemy. Just before impaling them with his spear.

He sprang from his seat and backed away from the table. On the defensive, he watched his father for his next move, taking in the most subtle shift in stance.

Someone at the table made a loud gasp.

In one fluid motion, King Saul raised the spear and hurled it. Jonathan leaped out of the way and sprinted through the dining hall. As he ran he could hear his father's voice resound through the palace, "You no good son of a harlot! You'll never be king!"

———

AFTER SPENDING ONE NIGHT AND MOST OF THE NEXT day with Mical, David made ready to go to the old training field to meet Jonathan. It was the second day of the New Moon Feast, and David expected him to arrive possibly tonight, or early the next morning. He hoped to learn what King Saul said when he didn't arrive at the feast. Would he be welcomed back to the palace? Or would he be on the run again? He donned a simple tunic and wool cloak and prepared to leave.

Mical tried to detain him by first crying, and then arguing, and finally pouting. David knew if he delayed he might not leave the comfort of his home and the company of his wife in time. But he had to leave, he had to speak to Jonathan and determine where he stood with King Saul.

In the end, Mical packed a basket of food for him and tucked a linen napkin she had embroidered around the food. David accepted the basket and hurried away amidst her tearful goodbye.

He spent that evening hiding behind the grouping of large boulders at the edge of the old overgrown training field, waiting for Jonathan. Several small stunted trees and bunches of tall grass grew near the boulders, providing cover. Jonathan didn't appear, however, and David had to spend a lonely night outdoors.

Waking up at dawn, he found himself wet with dew, leaning back on the rocks. In his half-awake state he experienced a moment of confusion. Then he began remembering. He recalled his conversation with Jonathan and how he was in hiding, awaiting a sign from his friend which would direct his next move.

He gnawed a piece of bread and took a last swig from the jug that he brought to sustain himself while waiting. He fingered the piece of embroidery his wife gave him and held to his lips—*it has her scent.* Hopefully he would be able to return it to her soon. Reaching for his belt he realized why something felt off—in his haste to leave his wife amidst her tears and attempts to make him stay, he forgot his sword. It would be too risky to try to get it now, but maybe it wouldn't matter, if he was able to go home soon. Nonetheless, he felt at a loss without it.

The sun rose to the middle of the sky and David's mood changed from anticipation to impatience, irritated that after nearly a whole day of waiting Jonathan hadn't arrived yet. He dozed in the warmth of the sun against the rocks. As shadows lengthened the raucous call of several ravens woke him, and he watched them land nearby to peck at insects on the hard, dry earth. They flew away when he stretched out his legs, settling onto a small bent tree.

As he sat watching them, the birds abruptly took wing and soon David heard Jonathan's voice.

"Okay, Daniel, when I shoot the arrows, you go and fetch them. Make sure you watch them fly—I don't want to lose them."

A small voice said, "Yes, your highness."

David listened, hypervigilant. He crouched behind the rocks and waited. He heard a hiss in the air and saw the arrow land far beyond his hiding place. Then he saw two more flying past. His heart leapt. This meant Jonathan would be able to talk to him about what happened at the feast. He hoped and prayed it would be good news.

He heard the sound of running—the short, light steps of a child—and saw the boy pass, slow down, and, with eyes cast down, search the ground for the arrows.

"Keep going, Daniel, they are further, past where you are. Go find them."

Jonathan appeared around the boulders holding a finger to his lips. "Let me get rid of the boy." Tramping to where he was searching, he helped him find the three arrows, and then sent Daniel back to town with his weapons.

David rose and greeted Jonathan. He saw the sadness in his eyes and knew it would be bad news.

Jonathan reported what happened at the New Moon celebration. "I told him what you said, that you went to a family reunion in Bethlehem."

"How'd he take that?"

"Not good. He grabbed that spear he always has with him, and threw it at me, saying I let you escape. I think he truly hoped to strike me. You'd think me being his son would mean something, but it doesn't. Did I ever tell you about that incident with the honey?"

David shook his head.

"It was one of the times we were at war with the Philistines, years ago. Even before you came to live here. I was leading my men through the woods to return to Gibeah after our victory against one of their divisions. I was so hungry, I was feeling faint, and so were all those with me. There was some honey dripping down from a beehive up in a tree, so I tasted it, and encouraged my men to eat some, too, as just that little bit of sweetness revived me. One of them told me he heard my father had made an oath that no one was to eat anything until nightfall, until our victory over the Philistines was complete.

"When my father found out I ate the honey, he said I must die!"

David shook his head. "I am not surprised."

"I'm certain he would have had me killed if my men hadn't rescued me." Jonathan leaned back against the boulders. He was silent for a moment, looking down at the scrub at his feet. "Last night, when he threw his spear, my father said he knew you were trying to start an uprising and take the throne from our family. He said our dynasty would be at an end because of you."

Wary, David glanced at Jonathan. "I already told you as much. Except, of course, the bit about starting an uprising. Gaining the throne…that will come at a time God appoints. It's not up to me."

"I know. I know. What I mean, is, *he* knows. He is suspicious of you, and views you as a rival. You have to be on your guard at all times."

David took a moment to absorb this. "Samuel said as much to me not long ago. He said it is all part of God's plan." He paused. "I just wonder how he knows."

Jonathan shook his head. "Maybe just his paranoid nature. But the point is, he may not rest until he triumphs over you." He grasped David by the shoulders and looked into his eyes. "Don't let him find you. *Be careful.*"

David nodded solemnly. He reached down for the basket from Mical and took a step away from the mound of boulders. The two friends strolled quietly to the end of the old training field. "I don't really know where to go," he said. He lifted his eyes to the sun on it's way to the Great Sea and spotted a lone stork in flight. Maybe a good sign.

"Before you leave," Jonathan said, "let's make a pact. Between you and me. And God."

"Yes, a pact."

They were both silent in their thoughts.

Finally, Jonathan said, "May the Lord always be with you. And with me. May you treat me with the faithful love of the Lord as long as I live. When I die, may you treat my family fairly, with love and compassion. And I will do to you likewise."

They grasped each other's right forearms in agreement.

David said, "And may the Lord destroy all our enemies." The two friends embraced in farewell. When they broke away, Jonathan returned to the city. David started out in the opposite direction, trudging away from the Gibeah with a heavy heart.

PART TWO

20

The Sword

━━━◆━━━

Journeying south seemed automatic for David. South was Bethlehem. The tents and pastures of home. It was drawing him—calling to him. His hurried departure from Gibeah left him without the basic essentials for survival in the Judean countryside: food and a weapon.

He formulated a loosely made plan—he could gather the needed supplies from home and continue traveling from there. How good it would be to see his father, mother, and brothers again. Maybe he could visit for awhile…

David cut through recently harvested barley fields to avoid the main roads. He gleaned what he could from fallen stalks. As he chewed on raw barley, he began to think better of his plan to return home. He practically gave his position away when he had Jonathan tell the King about the supposed family reunion. Why didn't he give some more remote region as his excuse for not being at the feast? He should have been more careful. King Saul would think nothing of sending armed guards to his hometown, to his father's tents, to capture him. Remember Ramah? No. He needed another strategy.

By evening he was nearing the town of Nob, halfway between Gibeah and Bethlehem, where the Tabernacle was now situated. From a distance he could already see the great surrounding curtain wall glowing in the setting sun. He approached the entry curtains—beautifully embroidered in red, gold and azure—feet dusty and weary in the sandals. A servant detained him.

Taking a deep breath, David said, "I wish to speak to the high priest."

The servant, bored at his uneventful daily post, murmured, "And you are?"

David looked at him through half-closed eyes. With effort, he straightened and said, "I am David. Captain of King Saul's army."

The servant raised an eyebrow at the figure before him, clad in simple garments, lacking any weapons. He ushered him through and bid him sit on one of several benches just within the entrance.

The grandeur of the great altar and building of The Holy Place shook David from his lethargy. He inhaled the scent of the daily burnt offering filling the sky with smoke ascending to heaven. Sweet incense drifted to him from The Holy Place, the building that stood beyond the altar. Gazing around, he felt protected within this enclosure and wished he could just rest here for a while.

Several priests, busy with daily duties, were unmindful of David, seated in the shadow of the curtain walls. He sat, thus, observing the activities, remembering the last time he came to sacrifice here, during his early years in Gibeah. It seemed so long ago now.

Soon, David was aware of the High Priest, Ahimelech, passing the altar and stepping toward him. He recognized the white turban surrounded by a circlet of gold, and the Ephod, a colorful vest worn over a long tunic of sky blue.

It was fronted by the Breastplate, an arrangement of twelve precious stones, signifying the twelve tribes of Israel. Tiny bells hung from the hem of the tunic, allowing the High Priest to be heard as he worked in the Holy Place.

David stood up and approached, bowing deeply. "I am David. Captain of King Saul's army."

Ahimelech lifted his chin and paused for a moment. "David? You don't look like you're with the King's army. Where's your armor? Your weapons?" He glanced toward the entrance and waved an arm. "Or troops?…Tell me who you really are." He stood with arms crossed over the breastplate, gazing down at him, waiting.

David hesitated. He didn't expect this. "It's *true*. I *am* David. I left in a hurry. That's why I appear unprepared."

Ahimilech took a step back. The tiny bells on the hem of his tunic tinkled.

He tried to think of how he could make the high priest believe him. "Ask Samuel. The prophet."

"Samuel?"

"Yes. I spent a month with him recently. He knows me."

"Hm. I worshipped with him last week. He told me of King Saul's captain staying with him. So, that was you?"

David let out a sigh. "Yes. Me."

Ahimilech waved a hand again. "Well, in that case, please tell me: why are you here alone? Where are your troops?"

David hedged. "Like I said, I had to leave quickly. But it's only because I'm…I'm on urgent business for King Saul."

"Urgent business?"

"Yes, a covert mission." He gained confidence as his story took shape in his mind. "And I need your help. *King Saul* needs your help."

"King Saul? Of course. How can I help his Highness?"

"Well, you can give me some food…for…for my men. For when they arrive to meet me. And a weapon. A spear or a sword. I left so abruptly, I left my sword. I'll need about ten loaves of bread and whatever else you have to give me—*us* to eat."

Ahimelech thought for a moment. "I have bread, but it's the holy bread, reserved for the priests. I will let your men have it…*only* if they haven't been with women for at least three days."

"Of course. My men are all business. They don't frolic with women when they are on assignment." David faltered briefly, remembering the night he just spent with his wife. But these were irregular times. He hoped God would understand the break in tradition.

Ahimelech left to get the bread.

While he was gone, an Edomite named Doeg was led through the entrance. He wore a black cloak and turban. His eyes, shaded by the turban, were hard to see. David tried to sidestep him.

Doeg turned toward David and asked, his voice harsh, "Where's the priest? I came for the ceremonial purification. He said he would be here…"

"He's here," David answered. "He just went to get me something."

Doeg stood around waiting. Ahimelech returned with a large basket full of flatbread, and a long object wrapped in a blanket.

"Here it is. Freshly baked. I hope this is enough bread for your men."

David reached out and grasped the basket of bread with both hands, mouth watering at the comforting scent of the warm bread.

"And this is the only spare weapon I have. You should be able to recognize it—it's the sword of the giant you slew as a young man. The sword of Goliath the Philistine."

David fell silent. He set the bread aside and accepted the weapon. He unwrapped it and pulled the sword out of the leather scabbard. Large as it was, the sword was not unwieldy, as when he first held it as a youth of sixteen. And it wasn't a thing of beauty—no, not this sword. This was a weapon of business—an efficient and powerful weapon. Although it was a bit tarnished from years of storage, he felt he could polish it and bring out the honest color of bronze of which it was made. He hefted it. It felt good in his hand, heavy and dependable. Yes, this would do. It would definitely do.

David was delighted with this unexpected find, and felt it was a good omen. "This will serve me well. There is nothing like it!" Bowing, he said, "I—and his Highness, King Saul—thank you." He passed his belt through the two slits in the leather scabbard and sheathed the sword. It felt good, suspended there against his leg. He could feel it as he moved, and the weight of it was reassuring.

After gathering the basket of bread and his other belongings, David said a final "thank you" to the high priest and turned toward the entrance. While exiting, he caught sight of Doeg, the Edomite, eyes like slits beneath the turban, watching him leave.

DAVID'S NEXT OBJECTIVE WAS TO GAIN ALLIES. He thought about gathering a group of supporters to help protect him against King Saul. But how would that help against an army of thousands? And how could he trust any of his countrymen to aid him once the King put out an order to capture him? They would turn him over to the King for a reward.

His only chance was to get support from other countries and make friends with some important officials as a way of protecting himself from further attacks by King Saul. His travels over the next two days took him west, to the land of the Philistines. King Saul would never think of looking for him there.

King Akish of the Philistines resided in Gath, one of the Five Cities, and may prove a valuable friend. David hoped he could convince him that since he was a fugitive from King Saul, he was no longer a threat to him. It was a reach, he knew, and he wasn't lost to the irony of seeking help among his enemies. But he was desperate.

A servant clad in a shiny blue robe left David seated on a bench in the large reception room of the palace in Gath. He gazed around the elegant space. It was sparely furnished, but each chair and bench was crafted of rich fabrics and ornately carved wood. The servant disappeared around a corner into the King's throne room and David relaxed on the soft upholstery as he heard himself being announced.

The next thing he heard made his blood run cold.

It was King Akish saying, "Isn't this the Captain David of whom they say, 'Saul has killed his thousands, and David his ten thousands' after a victory against *our people*? The gods have brought him to us. Arrest him!"

I've got to get out of here!

David sprang from the bench and whirled around, searching for the door by which he entered. He strode to the door and yanked it open, only to be met by a well-armed sentry. He shoved the door shut and spun back around to find four armed guards coming his way. His eyes darted to the exit behind him, and back to the guards advancing rapidly.

He was trapped.

His weapon was hidden outside—he had not wanted to appear a threat to those in the palace by bringing it with him. Now he wished had it. He would be no match in hand-to-hand combat against this group of well-trained men, who were now a mere five paces away. He imagined himself a prisoner in the chains they held in their hands.

Not waiting another second, David dropped down on all fours. He roared like a lion, baring his teeth. Everyone jumped back. He sprung onto one bench, still on all fours, and then onto another. Lunging for the door, he pounded at it. The sentry burst through the doorway, his weapon drawn. Quicker, David attacked him, scratching and biting. Before he could escape, however, the sentry fled back outside, slamming the door behind him.

Back down on the floor, he looked up to see King Akish, himself, gawking at him from the throne room entry. David shook his head and gave a mighty roar.

"What do you think you're doing, bringing me a madman?" King Akish said to his men, who by now all had their backs pressed against the wall on the other side of the room. "This person is obviously deluded, saying he's 'Captain David'. Get him out of here! Don't I have enough crazy people in my kingdom already?"

The guards opened the door and threw David out into the street, where he continued his charade until out of their sight. He then fell, weak from laughter, against a tree. *Wait till I tell Mical about this one.*

Mical. The sudden thought of her made him pause. When will he get the chance to tell her? His exile had just begun. His mood somber, he continued through the city, and eventually reclaimed his belongings, hidden among the foliage near the city wall. He sat on the ground and leaned back against the stone wall of a cistern as the sun set, casting an orange glow across the city. The evening breeze soothed his sunburnt arms. Exhausted from his travels and his experience at the palace, he went to sleep as night fell.

Before long, he heard Mical calling for him, bidding him walk with her in the cool evening air, something she always loved to do. She was leading him by the hand, her fine linen gown drifting against his leg.

His eyes sprang open and he shook his head, orienting himself. In the dim morning light, he glanced at his legs outstretched before him, and discovered that the basket was upended and the embroidered cloth from Mical draped on his leg. He reached for it, smiling, and brought it to his face.

The small memento of his wife cheered him, and he clutched it, feeling her with him in spirit, urging him on with her positive outlook. Focusing on his journey, he got up and packed his things together. He took a generous bite from a loaf of flatbread, filled his jug at the cistern, and buckled the sword of the giant more snugly around his waist. He strode out of the city gate and headed east, to the hill country bordering Philistia and Judah.

After a day's journey he secured a base camp for himself in the caves of Adullam.

21

The Caves of Adullam

────────◆────────

David's stomach rumbled as he crouched by the fire at the entrance of the cave. He had to eat. He had been staying in the cave for a week, and the bread he brought from Nob had long run out. He could no longer subsist on the sparse edible vegetation and herbs he was able to find—he had to go hunting.

The sword, as excellent as it was, wasn't suitable for catching wild game. A sling would serve him well. He tore a strip of cloth from the hem of his robe. It was about a cubit in length, as long as his arm from shoulder to tips of fingers. He wound a third of both ends with strong dried grass and left the middle free, forming the pocket of the sling. He located a few round stones in the arid soil near the cave.

Excelling in warfare with sword and bow, David had set the sling aside along with his youth. Today, he returned to it. A few practice shots at a small tree were successful. Now, to try a moving target.

Reclining by the campfire at the mouth of the cave, he had noticed lizards and rodents emerging in the evenings. There were also large scavenger birds and the occasional wild goat. As he waited, a few birds landed, one with the remains of an unidentifiable animal in its talons. The three birds took to fighting over it, each grabbing it in turn. They eventually settled down to a grudging feast of carrion, nipping at one another from time to time.

Occupied thus, the birds were unaware of the sling David swung at them. One shot and they were flying away, leaving their precious meal behind. He scurried out of the cave and examined the meat they were eating. A few tufts of soft fur remained on it—perhaps at one time it was a desert hare. The meat smelled fresh, so he decided it was worth saving, and set it aside carefully in a basket.

Looking out of the cave, David spied a young wild goat nibbling at scrub. He aimed his sling at the goat and, mercifully, downed the animal with one swift shot. He offered up a prayer of thanks as he slit the goat's neck with the sharpened tip of his sword, draining the animal of blood, in keeping with rules of Kosher eating.

He built up the fire a bit. Those days hanging out with his brother, Nate, as a child proved to be useful at last. He taught him how to make an excellent fire out of practically nothing. After skinning the goat he placed it on two forked sticks raised above the fire, allowing the animal to roast slowly.

The fresh meat the birds left could be prepared another way. He walked a half mile to a stream, filled his empty jug with water, and returned to the cave. Earlier that week, he had fashioned a bowl out of the clay he found near the stream. After letting it dry in the sun for a day, then baking it in the fire, it became a useful vessel to drink from, and even make a sort of tea by placing crushed herbs and water in it and heating it on the fire.

This would be just the thing in which to cook the meat. He covered the meat with water, added a sprig of herbs, and placed the bowl in the heart of the fire. Once it boiled for several minutes, David enjoyed the stew of unknown meat. Kosher? Probably not. Rabbits and hares were not. But his hunger was finally sated, and he was able to await the roasted goat with less impatience.

By sunset, the next course of his meal was finally done. He carefully lifted the goat from the forked branches and used a sharpened stick to separate the meat from the bones. He nibbled at the hot, dry meat, and found it satisfying. After he ate his fill, there was enough meat left for a couple more meals. He placed the leftovers into the basket and tossed the hide and the few bones into the back of the cave. His stomach full, he lay next to the fire in the waning twilight and fell asleep.

In this way, hunting and scavenging, he sustained himself for several more weeks, well into the dry season.

DURING THE EARLY WEEKS IN ADULLAM, DAVID ENJOYED the quiet solitude. The tension that had built up in his relationship with King Saul was exhausting, as was trying to dodge the King's efforts at harming him. Here, alone in the arid wilderness, he felt at peace. In limbo, he spent time in prayer and reflection.

> *Praise the Lord with melodies on the lyre;*
> *Make music for Him on the ten-stringed harp.*
> *Sing new songs of praise to Him;*
> *Play skillfully on the lyre and sing with joy.*
>
> *The Lord merely spoke,*
> *And the heavens were created.*

He breathed the word,
And all the stars were born.
He gave the sea its boundaries
And locked the oceans in vast reservoirs.

Psalm 33

David wished he had his lyre with him. Since that day King Saul attacked him with his spear, he was loathe to return to the throne room to retrieve his instrument. He pictured it, sad and forgotten, beneath a pile of cushions, or shoved behind one of the great tapestries that hung to the floor. How he would enjoy playing it now, while he had the time, and while he was undecided as to his next move.

Since he did have an abundance of free time, he thought he would try to craft a lyre out of the rough materials he had at hand. First, he searched the area for branches of suitable thickness, strength, and shape. He remembered a grove of olive trees near the stream. Olive branches were curvy, sturdy, and had lovely patterns in the wood. He broke off several branches and found two that were curved like the horns of a cow.

He stripped the bark from the branches and placed them on the ground, curving inward, with the bottom of the branches touching. The tops of the branches were separated from each other about a hand's breadth, and he connected them with a straight stick. He wound fresh sinew around the three branches that formed the frame of the lyre.

After a day of allowing it to dry in the sun, the sinew had tightened around the instrument, making it extremely sturdy. Dried sinews and tendons of the wild goats he killed were also useful as strings for the lyre. He suspended five strings between the connecting straight stick and the lower portions of the curved branches. He tuned it, and after a few hours' worth of experimentation with tension on the strings it sounded just right.

Making music was one of David's delights. He was pleased with his creation and spent many evenings writing songs and practicing his skill. Having left his box of writings back in Gibeah, he worked at remembering his favorites, like the one about God being our shepherd, and re-wrote them on flattened rolls of bark. It was his way to connect with God. In his songs were his prayers.

He reached out to God for guidance. Ambivalent, he knew he needed a plan, a timeline, some kind of strategy for reaching his goal—that of becoming the next king of Israel. This meant he had to live long enough to attain that goal, meaning he had to stay out of King Saul's way. He couldn't return to the royal city of Gibeah just yet.

Did reaching his goal mean waiting for God to show him what to do? Should he look for a sign? Or maybe God expected him to formulate his own scheme. He was starting to feel restless, just sitting around. He wanted to *do* something. He prayed, and waited for God to answer.

ANOTHER WEEK PASSED, AND DAVID SPENT YET ANOTHER evening seated near the mouth of the cave, playing the lyre and watching the sunset. He was feeling the effects of living by himself for an extended period, and at times loneliness overtook him. He began talking to the birds that visited his cave in the evenings, partaking of the scraps he offered.

"So you're back," he said to one he recognized by the broken wing feather that stuck up over his back. "Hope you like roast hare." The bird cocked its naked red head at him. It squawked and returned to the scraps, pecking at its companions who tried to share the food.

"Hm," he continued. "So you don't want to talk. Just want to eat. Not even a thank you for providing your meal." He situated himself more comfortably on the ground. The birds didn't shy away—they were used to his movements by now.

"Well, I'll try to have wild goat for you tomorrow. I need to start eating more Kosher anyway." The birds finished their meal as night fell. David lay down on a mat he had woven of rushes and went to sleep.

As he slept he dreamt—deep vivid dreams of his wife, his home, and his days training with Jonathan. The dreams of Mical were welcome, and sometimes he tried to stay asleep so he could be with her for a longer time. His body ached for her, and he missed their spirited conversations, and the way she said "Oh, David—" when she had something important to say. He hoped she was safe, and happy. How long has it been? Two months? He dared not try to contact her lest King Saul find him.

He imagined King Saul was still looking for him with the might of his many soldiers. Even after that month being gone in Ramah, when he stayed with Samuel, the King had sent them to capture him. And from what Jonathan said that last day in the old practice field, the King felt he had reason to distrust him and was suspicious of him starting a rebellion. David knew it wasn't true. He continued to respect the presently anointed King, and had no desire to overthrow his rule. He just wanted to bide his time until God directed him to act.

The next day he woke to a steady rain falling. This was a welcome change. His escape from Gibeah took place at the beginning of the dry season, so there was very little rain during the past weeks, with longer and longer periods between showers.

The creek from which he was getting water was running low. Underground springs and wells would have to suffice soon. But this morning, the sound of rain was soothing, a promise of grass and plants growing, which would attract goats and hares, ensuring he wouldn't starve. For now.

Looking around himself, David thought about the low he had sunk to: subsisting on scavenged meat, hiding, skittish, in a cave, and undecided on his next move. What kind of king would he be?

Samuel's words came to him: *"Man looks on the outward appearance, but God looks on the heart."* Good thing, too, as he had less resources at his disposal now than ever. He was doubtful God could make a king out of him in this condition. Did God even remember him?

That evening, he sat, as always, watching the golden orb of the sun sink past the horizon. He looked out over the wilderness before him and detected hints of green sprouting in many places thanks to the recent rain. Resting his head on his forearms, crossed over drawn-up knees, he looked down and observed the leather straps of his sandals were split and in need of mending. Just another sign of his destitute condition, like the frayed hem of his tunic and his tangled hair and beard.

Laughing bitterly, he wondered if all this was in God's plan, too. The palace, numerous feasts, trim military uniform, and well-groomed appearance all seemed a lifetime away. Was he ever to return to that lifestyle?

Lifting his head, he looked to the side and caught sight of the sword in its sheath, propped against the wall of the cave. The sword of the giant. He had such hopes back then, when he was victorious. He was the hero. He was popular. He had potential. And now? Hiding in a cave? He was obsolete. Useless. Forgotten.

David lay down before the dying cooking fire. Dejected, all he wanted to do was sleep. A breath of wind blew across the cave entrance, murmuring comfort, whispering peace. He slept a profound and dreamless sleep.

22

Reunion

———————

David awoke with the sunrise. The early morning sun shone off smooth stones and sprouting vegetation and cast oddly shaped long shadows across the land. Faint birdsong and the fresh scent of the recent rains greeted him as he stretched stiff limbs and rose from his woven mat. His depressed mood of the previous evening was lessened a little in the promise of the new day.

Maybe today he would hear from God. Maybe today there would be a sign.

While performing a few housekeeping tasks—collecting something to build a fire, clearing the cave of detritus, praying—he heard talking. At first he wasn't sure. Who else would be inhabiting this wasteland?

He scurried to the back of the cave. The voices were becoming louder and seemed to come from several people. Deep voices of men and a few lighter, younger voices, as well as the scuffing sound of animal hooves on the stony ground, and the braying of a donkey reached his hearing. He waited in the dimness, taking quick shallow breaths and staying very still.

The procession walked by the mouth of the cave. David unsheathed his sword and crept forward a bit to observe men in light colored knee-length robes and donkeys laden with overflowing baskets. He heard snatches of conversation.

"…around here somewhere…"

"How much more should we look?"

"I feel like we'll be finding him soon…"

Was someone was looking for him? They didn't look threatening, and something about their voices sounded familiar—an accent he recognized.

Finally, he stepped forward and revealed himself, sword in plain view.

One of the men came near. "David?"

"Who's asking?" he said.

The man tossed his head to allow his headscarf to fall back, and stood with arms crossed. "Nathan, of Bethlehem."

"Nate!" David exclaimed, and assaulted his brother with a vigorous embrace, nearly toppling him.

Nate grasped David's wrists and held him at arm's length. He gazed into the intense brown eyes. "It *is* you, little brother. We've been searching for you for days." At that moment a much older Ozzy and Rad joined the reunion.

David beheld the faces of his brothers, a broad smile forming on his lips. He shouted and ran around the assembly, his feet joyously beating the rhythm his heart felt at the sudden appearance of his family. The last few weeks of isolation were devastating, and here, as in a dream, were his brothers.

Returning to them, they all started speaking at once. As David listened, he was conscious of how much they had changed. Ozzy gained a few more pounds. He wore a leather headband around his dark curly hair. Rad, always the best-groomed of the brothers, wore a light brown robe that reached nearly to his feet. The matching headscarf covered reddish-brown hair that fell long over his lean shoulders. Nate had grown out of his extra weight and was the tallest and fittest of the brothers.

"Nice place you have here, Dave," said Ozzy. "Aren't you going to invite us in?" He play-punched David in the shoulder. David blocked a second strike, and landed one at Ozzy's midsection.

"Living in the desert hasn't dulled your reflexes any, I see," said Ozzy, rubbing his belly and smiling.

David grinned. He turned to see Nate approaching, holding the hands of two boys aged about seven and eight.

"You remember my sons, Caleb and Obed," Nate said.

David reached out and ruffled both boys' hair. "Obed. You know you were named after my grandfather?"

The taller boy nodded.

"I haven't seen you two since you were about this high." He held his hand, flat, at knee height. "You resemble your father. I hope you don't give him any trouble."

"Caleb does. I never do," Obed said, pointing a thumb into his own chest. His remark earned him a poke in the ribs by his younger brother.

"Okay, boys, go and help unpack. We're staying with Uncle Dave for a while," Nate said.

"What…what do you mean?" David said. "Is that why you're here?"

"What did you think?"

"I thought maybe you were on a trading journey…"

"Are you joking? I told you, we were looking for you," Nate said. "Your wife sent word to Bethlehem two weeks ago that she was still waiting for you to return. She was worried something happened. Is it true King Saul has a price on your head?"

David led the way to the cave entrance, Nate and Ozzy following. The rest of the company busied themselves in unpacking. "I didn't hear it that way, exactly, but he is trying to kill me."

"Why?"

"Jealousy. Insecurity. He may have figured out I'm to be the next king. He thinks I intend to overthrow him. He's mad as a wounded lion, thinking his sons won't succeed him, that his dynasty will end. So he's trying to get me out of the way. His actions are dictated by his moods, which change day by day, sometimes hourly. I don't trust him, so I'm staying away until I figure out what to do."

Nate grasped his arm. "You should come back to Bethlehem. We would love to have you back. Mother and Father miss you…We miss you."

A bitter thought struck David. "Funny, you never visited."

"Never visited? We were forbidden! We didn't visit Eliab or Abinidab either. General Abner didn't want his soldiers distracted, so he made a law against family members visiting those in his army. That's the only reason."

David nodded. "I know. I know." He scuffed a foot in the dirt. "It still seemed like you all forgot about me. Why do you think I never came home? I figured you didn't care."

"I'm sorry that happened." Nate spread his arms, palms out. "But you see, we're all here now. Ready to take you back, or support you in whatever your next move will be."

David looked out of his cave. Tents were in the process of being pitched, and the little boys had assembled a pile of camel chips and stray twigs, the rudiments of a campfire. He counted eight mules and donkeys and about fourteen people, all having come looking for *him*. Tears misted his eyes and he retired suddenly to the back recesses, weeping in secret.

He poured tears and heart out to God in the darkness. He considered the blessing of his brothers finding him, their changed opinion of him, and their kindness. The lonely years he spent in Gibeah, missing his family, welled up inside of him from where he had kept them buried deep within his heart.

He fell to his face and prayed, "God of my fathers, You have shown me how faithful You are to me, Your humble servant. I now know that You have been with me in the wilderness all this time. And when I felt like You had forgotten me, You already had my brothers on their journey, looking for me. I thank You in advance for fulfilling Your plan in my life. Take me, and make me the king You want me to be."

David stood up and straightened his clothes. He raked his fingers through his hair and beard, detangling it. He shook his head, getting rid of the dust and self-doubt that had hindered him on his quest. He reached for the jug and poured some water into his hands and wiped his face.

Looking at his hands open before him, he realized they were tingling, and he felt a rush of warmth go through him. This private sign from God reminded David of His presence and power in his life. Feeling it just now lightened his heart and steps. Even here, in this wasteland, in this cave, God was in control. God had not forgotten him.

David fastened the sword of the giant around his waist and stepped confidently to the cave entrance. When he finally emerged into the bright late morning sun, emotionally cleansed, he was amazed at the transformation.

The arid land before his cave had been changed into a well-organized campsite, with two tents arranged on either side of a campfire. Donkeys and mules were tethered nearby. Cooking pots on the fire promised his first decent meal in weeks.

The day and evening passed pleasantly. David filled himself with barley and leek stew and crispy flatbread. Wine was a welcome change from muddy water and weak tea. The brothers lounged on reed mats before the fire and caught up on family news.

David was surprised to find how many children had been born to the clan over the past six years and saddened to hear of some who had departed this earth.

He learned that his second oldest brother, Abinidab, died in battle. He suffered a sword strike while trying to back up one of his fellow soldiers. David took a few minutes to absorb losing this gentle brother, the one who encouraged him at the Valley of Elah when he took on Goliath. It was a noble death, but it left a void, just the same.

"I have to tell you something, Dave," Ozzy said.

"What's that?"

Ozzy swallowed a bite of flatbread. "There are others."

"Others?"

"More are coming."

David shook his head and gave his brothers a questioning look.

Nate jumped in. "He means that there are several men, perhaps many, who heard about our journey to find you. Whenever we mentioned your name, and that we were looking for you, people got excited. You have quite a following."

"I hope you didn't reveal you were looking for me to anyone with the King's army," David said.

"Of course not," said Nate. "We were careful."

"This place is really secluded," added Rad. "We almost went back home, but had a feeling that soon God would help us find you."

David laid a hand on Rad's shoulder. "I'm glad you didn't give up."

"In our encounters with surrounding clans, people kept asking if they could join us when we found you," said Nate. "So, you can probably expect more people arriving over the next days. Men who are dissatisfied with the King; some heavily in debt and dodging tax collectors or prison terms. Some whose family members were mistreated, or taken, by the King as punishment."

"Taken?"

Nate nodded gravely. "Yes. Children, mostly. They are returned when the person complies. You never heard about that?"

David shook his head.

"Just saying, there are many who hope to join up with you and your mission."

"My mission?" David said. He shifted his position on the reed mat and reached for a final bite of flatbread. He soaked it in the stew and popped it into his mouth. "I'm still trying to make up my mind what that is. And I don't know if I want a bunch of outlaws following me. I really just need time to think…"

Nate spoke up. "You've *had* time to think. We—Ozzy, Rad, and I—are ready to help you, to *defend* you."

David held up a hand, "Hold on, I don't want to start an uprising."

"It's not like that," said Nate. "King Saul will be looking for you with his army." He cut his outstretched hand onto the flattened palm of the other. "You should form an army of your own, if for nothing else but to defend against King Saul. If these men that are coming want to help you, we can train them. We can keep things organized, so you can protect yourself against King Saul, if you have to."

David thought it was a good plan. As it was, he was hiding for his life. If his brothers were able to find him, it was only a matter of time before King Saul would. And then he would be on the run again. That was no way to reach his goal of becoming king of Israel.

With a dependable group of men surrounding and protecting him, David could start planning for the future, for whenever God enacted His plan. And with his brothers at his side, he felt his stronghold in Adullam would be secure.

23

Four Hundred Outlaws

The following months were full of change. People came to David's settlement in Adullam by the dozens. Many men and even a few women arrived, offering help to the fugitive former captain of King Saul's army.

Some brought their own weapons, or arrived on horseback. All were tested to determine their strengths and placed in groups with those of like skills—archers, horsemen, and swordsmen.

David learned that Nate and Ozzy were running from the law themselves. They were defectors from the royal army, having just joined up that year. It was during their first visit home that a messenger arrived from Mical, begging help locating David. Shortly afterward they packed up and went searching for him, never returning to the barracks in Gibeah. They, along with David, taught the volunteer army the rudiments of warfare.

Some of the newcomers spread rumors that their purpose was to develop an army to take over the royal city and depose King Saul. When David heard about this, he called an assembly of the entire encampment.

He stood at the mouth of his cave and called everyone

to attention. "I want all of you who have joined me, and my brothers, Nate, Ozzy, and Rad, to know we value your help. However, I need to clear up some rumors about our reason for gathering together like this.

"Many of you are aware that I was a captain in King Saul's army. I have recently fallen into disfavor with the King. He is seeking my life, although I have done nothing to deserve the anger of his Highness. I have always been loyal to him, and *I still am*.

"When my brothers joined me here in Adullam, I was hiding in this cave. They let me know I had many followers of my own. I'm not sure why some of you decided to join me here. Just realize we are *not* here to start a revolution. No one is trying to overthrow the King. My brothers will be training many of you to be soldiers—soldiers in a *defensive* army to protect me against possible attacks by the King.

"Some of you may have military experience already, and we will be happy to perfect any training you have had, but that doesn't mean you will have higher rank than anyone else. We will award rank on merit and skill.

"To all non-military persons, we will make use of any talents you have. You will be needed to help take care of the daily running of our settlement. Together, we can support one another and remain safe here in the wilderness."

NATE'S WIFE, DEBORAH, JOINED HER HUSBAND IN ADULlam a few weeks after he arrived. Nate had sent for her in Bethlehem and she and her servants arrived with several donkeys loaded with much needed supplies: food, lengths of fabric, and earthenware jugs and cooking utensils. Obed and Caleb were happy to have their mother back with them again.

David usually had the morning meal with Nate and Deborah at their cooking fire. Deborah made the best barley porridge, sweetened with honey and almonds. The boys always came back for seconds.

Since Ozzy hadn't married yet, he ate his meals with Nate's family as well. He liked teasing Obed and Caleb, and they enjoyed their fun uncle. A favorite trick of his was 'finding' a stray locust in their bowl of porridge. It usually earned him an extra helping, as the nephew wouldn't finish the food after it had been tainted with the creature. How they squirmed when Ozzy crunched the still-wriggling locust between his teeth!

After breakfast one morning Ozzy and Nate readied to go on a hunting trip with several other young men. Deborah herded her sons into the tent to wash up for the day. As David had a last cup of mint tea by the fire, Rad strolled by.

"Rad," he called out. He patted his hand on the rug next to him. "Have a seat. I wanted to talk to you."

Rad sat down before the cooking fire. David poured a cup of hot tea from the jug on the fire and handed it to his brother, who sipped carefully. David observed how Rad unconsciously kept his right hand hidden, and once again felt a pang of guilt.

Rad glanced up and looked at him over the rim of his cup.

David paused a moment, gathering his thoughts. "There are some things I need you to do."

Rad took a sip of tea. "Anything you need, Dave, I'm yours."

"I know you weren't able to join the army. Because… because of your hand. So you don't have military training…"

Rad looked down to where his right hand was hidden beneath his robe. "Yeah…that's nothing new. So what?"

David hesitated. What happened was so long ago. They were just children. But it still pained him, and he felt remorse for the accident anew every time he thought about it.

He looked into Rad's eyes. "I'm sorry. Back then…with the wolf. I shouldn't have—"

"Don't. It's not *your fault.*"

David nodded, his mouth set. "Anyway…what I wanted to talk with you about is, I know you have talents in many other areas. You are a great communicator." He smiled. "Remember that time we—you, Nate, Ozzy, and I—wanted a tent of our own? We didn't want to sleep in the same tent as our old uncles, or the hired help?"

"I remember."

"It was you…*you* who convinced Father it was a good idea. Before I knew it we were moving into our own tent."

Rad's face brightened. "Yes. And then I got him to supply those thick fleece mattresses for us."

"Ha ha! Right. You told him we could work better and longer if we didn't wake up with sore backs." David sat quietly for a moment as he recalled, once again, the times with his family. How different was his relationship with his brothers back then, when he was misunderstood and often belittled by the older ones. How things have changed. He actually felt respected by them now.

David continued. "What I need around here is someone who will organize the food, and supplies. Someone who can allot tent space to newcomers. Someone who will obtain more food for us from surrounding towns."

"You want me to do that?"

"Not just you. But I'm asking you to organize the effort. I don't want to have to be concerned with the day-to-day running of our encampment. It takes so much of my time, and I'm no good at it. I need someone else, and I'm hoping that someone is you, to take over."

Rad took another sip of tea, and set the cup down. "If we are going to expect nearby towns to supply food to us, we will have to trade them for it. Some of the non-military newcomers are tentmakers, basket-weavers, and potters. If I can get enough of them to make, let's say, woven mats and clay pots, I'll have something to barter with for food."

"Exactly!" David reached out and gave Rad's shoulder a squeeze. "I can see I found the right man for the job. I need you to get started on this immediately." They stood up and moved on together.

"And, Rad," David said. "Develop some system for distributing the food fairly. We had a near-riot yesterday when the hunting party returned with two young goats. You'd think these people never saw fresh meat before."

Rad smiled. "I'm thinking of a scheme already."

"Good man. I have to concentrate on staying out of King Saul's way and helping Nate and Ozzy train our militia. I must to be ready to be king of Israel, when the time comes."

Rad turned and grasped his brother's forearm. "You will make an excellent king. God chose the right man for the job."

Before long, Rad had all non-military persons organized into task groups. Individuals who were too old, too young, or not physically fit enough to be in the volunteer army were given certain jobs. David's nephews and the few other youngsters among them were charged with keeping the cooking fires burning. They collected camel chips and any sticks or dry vegetation they could find. This was placed in piles by each of the fire rings.

The women among them took a morning's walk to the stream every day to bring jugs of water for cooking and watering the animals. The stream was getting low, but at the time was still a reliable source of water. They also baked bread daily on flat stones heated over campfires using grain and oil obtained through Rad's barter method.

Some of those who joined David in Adullam were workers in crafts and trades. There were iron-workers who could sharpen swords or forge arrowheads. Healers understood how to use herbs indigenous to the area to cure illnesses and heal injuries. Tentmakers mended tents with patches of woven goat's hair cloth. They also doubled as tailors and helped keep clothing in good repair.

Originally a small cluster of tents, the encampment became a well-organized community of dozens of tents and campsites. Before long, four hundred men joined David's cause. To most of them, it was enough to be part of a defensive army, protecting the famous Captain David, formerly of King Saul's military.

David continued to live in his cave, albeit in better conditions than when his brothers first found him. The dirt floor was now lined with woven wool rugs. He had a fleece mat to sleep on, and an oil lamp that allowed him to have meetings with his brothers late into the night.

It was at one of these meetings with Nate and Ozzy that David introduced the idea of a group of specially trained soldiers.

David served wine to his brothers, and joined them on the rug by the fire. "What I envision is a company of about twenty or thirty soldiers with special skills."

"We have a few who are able to hurl a spear with both left and right hand with equal accuracy," Nate said.

"And several who can shoot an arrow at a full gallop," added Ozzy.

"Good. Good. That's the kind of thing we need. Also spies. We need spies to infiltrate the surrounding towns to make sure we are still safe here, safe from King Saul's army."

Ozzy popped a few raisins into his mouth. He always had a snack handy. "Last week a fellow named Josh came to the camp with a few others from around Gibeah. Said he used to work with you. He's a spy."

"From King Saul's army?" David said.

"Yes…but it's not like that. He defected. He's one of us now."

"Nate? What do you think?"

Nate raised his chin and thought for a moment. "We could do worse. He's here, now, and I've met him. I believe we can trust him. If he was still working for the King, they would have already come for you."

"True. And I do remember him. He helped me with the two hundred sandals when I fought those Philistines for Mical. We got on well."

Ozzy stopped chewing. "Sandals?"

"Ha ha! Yes. Sandals. I'll have to tell you the story some other time. Point is, let's try him out. Bring him to our next meeting, tomorrow night. I'd like to question him, see where his loyalty lies. Maybe he would be the right man to lead our company of specialists."

Over the next few weeks David observed his volunteer army in military training exercises. He watched archers at target practice, swordsmen sparring with one another, and the small cavalry practicing throwing spears at a full gallop. Everyone was learning and perfecting new skills.

Having taken Josh into his confidence, David authorized him to form the group of specialists. Josh assumed the task wholeheartedly and soon had an elite company of warriors called "The Thirty".

David met with his three brothers and Josh, on a regular basis. They discussed training strategies and worked to marshal the outlaw army into a well-structured organization. David's authority over the group was absolute, and they followed him with dogged devotion.

24

Aʙɪᴀᴛʜᴀʀ

The dry season had come to an end. The rains that followed were a welcome relief to the unrelenting heat. Living in a cave had its advantages—cooler than out on the wilderness floor. And drier.

During a downpour, Ozzy ducked into David's cave followed by a visitor. It wasn't unusual to have a newcomer in the encampment, except this one wasn't looking to join his army.

David rose to greet the visitor, who was attired in a roughly woven cloak tied at the middle with a leather strap. A dirty white and blue fringed shawl hung limply around his shoulders, dripping onto the cave floor. It was the type of garment a priest would wear. He stepped rapidly from one foot to the other and wrapped his arms around himself.

"Come here and dry yourself by the fire," David said. "Ozzy, get him something to eat." David reached for a folded blanket and shook it out. He draped it across the priest's shoulders.

"What is your name? And from what city have you come?"

The newcomer looked up at David from his place on the rug. "My name…my name is Abiathar. And I…I come from Nob." The priest twisted a bit of fringe from the shawl around his finger as he spoke.

Ozzy returned from getting some food. After shaking out his bushy hair he placed a bowl of lentil stew and cup of wine before the priest. He then sat down on a rug nearby and nibbled on a section of dried venison.

Abiathar slurped the stew without stopping. When he finally looked up, David made light conversation. "I've been to Nob. Ahimelech, the high priest, helped me when I was in trouble once."

Abiathar swiped the inside of his bowl and licked his finger. "Do you know Ahimelech?"

The priest looked up at David. He blinked a couple times and nodded.

"Is he well?"

"Not…not really."

"Not really?"

Abiathar's breathing became rapid. His eyes darted from David to Ozzy and back to David again. "He's gone."

David felt impatient. He didn't like dragging information out of someone. He waved a hand. "Well, what do you mean? Was he sick? Did he leave Nob?"

"They're…they're all gone. All of them."

"Who?"

"Only I escaped."

"Escaped what?"

"The slaughter."

Ozzy stopped chewing and gazed at the priest.

David rose to his feet and stood over timid Abiathar. "What are you talking about?"

As if in a trance, Abiathar told the story, haltingly at first, then with more emotion. "It, it was Doeg, the camel herdsman from Edom. He told King Saul…He told King Saul that my father helped you. My father, Ahimelech.

Doeg told the King that my father gave you food, and a weapon.

"I heard about it when I was at the marketplace. That's how I knew about King Saul coming to the Tabernacle. He came…he came with his soldiers. Demanded to see my father. It was *awful*." The priest twisted the fringe so tight that the strands broke in his hand. He stopped his disjointed narrative and buried his face in his hands.

David knelt down in front of him. "It's okay. You're safe now. Please…tell me the rest."

Abiather looked up and saw the kindness in David's eyes. He glanced at Ozzy, who was listening, rapt, to the astonishing story.

He took a deep breath and continued. "I'm…I'm sorry. I just can't seem to tell it right. I've been in hiding for weeks. I…I haven't eaten. I'm the only one left." He took a long drink of sustaining wine. "When the King found out that my father helped you, he…he ordered that all priests be put to death. All eighty-five! Like I said, I was at the market that day. I came back to the Tabernacle fast as I could, just after it happened. I was a *coward*. I should have gone after them." Abiathar closed his eyes tight and sank into a pit of self-condemnation. "I should have been one of the ones that died."

"Come, now," David soothed. "It would have been suicide. There would be no priests left if you tried to fight. You were no match for the King's army."

Abiathar was silent for a moment. He blinked his eyes and said, "One of my brothers…my brother told me everything before he died. So I had to find you. I…I had to find the man my father died trying to help."

David got up and walked to the mouth of the cave. The slaughter of the priests was indirectly his fault, and he wondered at the devotion of the one that escaped. "Why, God?" he whispered severely, looking up to the dripping heavens. "Why did you let your servants be slaughtered?"

After a moment, he took a deep breath and joined Abiathar and Ozzy by the fire once again. "I knew when Doeg was there at the temple in Nob that day, I knew he was up to no good," David said through clenched teeth. "He probably followed me there to Nob. He's a zealot—always looking for a way to get in good with the King. Even if it costs innocent lives."

Abiathar sat on the rug, observing David. He brushed a few thin strands of hair out of his eyes. His weak chin trembled. Finally, he said, "I…I didn't know what else to do. Everyone's gone. It took me a long time to find you."

David took him gently by both shoulders. "Of course. Stay with us. I will protect you myself. It's the least I can do for the son of one who died for me. Besides, these men here with me…they need a chaplain to help us stay in line with God's will. Please remain with us."

He led Abiathar to the tent settlement just outside of his cave. Ozzy said his goodbyes and left to join Nate and his family for supper. The rain was letting up.

Finding Rad, David asked him to locate some provisions for the priest and allow him to sleep in his tent for now. He then returned to his own campfire.

As he sat on the rug, he felt distracted. Why did God allow this to happen to nervous Abiathar? And what was King Saul thinking, murdering a household of priests? He picked up a sharpened reed pen and his papyrus roll. He wrote with fervor, denouncing Doeg the Edomite.

You call yourself a hero, do you?
Why boast about this crime of yours,

You who have disgraced God's people?
All day long you plot destruction.
Your tongue cuts like a razor;
You're an expert at telling lies.
You love evil more than good,
And lies more than truth.

But God will strike you down once and for all.
He will pull you from your home
And drag you from the land of the living.

But I am like an olive tree,
Thriving in the house of God.
I trust in God's unfailing love
Forever and ever.

Psalm 52

David's purpose to become the next king of Israel grew that night. He envisioned a country where worship of the one true God was encouraged and the Priestly tribe of Levites held in respect, not controlled or punished at King Saul's whim. He couldn't allow him to terrorize the good people of his country, and he didn't want anyone else to suffer for his monomaniacal ambition—that of finding and killing him.

DAVID WAS TRUE TO HIS WORD, AND LET NO HARM BEFALL the priest. As for Abiathar, he was pleased to stay in the settlement in Adullam. Rad allowed him to sleep in his tent for the time being, and his calm temperament helped soothe his anxiety. He let the priest talk.

They talked while having their morning tea. They talked at night, as the fire died down. The priest talked about his family, and it helped him get through the grieving, having someone listen to him.

"My brothers and I, we were…we were always involved in the priesthood. It's all I remember. We are Levites," said Abiathar after supper.

"That's how it was with my family and sheep. Always sheep," Rad said. "And since I was second youngest, I had to do a lot of the hard work, and stay with the flocks more often. Of course, David had it worse than me, being youngest." He stirred the dying embers with a stick, sending up sparks.

Abiathar twisted the fringe of his shawl absently. "He's the youngest?"

"Yes, and our older brothers never let him forget it. They always think they're better than him. And me."

"I'm the youngest, too. I hated it. And now…now I'm all that's left." Abiathar concentrated on the fringe. He combed his fingers through it, straightening it.

Rad was silent for a moment, trying to think of an appropriate comment to comfort the priest, who just lost every one of his family members. "You're safe here—my brother won't let anything happen to you. Consider us your family now."

Abiathar looked up at Rad and smiled. "It seems…it seems that David, though youngest, is your leader now. You and your brothers. And this group."

Rad considered this. "Yes, that's true. And it's about time. He worked hard to win our, and our father's approval. And since he was chosen by God to be the next—I mean—" He closed his mouth abruptly—*that was close*—and caught Abiathar's eye, waiting for him to finish his sentence.

"That is…um…you know he killed that giant years ago. Proves God is with him." He hoped he didn't give anything away as he continued to hold David's secret close to his heart, until allowed to reveal it.

"Yes. He has favor with God," the priest said simply.

During the following weeks Abiathar made a habit of walking to the edge of the encampment daily for a time alone with God. He prayed for David and the people of his clan. He prayed for guidance and for safety.

Abiathar hoped he would be a godly influence to the kind people here who embraced him in his distress. And also to the outlaws and renegades who made up most of the 'volunteer army'. He planned to arrange regular religious observances. He would guide David in God's will for the settlement. He would prove his value as a priest, something he hadn't been able to do at home, being youngest. He began to feel he had a purpose. And this started to heal the hole in his heart. It gave him confidence. Soon he regained his strength and resolve.

25

The Forest of Hereth

·········•·········

It was only a month before Abiathar proved his worth as a priest. He rushed into David's cave one morning, and, running headlong into Nate, stumbled to the ground. Nate and Ozzy were just leaving, having finished their morning meeting with David. He got back onto his feet and blurted out, "I have…I have—"

"Hang on," David said, holding out a hand. "Hey, Ozzy," he called as his brothers stepped away. Ozzy turned. "Be on time tomorrow morning. *Early*, even."

Ozzy winked and said, "The problem with being early is no one is there to appreciate it." He chuckled and left the cave with Nate.

"Hmph," David said, shaking his head. He looked at the priest and gave him his full attention.

Abiathar blinked his eyes. "I have an urgent message from… from God. He says now is the time…*now* is the time for you to leave Adullam and return to Judah. We must leave immediately."

David tossed the last crust of his breakfast flatbread into the fire and took a few minutes to absorb this information. Was this the direction he had been waiting for? Is this part of his mission? And why the urgency?

Moving back east to Judah meant being near Gibeah. And Mical. Mical who sent his brothers to find him in this wasteland. Who visited him in his dreams, leaving him breathless when he awoke. Maybe this meant he would be able to return to her soon.

Over six months had passed since David fled to Adullam and things have been pretty quiet lately. Perhaps King Saul had given up hunting for David. He was definitely ready to move back home.

"Okay…" David replied. "Any particular reason, just now?"

Abiathar shook his head. "I…I just know during prayer this morning God told me it was time to move."

David walked through the encampment with Abiathar and sought out his three brothers. They found Nate and Rad, and eventually located Ozzy, sparring with young Obed with wooden swords at the edge of the encampment. Nate sent his son home, and the men moved to the shade of a cluster of thorn trees.

"Abiathar has heard from God," David said, indicating the priest at his side. "It's time to leave Adullam. We must all work together to get this done."

The brothers nodded their heads and listened closely.

"So, tomorrow," David said, "Nate and Ozzy, organize the men into companies and gather all weapons and horse gear. Rad, have the women and non-military men load the tents and supplies onto pack animals, and make ready to move. We are all moving to Judah."

"Where to?" said Rad.

"Hm?"

"Where? What city? Back to Gibeah? Because I know our brothers," he indicated Nate and Ozzy to his side, "they face prison for leaving the King's army without permission. So, too, might many of the volunteers."

David walked a few paces away, chin in hand. He returned and said, "I was so excited about seeing my wife again, I gave no thought as to how this would affect everyone else. I certainly don't want to jeopardize our brothers' freedom." He looked at Rad. "What do you suggest?"

"The great forest of Hereth is between us, here, and Gibeah. I've travelled through it several times obtaining supplies. I say we settle there. It's large, two or three days' journey through, and we are used to living rough," Rad said. "Plus it will have resources we need, like water, wood for cooking fires, and—"

Nate cut in. "Good thinking. Just what I was going to say. While there we can determine the mood nearer Gibeah. See how much of a threat it would be for you to return, Dave."

"*And…*" Rad continued, looking sidelong at Nate. "We will still be following the priest's direction. We'll be in Judah. Just keeping our distance."

David was silent for a moment. "If—and I say 'if' because I still don't trust the King—*if* it's safe for me to return, the rest of our group can disperse to wherever they came from originally. You three can go back to home to Bethlehem, if you want, and the volunteers can go where they wish. Abiathar, you can always stay with me." He smiled at the priest.

He nodded at Rad. "It's a good plan. Well done."

Rad's eyes glowed at the compliment.

Nate muttered a slur under his breath.

They disbanded to begin packing.

OVER THE FOLLOWING WEEK ALL FOUR HUNDRED VOL-unteer soldiers as well as the many other helpers moved east into Judah, settling in the Forest of Hereth. Remaining hidden in this vast forest, David wasn't ready to reveal himself just yet. He wanted to test the waters, determine if King Saul was pursuing him.

After they were settled in Hereth, David sent Josh and a few of The Thirty to survey the surrounding territory to make certain of their safety in the middle of the forest. They went all the way back to the caves in Adullam.

Two days later, Josh came to report his findings. David had been busy all day working on his handmade lyre. First, he removed the old sinew wrapped around it, and then, using tools he now had at his disposal, he connected the two curved olive-wood pieces and the cross piece with tightly fitting wooden pegs, stabilizing it. He rubbed the wood smooth with handfuls of sand and worked flaxseed oil into the grain. Lengths of new sinew would be left to dry before he used them as strings for the lyre. He was applying a final coat of flaxseed oil as Josh strode in past the tent flap.

"Just thought you might want to know," he said, standing before David, "what happened last night."

David looked up at Josh and waved a hand.

Josh squatted on the rug across from David and balanced himself with a finger. "I took a group from The Thirty as you requested. We searched the towns surrounding the forest. No sign of military activity."

"Good. Good," David said, nodding.

Josh lowered his voice and leaned in closer. "However, when we went to Adullam, where we had been living, there was an army encamped across the whole region. Hundreds of tents. Many horses. Camels. Mules. About a thousand soldiers. It was King Saul's army."

David raised his eyebrows.

"Some of them were in *your cave*," Josh said.

"Looking for me?"

"That's the information I got from my men."

David was at once wary. "How did he know where I was?"

Josh shrugged and shook his head.

"We have no choice, then, but to remain hidden here, in Hereth, until we hear from God again," David said. "So much for returning to Gibeah. The King was just biding his time. He's *still* on the hunt for me." He picked up his lyre and rubbed it absently with a handful of fleece dampened with flaxseed oil, thinking for a moment. Glancing back at Josh, he said, "I need you and The Thirty to keep watch around our encampment at all times. Work in shifts. Let me know if you see anything irregular."

Josh gave a solemn nod and exited the tent.

The rainy season was over and the days of endless sunshine began. David and the volunteer army subsisted quite well in their settlement in the Forest of Hereth. Game such as roebuck and wild goat, as well as quail and geese were plentiful among the pines and olive trees. Whatever they needed, apart from fresh game, they traded for or bought in nearby towns.

David himself had earned a reputation of fairness in the region in all business and trading deals. It wasn't unusual, therefore, that officials from the city of Keilah came to him for help.

Rad and his assistants set out early in the morning en route to Keilah to obtain supplies for the settlement. He continued to act in his capacity as negotiator with those in authority in the nearby villages, trading services and goods for food and other necessities.

As Rad approached the walls of Keilah, they were met by officials from the city traveling the other way. The city was situated just outside the forest, and had access to fertile farmland south of them, which made them a great resource for the volunteer army.

"How goes it, brothers?" he said as he dismounted.

The officials stopped on the path and the lead man approached. He cast a furtive look at his companions, then said to Rad, "I am Joeheb. City council leader."

"Yes," said Rad. "We had dealings together last month, when we helped with the barley harvest."

Joeheb nodded. "Of course. I'm sorry, this is just so worrying…I can't even think."

Rad kept silent as Joeheb explained the dilemma the people of Keilah faced, and why he was on his way to see David.

"Our city has been under harassment by the Philistines," he said. "This time they stole our grain. Right from the threshing floor. Next time it may be our livestock. Or our *women*. The council decided since we are a small city, mainly relying on our strong walls and barred gates for protection, that we should beg help of David and his army. We have always been fair in trading with him, and have denied him nothing he or his men needed."

"Of course," Rad said. "If you come back with us, I will take you to David personally." The officials from Keilah returned to their city. Rad and Joeheb traveled back to the settlement, where they found David exiting the weapons tent. He had been inspecting the collection of weapons and armor that had accumulated since the formation of the volunteer army. It was time to arrange the items in a more organized manner, catalogue what they had, and seek to obtain any missing pieces.

"Dave," Rad said. "This is our neighbor, Joeheb. He hails from Keilah."

David reached out to greet him. "Welcome, welcome. Now you see how we live, like nomads, and why we are so grateful for all the things you provide for us. What can I do for the people of Keilah?"

Joeheb explained the predicament the city was in—the recent harassment by the Philistines.

"Were they seen?" asked David.

"Who?"

"The Philistines. You said they stole the grain at night. How do you know it was them?"

Joeheb looked down. His voice got quiet. "Some of our older men who had been threshing that day slept in the barn. They saw them." Joeheb kicked a pebble and looked back up at David. "They were no match for the Philistines, who were well-armed. They remained hidden."

"I don't blame them. They would have been killed." David turned to Rad. "Is Abiathar still staying with you?"

"He wanted it that way, so I was happy to let him."

"I need to ask him about this. He can pray to God and find out if we might be successful in ridding Keilah of the Philistines."

Abiathar came to David's tent after the evening meal.

"Sit here, Abiathar. Have some tea." David poured the last of the tea into a cup and handed it to Abiathar.

The priest sat on a log in front of the fire and curled his hands around the warm cup. "Thank you for meeting with me," said David. "We have been asked for help by our neighbors outside the forest. The people of Keilah."

"Yes. Rad told me about it."

"The question is if we should help them. Should we risk protecting them from the Philistines? Will God help us be successful?"

Abiathar plucked at the fringe of his shawl. "I…I already prayed. I asked God if…if we should fight. God said 'Yes', we will be successful against the Philistines."

"Thank you, Abiathar." David looked at the priest, his eyes earnest. "I hope you know how much we appreciate you around here. I am happy to know you will keep us in line with God's will. That means everything to me."

Abiathar lowered his eyes, a pleased smile on his lips. He stole away from the fire and headed toward his tent.

Nate and Ozzy met with David as usual the next morning.

"Good news, brothers, good news," David said as they joined him on rugs inside his tent. "Looks like we will have a chance to try out our new troops. Seems our friends in Keilah are having a problem with the Philistines—breaking into the city at night and robbing them. They need our help."

Nate sat up tall and crossed his arms. "Our men will set a guard around the perimeter of the city and rotate watches throughout the night."

"I really think this time we need to be on the offensive," David said. "This is very brazen of them, assaulting these smaller towns in Judah. If we don't send them back to their own country, they will overrun our land again, possibly even striking against our own settlement. I cleared them out once before, back when I was with King Saul. We can't let them advance again." He placed a hand on Nate's shoulder.

"The priest said God will help us be victorious against the Philistines. This is a great opportunity. It will give our army something to work for."

"No," said Ozzy, shaking his head. He popped a date into his mouth and chewed slowly.

David shot Nate a puzzled look. "What does he mean?"

Nate glanced at Ozzy, next to him. "He means the troops aren't ready for this yet. For combat, and possible exposure to other armies, maybe even King Saul's men. They are afraid of being found out as traitors or renegades."

"But it won't be King Saul's army—just us. And the Philistines."

"Look," Nate said, lifting his chin. "It's just a bad idea to strike against the Philistine army right now. We shouldn't do it. It's too public. And dangerous."

David rubbed the back of his neck. *How to approach this?* He looked up and said, "Your men have gone soft, living it up here in the forest. You have to drill them harder. And have the more experienced men work with the younger ones, so they can perfect their skills. You think we are just living in the woods for a camping trip? I have a *mission*." David glanced at Ozzy, then back at Nate. "That's why you came to help me in the first place.

"If God says to go, we shall go. It will be good for the men to have a taste of warfare. To use the skills they have been learning of you two." He looked with steely eyes at Nate. "God *will* help us conquer the Philistines and defend the people of Keilah."

The volunteer army intensified training over the next week, with many hours spent each day on drills: target practice, hand-to-hand combat, and sword fighting. Shirkers among them were disciplined. A few deserted. The rest of the soldiers were newly energized. Despite Nate's misgivings, they felt purpose, a goal, and they worked harder than ever to be in top shape, physically and mentally.

Everyone in the settlement got involved in the effort. The women made and repaired the tightly woven tunics the soldiers wore beneath their armor. Caleb and Obed kept busy fetching items for the workers and delivering messages around the community. Rad had his hands full organizing the weapons tent, making sure each soldier was completely outfitted with armor, and bow and arrow, or sword and shield. The metalworkers among them worked day and night, sharpening swords and spearheads and fitting armor to the individual soldiers.

David took the opportunity to attend to a task he had been meaning to do. He strode to the clay furnace in the center of the encampment and greeted the metalworker, Ethan. "How goes it, brother?"

Ethan turned from placing fuel into the bottom of the furnace. His reddened face spread into a wide grin. "David! Good to see you. It's been a while." He mopped his forehead with a rag.

"I have a special job for you." David drew his sword and handed it to Ethan. "I need this cleaned, polished, and sharpened."

Ethan grasped the hilt. "Is this…?"

David grinned. "Goliath's sword. The very sword I used as a youth to kill that Philistine."

Ethan hefted it. It was a large sword. A *Philistine* sword. But it looked diminutive in his beefy hand. He spit on the blade and shined it on the rag tucked into his leather apron. The color of bronze shone through.

"A beautiful weapon," Ethan said. "I'll take care of it."

"As long as you are caught up on your other work. This battle we are preparing for takes priority."

Ethan indicated a group of young men behind him, diligently working at stations of their own. They were sharpening swords, working the bellows of the furnace, or plunging glowing arrowheads into water. "I have time. Come back tonight."

David returned to the metalworking station after supper. He brought a thick slice of roast venison wrapped in a loaf of flatbread to give to Ethan.

"Ah! This looks good," Ethan said, reaching for the food. He took a large bite, chewed, and swallowed. "I just finished with your sword. Look." He produced the sword of the giant loosely wrapped in a linen cloth.

David unwrapped it and beheld the gleaming bronze weapon. It looked beautiful. And deadly. A ray of sunshine shone off the blade and into his eyes. He bounced the reflection back onto Ethan. "Shiny!"

He closely inspected the workmanship of the sword. It was almost like seeing it for the first time. The blade and hilt had been forged as a single unit. There was very little guard, enabling it to have less drag and be swifter in a down-strike from astride a horse. The hilt was decorated with a delicate filigree of grapes and grapevines, something David didn't notice before, as it had been encrusted with dirt and blood. Not only beautiful, the raised design gave great hold. No chance for this weapon to slip out of his hand.

"Hold it out," Ethan said. David pointed the sword out before him, blade in an up-and-down position. Ethan suspended the linen cloth above the sword. "Watch this…" he said, grinning.

He dropped the cloth onto the blade of the sword. It drifted to the ground, neatly sliced in two.

David's eyes widened with admiration. He carefully slipped the sword of the giant into the leather scabbard buckled around his waist. Grasping Ethan's forearm, he said, "Thank you. I know when called upon, this weapon will serve me well."

After two weeks of rigorous training, the volunteer army was ready to aid the people of Keilah.

It had been a week since Josh and his team were in communication with Joeheb, and they still were unaware of how the Philistines were getting into the city. Perhaps they had someone on the inside helping them, or maybe there was a secret tunnel.

David sent Nate and Ozzy to Keilah early in the morning to feel out the current situation. As the sun began it's descent in the west, they returned to David, seated on a crude bench by his tent, his lyre in his lap.

"We didn't get very close to the city. If the enemy was in range, we would be, too." Ozzy said. He bit into a fig.

"What do you mean?" asked David, his fingers stopped in mid-strum.

"We watched from behind the trees," said Nate. "It's worse than before. About three hundred Philistine soldiers have *laid siege* on Keilah." He let this pronouncement sink in. "This, however, works out well for us. We should attack them by night, as they will not be expecting us, coming from behind. They don't know we're here in the forest. Our troops are ready." He rapped his fist into his open palm. "Let's finish this *tonight*."

"Last time I fought the Philistines they were laying siege against Zorah," David said. "It was when I fought for Mical's dowry." Suddenly remembering his wife caused him to falter. He looked up and gazed at the clouds, her face appearing before him. He heard her call his name…

"Dave," a voice called. A hand grasped his arm. "Dave!" It was Ozzy.

David looked at Ozzy. He shook his head. "Sorry. Thought I saw something…What was I saying? Oh, right— remember the two hundred sandals?"

Ozzy's face brightened as he remembered the reference. "You never explained that to me."

"Another time, perhaps. The point is, the Philistines were so focused on the city they were encamped against, they didn't expect our attack. It was an easy win." He gave a resolute nod of his head toward both brothers. "We can do this."

26

Freeing Keilah

⸻❖⸻

David entrusted his brothers and Josh to handle the operation to free Keilah. He planned to remain behind with one hundred soldiers as protection for the encampment. Now that there were several women and even some children among them, including his nephews, Caleb and Obed, he felt a keen responsibility for them.

After briefing the volunteer army of the plans, Nate took the lead regiment, Ozzy and Josh the second. They traveled south, through the forest, to Keilah, and reached the city as the sun was setting. Nate and his men circled east, towards the hill country. Ozzy and Josh led their regiment west, remaining hidden in the outer perimeter of the forest. Pine needles cushioned and quieted their approach. Peering from behind stands of trees, Ozzy could see the stone walls of Keilah about a hundred paces away, surrounded by Philistine campsites.

Ozzy motioned to his men. "We wait till dark. And, remember," he winked at them, "incoming arrows always have the right of way." The smell of cooking food still lingered in the air from the Philistine army campsites and drove him to distraction. He reached into his pouch for the last bit of dried venison and chewed it slowly, savoring it.

They had agreed on a signal—two hawk shrieks. The plan was to attack together, from both sides. As shadows lengthened and faces became clouded in darkness, Josh took his position between the regiments and sounded the signal.

The volunteer army charged the enemy.

Ozzy scrambled in the lead for about fifty paces. He encountered a Philistine sentry who hacked at him with a sword. He ducked, sliced upward, and made a final slash against his throat.

Wiping the spray of blood from his face, he continued with his men, battling the surrounding guard. When they broke through the line of defense, they raced to the campsites. Ozzy entered a tent and roused those within. He roared, arms raised and sword brandished. The four Philistine soldiers burst out through the back tent flap. They fled toward the forest, leaving their weapons behind. Ozzy had a detachment there that would finish them off.

In the darkness of the tent, he heard Philistine commanding officers rousing soldiers from sleep. He heard the whizzing of arrows, clanging of swords, and the death-cries of men. He hoped most of those would be from the enemy, but he knew the reality was he would lose some of his own.

After chasing the inhabitants out of a few more tents, Ozzy left his troops in Josh's charge and stole back to the forest. He wanted to meet up with Nate.

He tripped over a fallen soldier. Looking down in the dim starlight and seeing it was a Philistine, he snatched up the man's dagger and tucked it into his belt.

He heard the swift whine of the arrow just as it pierced his arm.

Stumbling backwards, Ozzy grasped the arrow jammed into the muscle of his upper arm. Biting down on his lower lip, he resisted crying out. He staggered into the forest and slunk down against a tree.

In the darkness he could feel his left hand, wet with blood, as he clutched his wounded right arm. The puncture pulsated. He knew he could inflict far more damage if he pulled the arrow out. He had seen these wounds. They usually ended in unrelenting bleeding.

He felt dizzy. The sounds of warfare around him grew faint. His eyes closed and he slumped back against the tree.

———————

DAVID MOUNTED HIS HORSE IN THE EVENING, AFTER supper. The troops had left that afternoon and, despite formerly deciding not to get involved, he felt a calling to arms. He strapped on his newly refurbished sword—the sword of the giant. Great potential emanated from within the scabbard. He knew it would serve him well.

He had a personal grudge against the Philistines—attacking the peaceful people of Keilah, invading the land of Judah again after he sent them packing several years ago.

Riding through camp, he located Rad taking an evening walk with Abiathar. "You're in charge," he said, pointing to Rad.

Rad looked around behind himself, then back to David. "Me?"

"*You*. I'm going to Keilah." He spurred his horse and rode away swiftly.

Traveling south through the forest, David unexpectedly thought of Jonathan. How many times he and Jonathan rode together—on the way to battle, overseeing the training of troops, or just as a way to relax. How long ago was that? He thought back and realized it was a year since he left Jonathan in the old training field after the New Moon Feast. As he let his horse pick his way through the forest, he wondered if he would ever see his friend again.

In the moonlight, he followed the trail of broken branches and trodden down vegetation created by his troops, marching to Keilah earlier that day. His excitement at being involved in warfare again quickened his senses, attuned to the atmosphere around him. Before long he could hear the faint sounds of the battle—men shouting and swords ringing against metal. He rode at a slow walk toward the edge of the forest, avoiding branches that could snap. He sidestepped someone lying—dead?—against a tree. He continued a few paces…and abruptly spun his horse around.

It was Ozzy.

David dismounted and knelt before him. Leaning in close, he could feel his brother's hot breath against his cheek. *Still alive.* He grasped him under the shoulders and felt the arrow protruding from his upper arm. Drying blood was sticky around it.

He looked around. They were alone. And the sounds of fighting were becoming more distant as his men chased the Philistines west, back into their own land.

He couldn't lift his brother, hefty in build and laden with armor, onto his horse. He needed help. Stepping to the edge of the forest, he peered through the branches to the Philistine campsites surrounding Keilah, and saw a few of his own men stripping the fallen enemy of their weapons.

He called out to them.

The three soldiers drew near, laden with swords and armor.

"It's Ozzy. He took an arrow. I need to get him on my horse."

One of them was skilled in healing battle wounds and removed the arrowhead by twisting it out slowly. He immediately placed pressure on the cavity it created, stopping further blood loss, and tied a band of cloth tightly around Ozzy's upper arm, covering the wound. The four men were able to drape Ozzy's still unconscious body over David's saddle. They started back through the night to their camp in Hereth.

Making several rest stops along the way, it took till morning for them to reach the encampment.

Most of the soldiers had returned by now, and Nate was numbering them, accounting for those they lost. He become aware of David returning and hailed him. "Hey Dave! So you decided to join us—" He then noticed the body of his twin brother lying on David's horse and raced to his side.

"He took an arrow," David said to Nate. "He's alive, but lost a lot of blood."

Nate nodded, comprehending. He addressed the three soldiers with David, "Take him to my tent. Deborah will look after him."

By that evening, Ozzy was lifting his head to receive nourishing broth from the hand of Deborah. She bathed and bandaged the deep puncture in his upper arm twice daily.

Abiathar visited Ozzy every morning and said special prayers for his recovery. Battle wounds festered. They caused fevers and draining sores. David knew as many warriors died after the battle from the wounds they received, as during the fighting. He hoped Ozzy wouldn't be one of them.

27

Escape To Ziph

David and his lead men were invited to Keilah to celebrate the conquest over the Philistines. Among the spoils of battle were numerous horses and pack animals. These were presented to the leaders of Keilah. Grateful to David and his army, city council leader Joeheb insisted they take half of them back to the encampment, which served to strengthen their cavalry with a number of well-trained mounts.

During the following days, David, Rad, and several others spent time in Keilah, organizing the livestock, and preparing to go back to Hereth.

Rad rode back to the settlement to deliver a group of four Philistine pack mules. When he returned to Keilah that afternoon, David called out to him from the door of his temporary quarters.

"I was just leaving to meet with Josh. Walk with me?" David said.

They ambled along the street together. "Did you see Ozzy while you were in Hereth?" David asked.

"Hm. I did. He's in bad shape."

David stopped by a stone watering trough and turned to Rad. "I thought he was recovering."

"He was. Deborah said he was even eating better. But this morning he was sweaty. And his skin was cold. He was shivering. And the wound…the wound is draining through the dressing and constantly covered with flies, no matter how often Deborah cleans it. Caleb and Obed take turns sitting with him to chase the flies away."

David gnawed his lower lip. "I don't know what else can be done. Deborah is doing her best, I'm sure."

"She is. But even she is worried. Especially since he quit eating today." Rad placed a sandal-shod foot on the stone trough and leaned into his leg, his face grim.

"That is concerning," said David.

Rad was silent for a moment, then he turned to face David. "He said something to me. He could barely talk. I had to get close, like this." He leaned in nearer to David. "He said, 'Live each day as if it were your last, for one day it shall be.'"

David pressed his lips together. He felt a tightness in his throat. "When will you be returning?"

"I can go back day after tomorrow. When I take the last group of mules. I'll check on Ozzy then."

"Thanks. Please report to me immediately when you come back."

He left Rad in search of Josh again. When he found him, he dispatched The Thirty, who had been keeping watch around the walls of the city, to travel further into the forest to ensure the Philistines weren't returning. They set out on their mission that evening.

After sunset, Josh rode into the city at a gallop, nearly trampling David, who was walking with Abiathar.

"Sorry!" Josh shouted. He dismounted roughly. The horse pranced and reared at the end of the reins in his hand.

Winded, he said, "King Saul's army has been sighted."

David's eyes flashed. "*King Saul*. Where is he?"

"My scout told me they are encamped a few miles east of Keilah. About eight hundred strong."

"Are they coming *here*? For *me*? Or going somewhere else?"

Josh squeezed his eyes shut. "Does it really matter?" He looked at David. "Point is, he's close, possibly headed this way. We have to leave *now*."

David could hear the urgency in Josh's voice. He knew they didn't have much time if King Saul was indeed advancing. But he also was becoming more attuned to God's will and plan for his and his followers' lives. He addressed the priest, next to him. "What do you think? Will you ask God if King Saul is coming for me? And if the people of Keilah will protect us?"

Josh cleared his throat. David glanced at him and waved his hand impatiently.

"These people can't defend you," Josh said. "This is a small city. No army. No match for King Saul. Why do you think they needed us to help against the Philistines? If the King is coming here, we can't depend on Keilah to help us."

David and Abiathar returned to their temporary housing. It would just take a few moments for the priest to get him the information he needed. He paced the floor as Abiathar spent a moment in prayer on the rooftop.

He stepped down the ladder, his face grim. "God said, 'King Saul will come.'" He blinked his eyes rapidly.

"Of course." David studied the ground for a moment. He looked back at the priest. "Anything else?"

"Yes. The people of Keilah will betray you. They will… they will turn you over to King Saul. We must leave at once!"

David turned and stormed out of the house. He went in search of Josh and his brothers. *How could they betray us after we put our lives on the line for them?* What a waste that Ozzy incurred a possible life altering injury because of the people of Keilah.

David felt he was such a fool to think they could win this. It was pure arrogance that drove him. *His army*. How proud he was of them, victorious against such a formidable enemy as the Philistines. And now he couldn't even ask them to defend against King Saul, who, with just a few regiments outnumbered his entire army.

Maybe Nate was right. It was too public to be going to battle. Why didn't he just remain hidden in the wilderness?

Somehow King Saul found out where they are.

When David found Josh and his brothers, he instructed them to evacuate any of their soldiers who were in Keilah and head back to the Forest of Hereth. They all left in a hurry under the cover of night.

During the following day, the settlement in the Forest of Hereth packed up and was on the move once again. Now that King Saul was nearby, David's brothers advised him to seek safety and anonymity by moving to an even more remote part of the Judah, to the wilderness south of Ziph.

There was an unseasonable cloudburst. The departure was a hurried jumble of pack animals, carts, and soldiers all laden with bundles, tromping through slick mud. At one time Caleb came up missing. Deborah was in a panic. She found him peacefully leading his own donkey at the rear of the company, singing to himself.

Four soldiers carried Ozzy on a litter. By the time they reached Ziph he breathed his last.

That first night in Ziph everyone slept rough, on damp ground in makeshift campsites. David was seated at the entry of an improvised shelter, nibbling on stale flatbread, unable to sleep. He looked up to see Nate and Deborah approaching.

Deborah looked back at Nate, then at David. She lowered her head "David. Your brother, Ozzy. He…he didn't make it."

David's eyes got big. "No!"

Nate pressed his lips together and squeezed his eyes shut against his tears. David stood and embraced them, weeping together, knowing Nate's loss was greater then his own. He lost a twin, a life-long friend.

David released Nate and stepped back. "Nate, I'm sorry. I know it's harder for you…"

"I should have been there. I shouldn't have let him take his own regiment. Why didn't he stay with me?" Nate said. He sniffled loudly and wiped his nose on the back of his hand. "He insisted we split up. He said we could surround them."

"Don't blame yourself," David said, reaching out to grasp Nate's forearm. "It could have been any of us. And it may still be. We have all put our lives on the line, but have to believe somehow that God is still in control."

Nate slowly moved his head from side to side. "I can't believe that. Why would God let this happen?"

David didn't know. He didn't have the answer.

Nate glared at him. "And why did you make us run from Hereth while my brother was so sick? We should have stayed there. He could have rested…."

"But we couldn't stay. You know that," David said gently. "King Saul was coming for us. He was closing in. We had to leave."

Nate was out of words. The best David could do was allow him to grieve. Deborah squeezed her husband's hand and led him away.

As they left, David's mind went to his friend and spiritual mentor, Samuel. Samuel would have the answer to the question, "Why would God let this happen?" Samuel would know how to explain it in a way they could accept.

David hoped he would have the chance to see the prophet again, soon. Every purpose he had was calling him north, through Judah. Back to Samuel. Jonathan. Mical. And yet, his enemy, King Saul, continued chasing him south.

The only thing David could think, was, *Is God still in control?*

28

In the Wilderness

David sat on a flat table rock and looked out over the encampment in the wilderness of Ziph late one evening.

Large sandstone rocks lay in a tumble at his feet, their smooth surfaces sparkling in the setting sun. The entire area was surrounded by high rocky hills, part of the Judean mountains, shielding David's volunteer army from outsiders. Pockets of green scrub and tall grass fed by underground sources of water provided fresh fodder for the animals. Caves furnished shelter from the heat of the day and sometimes plummeting temperatures at night.

It was in one of these caves they buried Ozzy.

They buried Ozzy about two weeks ago, when they first arrived in Ziph. Abiathar spoke at the burial place, reading something David wrote. Despite having halting speech, when reading the written word out loud, the priest did it beautifully.

"Hear my prayer, Lord; let my cry for help come to you.
Do not hide your face from me when I am in distress.
Turn your ear to me and answer quickly when I call.

For my days vanish like smoke;
My bones burn like glowing embers.
My heart is blighted and withered like grass.
I groan aloud and am reduced to skin and bones.

I am like a desert owl, like an owl among the ruins.
I am alone as a bird on the roof."

Psalm 102

The days of mourning following Ozzy's death had delayed setting up the encampment in Ziph. Everyone felt the sting of losing one of their captains. David walked in bare feet and dressed in a coarse tunic all week, the dust of the wilderness rubbed into his hair.

As David watched the western sky from his perch on the flat rock, he thought about his journey from Gibeah, and how much he wanted to return to the royal city and his wife. He missed her laughter and ever-positive attitude, and even her sometimes hotheaded temper. He pictured her in their airy courtyard playing with the lamb (by now a grown sheep), or cleaning house with Lydia. Hopefully Jonathan was spending time with her to ease her loneliness, as he wouldn't be able to return to her soon.

He was grateful she had thought to send word to his family when he was in Adullam, destitute and starving, living in a cave, depressed, hopeless. Even then, when his faith was weak, God was with him. God brought his brothers to him.

Having had the chance to reconnect with Ozzy in such a friendly, constructive way over the past months was a source of comfort. He had grown to admire and enjoy him, full of witticisms and humor. Ozzy's death renewed his resolve to pursue becoming king of Israel. Because King Saul was relentless in dogging him in Hereth, David and his clan had to leave their encampment in a hurry, tipping the very delicate scales of Ozzy's recovery finally in the wrong direction. Perhaps if they had stayed, he would have recovered. He owed it to his brother to be successful in his mission, to replace King Saul on the throne, put an end to Philistine tyranny, and secure the borders of their land.

The kinship David felt with his brothers grew daily. They believed in him, and his calling. Nate and Rad were among the few who knew about his appointment by God to be the next king of Israel. Not even Josh or The Thirty were aware. And certainly not the volunteer army. He knew many of them still expected him to start a revolution despite advising them differently. But that was for God to decide. He would make no move unless he knew God was behind it.

<hr />

DURING A BREAK IN THE CONSTANT DRIZZLE OF THE rainy season one evening, a visitor entered the encampment in Ziph, seated tall in the saddle of his bay stallion. His hair fell dark and thick over his simple wool robe as he glanced down at Nate and his companions. "I'm here to see David."

Nate blocked the path, arms crossed over his chest. "I am David's brother and commander of his army. What is your purpose for seeing him?"

The visitor dismounted and handed the reins to one of the men with Nate. He adjusted the belt around his fine linen tunic and said, "Please, take me to David. I can promise you he will be very happy to see me."

"I will present you. Then he can decide for himself. Whom should I say seeks an audience with David?"

"My name is Jonathan."

As Nate led Jonathan through the camp, David was meeting with Josh. The Thirty had discovered King Saul's army about a day's journey north of the city of Ziph. David's heart sank. They were settled here, in the wilderness. It had everything they needed to survive: underground springs that provided water, ibex and mountain goats for fresh game, and cover. It was a good place to hide out.

And now, after only a few months, King Saul was on the move and headed in their direction again.

They discussed their options. The only realistic one was to pack up and leave. As Josh stepped out of the tent, David could see Nate approaching with someone. Someone asking for a favor, no doubt, or another volunteer wishing to join up. They had to turn several away lately, as the volunteer army was becoming almost too big to manage and take care of.

In the shadow of the tent opening, David was unable to make out the identity of his visitor, who bowed at the waist as he was presented.

"Someone to see you, Dave," Nate said. "Says his name is Jonathan."

David looked up as Jonathan straightened his back, standing tall and regal before him. The evening sun shone around his form and through his dark wavy hair, so like his father's. David's eyes misted as he recognized his old friend.

"Jonathan, my brother. How good to see you!" The two embraced and thumped each others' backs. David stepped back and clasped his arms, gazing at him for a moment, at once absorbed in his old friend's personality, dependable and steadfast. He drew him into the tent.

David turned to his brother. "Nate, this is King Saul's son, Jonathan—"

"King Saul's son?"

"Yes," he said, turning back to Jonathan. "He's been my mentor since I moved to Gibeah as a youth."

Nate bowed low. "It's a privilege to meet you. I'm sorry I didn't recognize you."

Jonathan laughed gently. "I don't know how you would, dressed in these plain clothes. It seems I've been influenced by your brother in that respect."

Nate glanced at David, and back at Jonathan. "The fact is, our family has always followed all reports of your victories with great admiration. I am honored to finally meet you." He indicated a small padded stool. "Please, sit here."

David sat across from Jonathan on the rug. It was unbelievable, having a surprise visit by his friend. But what kind of visit was this? Did Jonathan simply stumble on the encampment, or did he really know where to find him? Was King Saul close behind, closer than Josh reported?

Nate left for a moment and returned with a fig cake and cup of wine. Jonathan received these with a smile of thanks as Nate bowed again, backing out of the tent.

"Forgive me…" David said. "But I have to ask—why are you here?"

Jonathan took a sip of wine. "My father has me installing army regiments in all the major towns in Judah, to keep them protected against the Philistines. They have become a serious threat again. Even small towns like Keilah are experiencing raids. I had knowledge of your general whereabouts, and decided to visit you."

David's eyes widened. "You knew where to find me?"

Jonathan nodded. "I have my sources." He held up a hand, palm out. "But just so you know, I am selective with information I share with my father. Of course I never told him where you are."

The two talked for awhile, catching up on events in both of their lives. Merab was expecting a second child, not that she was able to even properly care for the first one. David told Jonathan about Ozzy and his battle injury and death. Jonathan nodded gravely, empathizing about the loss.

At length, Jonathan said, grinning, "So it was you who chased the Philistines away from Keilah?"

"It was us. Our first military campaign. And it went well, except, of course…"

"Yes. An unfortunate consequence of battle. No matter how well you plan, you lose soldiers. I'm so sorry it was your brother."

David nodded and kept silent for a moment.

Jonathan looked around the well-appointed tent. He observed the colorful rugs on the floor and the reed sleeping mat padded with sheepskin. "You have made yourself very comfortable here."

"It is nice here, all right. And this region supplies everything we need. But it looks like we have to move again."

"Why?"

"I'm surprised you don't know King Saul and his army are coming this way."

Jonathan shook his head. "I didn't know that. I've been in Hebron for the past month."

David sighed. "It's been a full-time job, trying to stay out of his way."

"Don't be afraid," Jonathan said. Hearty enthusiasm echoed in his voice. "My father may try to harm you. But he will never succeed. You *shall* be the next King of Israel, and I will be your right hand man."

Jonathan's words were a bright burst of sunlight amidst an overcast sky, blazing down between dark gray clouds, illuminating David's world. "You always have encouraging words for me," he said with a smile. "I am so glad you have come."

"You have to remain strong in your faith in God. Don't waver. He has commissioned you to do something exceptional. He will see you through it."

Something was weighing deep in David's mind. Seeing Jonathan again brought him back to his old life in Gibeah. To his home. To Mical.

"How's your sister…my wife, doing? How's Mical?"

Jonathan took a breath and hesitated.

"You know it was her doing that my brothers found me," David said. "I was living in a cave in Adullam, nearly starving to death. She sent word to Bethlehem that I needed help. I'll always be grateful to her for that. I really miss her. I hope to return home soon."

Hedging, Jonathan began, "Well, I'm sure she misses you, too. I mean, it's been a long time, and…" He avoided looking directly at David.

A cold shudder of warning shot through David. He looked at Jonathan, eyes flashing. "What's happened?"

Jonathan shifted on his seat. "Well…it's been what? One…two years since you left? You know how she is—rash, hotheaded." Finally, like someone trying to down bitter medicine, he said, "My father married her to someone else. He annulled your marriage, and wed her to a man named Palti."

David coughed. The news hit him like a spear thrust and he felt suddenly out of breath. He got up and paced the length of the tent.

All this time he had been thinking of her. Her soft skin, the color of the desert sand, her sweet scent. He longed to hold her shapely body and bury his face in her hair. He dreamed of her, and woke up in a sweat. And now someone else was holding her.

He whirled back and said, "Why? Was it her idea since I've been gone this long? Or your father's way of getting back at me?"

Jonathan considered this question. Gently, he said, "Both, I think…But don't blame yourself. She's young, impulsive. She doesn't know what she's doing."

"But King Saul does. He wanted to pick the one thing that would really hurt me, and he did." His voice caught. Jonathan let him brood.

At length, David said, "Who's the guy?"

"It's no one. Someone from Gallim. A trader."

"What did he give in return for her?" David asked sullenly, remembering the lives of two hundred Philistines he took to win the King's daughter.

"I don't know…" Jonathan stood up. "Anyway, I didn't come here to give you bad news. I came to encourage you. To let you know I support you." He took a final sip of wine and set the cup down on the rug. Looking into David's eyes, he said, "Your outlook must be more extensive. God is guiding and protecting you. Teaching you. Even here, in the wilderness. This thing with Mical, though you don't understand it—and it hurts, I know—must still be part of God's plan for you."

David attempted to shake himself out of his sour mood. He was sincerely happy to see Jonathan, and appreciated his words, but this news about his wife was difficult to set aside.

"You're right," David said, his lips pressed together. "And that sounds like something Samuel the prophet would say. He told me something like that when I spent time with him in

Ramah. When your father first started harassing me. He said even that was in God's plan."

He moved toward the tent flap and exited, followed by Jonathan.

"Please know that I am really glad you came to see me," David said. "We'll have a feast for you while you're here. You can meet my brothers and my nephews."

Nate and Deborah arranged for a banquet of indigenous game to celebrate their distinguished visitor. David, Jonathan, and the entire clan feasted heartily. Caleb and Obed were thrilled to meet King Saul's son. They sat at his feet and listened to war stories with rapt attention. Talk between David and Jonathan was lighthearted, superficial, avoiding the real issues that crowded their hearts—the betrayal by the King and Mical, and the value of even that experience in preparing David for his destiny.

Later that night, David lay in his tent looking up at the pitched roof. He focused on tiny flashes of moonlight coming through the weave in the fabric. He could hear the sounds of sleeping men—coarse raspy breathing—coming from neighboring tents and campsites. He glanced across at the sleeping form of his friend, Jonathan.

It was good he came, although the whole visit, sadly, was dampened by the news about Mical. She was to be his partner, his queen. She was meant to support him as God fulfilled His plan in his life.

And now she was in the arms of another man. Holding him…*laying* with him.

He shook his head. He couldn't stop thinking about it. Mical with someone else.

His thoughts went to King Saul—who betrayed him once again. And who was still hunting him. Coming for him with the might of his whole army. He visualized the ivory-shafted spear hurtling toward him.

He thought about Ozzy.

Ozzy wrapped in linen, lying in a cave.

Ozzy…

I never told him the story of the two hundred sandals.

He looked up and mouthed, "I'm sorry."

He choked back a sob. Rising from his bed, he crept outside and sat before the spent campfire. His grief came to him like a river at the end of the rainy season. He wept silently, shoulders shaking and tears falling, creating little pools among the ashes. He wept for Ozzy. And Mical. And the slaughtered priests of Nob. And even his brother, Abinidab. So many losses. When would it end?

He couldn't understand why God would allow King Saul to chase them all over the Judean wilderness. Was God really in control, like he told Nate? Like Jonathan told him? He wondered if God even remembered him.

In his despair, he prayed:

> *How long Lord?*
> *Will you forget me forever?*
> *How long will you hide your face from me?*
> *How long will my enemy triumph over me?*

He gazed up to the wide expanse of sky. Searching for God. For a sign.

> *Save me, O God, by your name;*
> *Vindicate me by your might.*
> *Look on me and answer, Lord my God.*

And I will trust in your unfailing love and salvation.
Surely God will be my help;
The Lord will sustain me.

Psalm 13 & 54

Several gathering clouds began to dim the light of the moon and stars. The call of an owl broke the silence, as did the sudden rustling of a desert mouse across the cinders, cold in the fire pit at David's feet.

He was out of tears. He looked about him, focusing on the other campsites and supply wagons, already partially packed for the move from Ziph. Escaping for their lives once again.

He heard Jonathan murmuring in sleep within the tent. His encouraging words from earlier that day came back to David: *You shall be the next King of Israel and I will be your right hand man.*

This is what he must believe. On this he must base his hope.

The next morning, before leaving, Jonathan and David renewed the pact of friendship they originally made in the old training field, the day David went on the run from King Saul.

"You will fulfill your destiny. God is with you," Jonathan said as he mounted his horse.

"Remember…" he said as he rode away. He was holding up his right hand.

David walked back to the encampment, smiling to himself. *My right hand man.*

David felt emotionally drained that morning. He wished he could stroll in the forest, eating berries and observing little birds. He wanted to sit by a creek and listen to the burbling water wash over stones. He wanted to let his thoughts wander. He wanted to do nothing at all.

But it wasn't to be—the morning lay heavy on his shoulders. He kept hearing reports of King Saul's army getting closer to their settlement. Josh found out that clans of Ziphite people had informed King Saul where they were. Feeling the weight of responsibility of the volunteers' and his brothers' lives, he knew they had to keep moving.

Time was short. King Saul was coming.

David charged Rad with making rounds of all groups of volunteers. Rad urged them to pack more quickly to hasten their departure. Deborah was a great organizer and helped Rad in this effort.

"Roll, don't fold, your clothes. It's quicker," she advised.

David grimaced. Did she really think the soldiers were folding their clothes? They threw their belongings into sacks and piled them onto supply carts.

Caleb and Obed helped load baskets and bundles onto donkeys. Pairs of mules were hurriedly hitched to supply wagons. Women and children rode among the supplies on carts to hasten their departure. Dirt was thrown over campfires. Every soldier was fully armed as they fled. The cavalry rode alongside the entire company for protection. It was time to leave.

While fleeing, David received frequent accounts from Josh about the activities and whereabouts of King Saul's army. Before long, the two armies were on opposite sides of the mountain from each other.

David could hear the King's army getting closer. He heard the clanging of armor and weapons, orders shouted by officers, and manly shouts of encouragement one soldier to another across the steep rocky land. The volunteer army moved on silently, keeping the mountain between them and King Saul's army. David wanted to avoid direct confrontation if at all possible.

Eventually, they had to stop for the night. The thick layer of clouds prevented any light from reaching the paths to guide their way. David and the troops settled in for an uneasy night, encamped on the mountainside. They fairly dropped where they stood, sleeping on the ground wrapped in cloaks, unable to build fires lest they give away their position. The women and children remained on the supply carts, told to keep quiet.

Hypervigilant, David thought he could make out individual voices of the Israelite army from where they camped on the other side of the mountain. Barely distinguishable words and phrases drifted to him in the misty darkness.

"Mount up!" David thought he heard. Could that be right? He sat up and bent an ear in the direction of the command, willing himself to hear what was being said.

Could they be coming?

He sprang up, about to give the order for his men to regain formation, about to order their retreat. He looked wildly about. Where was Josh? Where was Nate? He trod around the groupings of soldiers on the ground, disturbing their slumber, looking for his lead men.

As he searched, he heard the faint rasping sound of horses' hooves tramping on stony ground. It was coming from the Israelite camp. He paused to listen, gazing wide-eyed into the blackness for signs of movement from them. The sound was becoming indistinguishable. Soon he heard nothing.

It seemed they weren't *returning*.

David sat on the ground and leaned back against the wheel of a supply wagon, trying to stay awake and occasionally dozing fitfully. His eyes shot open just as the sun was showing the next morning. He sat upright, leaning an ear, listening for any sound from the enemy army.

He was startled to see Josh striding toward him, weaving in an out among the other soldiers still sleeping on the ground or just waking up. Josh was smiling.

David stood up and leaned backwards to stretch his back. Josh came near and burst out in laughter.

"What? What's so funny?"

"Good news!"

"And…?" David waved a hand.

"King Saul's army…they're not there anymore."

David narrowed his eyes. "What?"

"The *Philistine* army was seen near Gibeah. King Saul had to give up searching for you so he could defend his own city. Saved by the Philistines!"

Saved by the Philistines? Not likely. David knew this was salvation from another source. This proved God *was* still in control. He *did* remember them, and was working out His plan for David by delivering them from King Saul's army once again.

Joyfully, David and Josh began rousing their fellows to resume their journey.

29

The Rocks of the Wild Goats

Jonathan's news about Mical helped David decide what to do next. He had no reason to return to Gibeah. As risky as it was, he had been willing to chance visiting his wife. But now…he decided to continue south-east, across the lower Judean mountains. There he could await further direction from God concerning his mission.

David led the volunteer army to the Rocks of the Wild Goats, in En Gedi. This untamed area of backwoods country was the location of the only fresh water oasis this side of the Salt Sea. They settled among the caves in groups of twenty to fifty. For the rest of the rainy season and into the dry, he continued to wait for guidance, and had Abiathar pray to God daily on his behalf.

Jonathan's encouraging words rang in his ears: '*You shall be the next King of Israel, and I will be your right hand man.*'

Could this be true after so many years? At age twenty-five, it had been fourteen years since he was anointed king, and he felt restless, ready to take on his destiny. Hiding out in this wilderness was tiresome. Time was wasting. Some days he just wanted something to *happen*, something that would help him be victorious over his enemy, King Saul, and stop his unceasing efforts at pursuing him. He needed a sign, or word from God. And the chance to *do* something.

The waiting in limbo made it challenging to keep the volunteer army interested in supporting him. David encouraged them to remain loyal despite being always on the run from King Saul, telling them how much he depended on their support and protection, and rewarding those who showed significant improvement in their skills as warriors.

At least living in En Gedi provided plenty of fresh water, the abundant fruit of date palms, and large caverns to reside in instead of tents. They were even able to house the horses and livestock in caves, keeping them concealed. Having the King find them every time they moved made David passionate about keeping everyone out of sight, which was becoming harder and harder the larger in number they grew.

DAVID SETTLED IN ONE OF THE CAVES WITH JOSH, RAD, Abiathar, and a number of volunteers. It was a generous cavern with many rooms and a subterranean pool of clear water. Daylight filtered in through narrow shafts in the ceiling, illuminating strange configurations formed by dripping elements. Sightless reptiles scurried into dark corners of the cave, out of the revealing light of day.

The group was just rising and rolling up their sleeping mats; all gear was to be packed daily and ready to move at any time. They heard a voice, several voices, coming from the entrance to the cave. Since the newcomers didn't use the pre-arranged signal—three strikes, then two, with a staff against the wall of the cave—David was sure this was someone he didn't know. He sent Josh to spy on the intruders.

Josh came back to the rear cavern. "Someone from the Israelite army," he said, his voice sharp with warning. "He relieved himself against the cave wall, then sat down near the opening."

The Israelite army—again! And here they were, like rats in a trap, with no way of exiting the cave except to go past the enemy. As David paced back and forth he could hear the sounds of war horses stamping on the hard earth outside the cave. The rattling of armor and call of the ram's horn indicated a military situation—possibly renewing the pursuit after David himself.

"Who was it?" David whispered to Josh.

Josh shook his head. "He was in the shadows."

"How many are there?"

"Couldn't get near the cave opening, but I could see about a dozen armed men from where I was hidden."

"Were they advancing?"

"No. They were—"

"Don't spare me, Josh. I need to know! Should we be on the defensive?"

Josh was about to answer, but David broke in. "Forget it. I'll have a look myself."

He crept carefully along the damp wall of the cavern until he was near the outer chamber. The acrid smell of fresh urine stung his nose. He kept himself within the shadows of the cave wall as he observed the trespasser, who was seated on the floor of the cave.

The intruder was wearing full army gear, and there was a spear thrust into the earth nearby. His face was hidden by shoulder length black hair and a generous beard. The early morning sun cast down a beam of light, illuminating a wide streak of white hair falling over his forehead.

King Saul!

David shrank back against the cave wall. His breaths came choppy and shallow. An official appeared in the cave entrance. "Your Highness, shall we mobilize the troops?"

King Saul replied, "Hold on, hold on, eh? I just want to take a short break. Traveling all night—it's harder on me than it used to be, you know? I'll let you know when I'm ready."

The soldier exited the cave. King Saul closed his eyes and rested his head back against the cave wall. Soon, heavy and regular breathing indicated that he was asleep.

David returned to his comrades. His face was bright with excitement. "It's King Saul! He's come to me at last. And he's asleep in the cave."

Abiathar blinked rapidly. "Now's your chance. Maybe… maybe God has led him into your hands."

David grasped the hilt of the sword of the giant he had on him, as always, and withdrew it from the scabbard. What irony, if he would kill King Saul with it. What a way to finally fulfill his destiny.

What a way to finally fulfill his destiny? No—it was not the way to fulfill his destiny. Not with the shedding of blood. And not with harming God's anointed one. Despite the fact that God's Spirit left Saul years ago, he was still presently the King of Israel, and David would not have his life on his hands.

And, yet—*what an opportunity.*

He wasn't sure what to do. Abiathar fingered the fringe of his priest's shawl. He had his own grudge against King Saul, so he let David work this one out for himself. Finally, David took up the sword and stole forward to the outer chamber. He held out a hand to his companions, and they remained where they were.

Keeping to the dimness against the cave wall, he crept close to where King Saul was sleeping. His heart pounded faster and faster. He felt dizzy. He was relieved to observe no one in particular on guard nearby—the soldiers were chatting among themselves outside.

He edged closer. Close enough to sense the slow, regular breaths and the smell of sweat from the weary body of the King. He raised the sword and sliced it through the air, onto the King's robe that draped on the ground, severing it. Quickly, David grasped the fragment of fabric and scurried back to the cavern.

Josh rushed to him. He grasped his arm and said, "Let us attack him for you. If he's still asleep, it would be easy. Like slaughtering a lamb. Then the Kingdom would be yours."

David jerked his arm from his hold. "What do you mean?"

"Just…just…Isn't that what you want? You're waiting to take over the Kingdom, right?"

"*No,*" David said sharply. He glared at Rad. "What did you tell him?"

Rad held up his hands defensively. "Hey, Dave, I didn't tell him anything."

Josh broke in, "I don't need to be *told*. I'm a spy, remember?"

"Hang on," David said, pointing at Josh. "We'll talk about it later."

David paced the length of the cavern, fingering the section of King Saul's robe. He spoke a few words to a scout, sending him forward to the chamber to keep watch while the King was napping.

He turned abruptly to face Josh. "I already feel bad enough that I cut the King's robe. But I have a plan. And it doesn't include killing anyone. *No one's* trying to overthrow the King."

Several moments later the scout returned. "The King is on the move."

Quickly, David tightened his belt and threw on his cloak. He strode to the entrance of the cave and looked out, spotting the King riding away from him with his army. Should he risk it? He wanted to take action, and he had a plan. But what if it didn't go as he hoped? It would be easy for the King to capture him, take him back to Gibeah in disgrace, and have him put to death, a traitor. Maybe he should just let them be on their way, and he could continue living in En Gedi. Hiding in a cave with his followers. Wasting time.

He was tired of wasting time. He wanted to do something, and this was his chance to face up to the King and make his position known. Despite his misgivings, he pushed himself to move on, trotting out to catch up to them, finally facing his enemy, his stalker, the one who chased him from his home and all over Judah. The one who stole his wife from him. It was time for a confrontation.

Still several paces from the withdrawing army troops, he called out, "My lord the King!"

King Saul reined in his horse and wheeled around. David could see the King studying him, eyeing the simple garments he wore and the sword he brandished. Recognition dawned on the his face.

David took a deep bow. Straightening, he said in a loud voice, "Why do you listen to those who say I wish to harm you? This very day you have been given into my hands." He pointed behind himself. "You fell asleep in my cave, in the very place I was staying. I watched you sleep, deciding to let you live or die. And to prove I would never harm the anointed one of Israel" he waved the section of dark brown fabric edged in gold braid "—see? It is a piece of your robe. I cut it off as you slept."

King Saul quickly reached down and took up the hem of his outer garment. Seeing the irregularity, he glanced back at David, eyes full of alarm.

David continued, "My men urged me to kill you then and there, but I said I would never hurt the Lord's anointed one. This proves that I am not trying to harm you, even though you have been hunting me for over two years."

Finally, King Saul called back, "Is that really you, my son, David?"

"Yes, it is me, David. I'm just a dog. Or a flea on a dead dog. Why should the mighty King of Israel waste his time chasing me? May the Lord judge which of us is right, and punish the guilty one. He will rescue me from your power!"

Overcome, King Saul dismounted and handed the reins to his attendant. He stepped carefully, alone, over the uneven ground between himself and David.

Drawing nearer with clasped hands, he said, "You are a better man than I am. You have repaid my evil intentions with good, sparing my life. That's just like you. Righteous and just. Always doing the will of God, eh? You put me to shame."

David was still apprehensive about approaching the King, so he held his ground. King Saul continued speaking softly, his voice thick with regret, "May the Lord reward you for the kindness you have shown me today. Now I know what a good king you will be, and how Israel will prosper under your rule. Just promise me that when that happens you will treat my family with kindness. Promise you will not wipe out my descendants."

"I have already promised as much to your son, Jonathan. I make the same promise to you." David sheathed his sword and began moving back to the cave. He glanced behind himself and observed King Saul mount his horse with difficulty and settle into his saddle. The King turned his horse and retreated with his army. David watched them disappear over a bank of earth and into the early morning sun.

As he stepped toward the cave, he paused a moment and looked up, gazing past the sunlight filtering through the trees, splashing on leaves, illuminating them, and said, "I praise Your name, oh God, for delivering me from my persecutor, who is stronger than I. May honorable men surround me, and may You continue to bless and protect me." (Psalm 142:6–7)

David returned to the cave to find Josh and Rad waiting for him.

"Josh," he said. "I need you to go back with the men. Make sure they are all getting packed." Josh and Rad began moving toward the rear of the cave.

"Rad," David called out, "A word." He pulled Rad to the cave opening and whispered harshly, "Who told him I am preparing to be the next king of Israel?"

"Hold on, Dave. We, that is, Nate and I, have said nothing. We honor your secret. I don't know what he meant by that remark about 'taking over the Kingdom.'"

"All the same, I don't trust him." David paced away from Rad, then returned. "Where did he come from? He was in the King's service before showing up in Adullam, right?"

Rad shook his head. "So many came to us then, I really don't remember."

"*Think*, Rad! Could he be here, infiltrating for King Saul?"

"Dave, calm down. Then why would he suggest we strike the King down?"

"Don't you see? Maybe it was a test, to see if I would really try it. Then he could have alerted the King's troops to capture me."

Rad hedged. "That's something you should ask Nate. I don't know anything about that."

Later that morning, when the various groups from the caves gathered outside by campfires for the early meal, David found Nate sitting on a large rock with several others, drinking tea made by the healers out of indigenous herbs. It was supposed to improve strength, and all soldiers were ordered to drink it daily.

David motioned to Nate to follow him. The two made their way through clusters of breakfasting men and women. Nearing the edge of the encampment, David leaned in confidentially, "What do you know about Josh?"

"The spy?" Nate thought for a moment. "He came when we were in Adullam, along with a few others. They are Benjamites."

"Hm. Yes. I should have known. He's one of those left-handed warriors." They walked a few more paces. "So, he belongs to the *same tribe* as King Saul? Why wasn't I informed of this? You should have told me."

Nate stopped in the path and looked at David. He crossed his arms and said, "*You* said you worked with him once, remember? And we weren't too choosy who we let join us in the beginning. A lot of the men would rather not have others know where they came from, or what they did before they arrived. But as far as Josh is concerned, I've found him to be quite skilled, and loyal."

David nodded. "He has been, that's true. But he *is* a spy, and *was* one for King Saul. *And* coming from the same tribe—how do I know he won't double-cross me? How do I know *he* wasn't the one who told King Saul when we were in Keilah? Or Ziph?" David's voice grew tense. "Or here? Someone is informing on us."

"Hm. I see what you mean."

"…And, for some reason he is privy to the fact that I am to be king!"

Nate raised his eyebrows. "That's concerning. I can assure you we didn't say anything. All we need is for the troops to get wind of that. They would love to start a revolution against King Saul."

"Watch him closely. Let me know if you suspect anything," David said.

Nate raised his chin and gave a nod.

Over the next few days, David and the volunteer army made ready to leave En Gedi. It was just too close for comfort, having King Saul know where they were settled. When David thought about it, his apology just didn't ring true. He didn't trust him. Why would he give up so easily? An emotional moment, that's all it was.

They made plans to retreat even further south, toward Maon. The gentle hills of this land would support the clan well. Pastureland and plentiful streams would allow some to graze their own small groups of sheep and goats. The wooded valleys offered cover and protection from inclement weather, as well as providing building material. By now, several of the men had taken wives from the surrounding areas. Families were forming. Whenever they moved, it was like moving a whole city.

Riding in the lead, as always, David bid Rad ride alongside him on the way to Maon. The two picked their way along the stony paths.

"Last night when I was packing, I realized how tired I am," David said.

"Tired? You don't sleep well in a cave?"

"That's not it. This life. I'm not a nomad anymore. I've grown used to houses, cities. I don't want to live this way. In caves and tents."

Rad smiled. "Remember when we were young, and we set up a tent in the pastures when it was our turn to stay with the sheep?"

"Playing 'Sheiks', Ha ha!" David chuckled at the memory. "And Father was so mad the time we snuck one of his camels to take with us."

"*Right*. Didn't he know a sheik has to have a camel?"

They rode a few more paces, both lost in the reverie of the fond memory.

"I'm not having fun now," David said at length. "It's not a game anymore."

"It will be over soon," Rad said with a hopeful glance.

David pressed his lips together. Would it be over soon? Or would he just keep wandering in the wilderness until finally, in the end, King Saul prevailed against him?

PART THREE

30

A Caravan

A year passed. The volunteer army and their families lived in relative peace in Maon. This southern-most part of Judah was too remote for King Saul to bother with, it seemed. They settled among the gentle hills and streams, family groups or troops of soldiers sharing campsites. David and his brothers pitched their tents close to one another, near the abandoned stone sheepfold of a forgotten settlement, and took their meals together. Since the clans of Maon relied on sheep farming for their livelihood, the area felt familiar to David. Like home.

The volunteer army and their families were still dependent on trade and barter for many things, so Rad arranged to provide something the surrounding clans had need of—protection. Raiding parties of Edomites from the south, and Philistines from the west, were a constant threat. Josh organized the volunteer army to work in shifts, patrolling the entire region. Not only did they protect the local shepherds, they provided safety to their own settlement, as well.

David continued to hold Josh at arm's length, secure in the knowledge that Nate kept him under observation. Let *him* handle the spy. Thus far, Nate reported no reason to doubt Josh's loyalty. In addition, he was a great asset by organizing the patrol around the pastures of Maon.

In return for offering protection, David sought help from several of the wealthier clans when provisions got tight. He sent Rad and his team to visit a clan in Carmel.

A day later Rad returned from Carmel and met David at his tent "Dave, those people couldn't spare anything for us," he said.

"Is that so?" David said. He was busy adjusting the center pole keeping the entry aloft. With a final thrust, he secured the pole into the ground. Testing it, it held fast. He turned to face Rad.

Rad sat on the wall of the stone sheepfold and kicked his sandal in the dirt. "More like *wouldn't*. The chief of the clan, Nabal, sent us away empty-handed."

"Hm. I know for a fact they have plenty to spare," David said. His jaw clenched. "And they owe us! We've guarded their pastures this entire season. We even helped with the shearing."

Rad looked up at David. "That Nabal. He's a jackal. He has these huge bodyguards. When he refused our request, he turned them on us. We had to get out of there—fast."

David's expression grew dark. He sent Rad to find Nate and Josh.

Rad brought the two captains to David's tent that evening, having already told them what happened in Carmel.

Full of himself, David proclaimed, "We have to teach those Carmelites a lesson. We can't allow the clans around here to disrespect us." He fixed his eyes on Nate and Josh. "We'll visit them again tomorrow. This time we'll bring a few more 'guests.'"

Despite the peacefulness of the time, Nate and Josh had continued to drill the volunteer army daily. Monthly contests in the form of games, races, and tournaments showed off the soldiers' improvement in their skills, and gave them incentive to work hard. They aspired to always be in top shape, able to defend against King Saul if needed.

They would be ready for this undertaking.

The next day, David mounted his horse and led a company of fifty cavalry soldiers on the road to Carmel. He sat tall and confident in the saddle, the sword of the giant at his side. As he led the way down the hill, he became aware of movement coming toward him—a group of people and pack animals. He held out a hand, bringing his men to a stop.

David gazed at the caravan. Who was this coming to meet him? A woman—riding a donkey. Several more donkeys and servants followed her. Their passage up the ravine was laborsome, weighed down as they were with heavily laden baskets. When the woman was within hearing distance, she dismounted and bowed deeply before him.

"Well? What is it?" he said.

She stood to face him, eyes lowered. He recognized her as Abigail, the handsome wife of Nabal. She wore the typically modest garments of the local women, but even the head scarf and long gown she wore couldn't hide her mature beauty. Despite the hostility he felt toward her people, he descended from his horse and prepared to listen to what she had to say.

"My lord, I am your humble servant. From…from Carmel." She glanced up nervously. "Please don't hold what my husband has done to you against me, or against my people. He is a fool! So tightfisted, and—and…"

David saw a brief flash of passion and anger in the gentle woman's face.

Abigail cleared her throat and paused for a moment. She looked up to David. "I was not aware your men came to us for help and provisions yesterday. If I had been there, I would have given them all they needed."

At this, she indicated the pack animals behind her. "See? I hope this makes up for how stupid Nabal was in refusing to assist you. I have brought two hundred loaves of bread, wine, five roasted sheep, raisin and fig cakes. Enough for all your army. Please accept this gift as an apology for my husband's rash behavior."

As she finished her discourse she looked at the line of cavalry behind David—soldiers dressed in full combat gear, swords and archery equipment at their sides.

Her voice cracked. "Please…please promise me you will reconsider what you have planned to do. Please accept this gift and don't attack our settlement."

"Why? Why shouldn't I attack your husband?" David said. "I told my men just this morning, 'May God strike me dead if we don't have our revenge on Nabal today.' And now you want me to go back on my word. He has repaid my good with evil. He would be getting what he deserves."

She considered this for a moment, and began again, choosing her words carefully. "You're right. He would be. He is dishonest. Grasping. *A fool!* No one would miss him, believe me. But why punish *all* of our people for his wickedness?" She took a step forward. "Think of it, and please forgive me if I offend you. Don't let this act of vengeance be a blemish on your record. Everyone knows you have always treated the clans here in Maon with integrity and honesty. All this needless bloodshed—it will bother your conscience and perhaps hinder God's full blessing upon you."

She stepped back and watched David, her face hopeful. David listened carefully to the woman's statement. He recalled how angry he was yesterday. He turned to look at his troops, eager to back him up, impatient horses snorting and pawing the ground, soldiers reining them in. He raised his eyes to gaze at the caravan before him—at the rough-faced, unarmed servants, at the donkeys bearing generous gifts of food, and back at the lovely Abigail. His heart softened.

This undertaking, attacking Carmel, this was nothing but a hot-headed response to an affront he suffered. Rather than have his volunteer army, and his brothers, think him an ineffective leader, David determined to confront and punish those who offended him. But now he realized he was taking this way too personally, and this woman called him on it. She was right—this was no way to maintain favor with God. It was time to back down.

David laughed gently. He turned to his soldiers, and said, "Who can argue with that reasoning? She's got me beat!"

He faced Abigail and gave a nod. "I accept your gift. Thank God for your shrewdness and generosity, for you have kept me from making a big mistake, harming innocent people just to take revenge on your husband. He should thank you."

She let out a cynical laugh. "That's not going to happen."

David felt a twinge of sentiment pass through him as Abigail held his gaze. He bowed gallantly, maintaining eye contact with her beneath his generous eyebrows. "Once again, we accept your gifts. And you may return in peace, knowing you saved your people."

Abigail let out a relieved sigh. "Thank you," she said, lowering her eyes. She mounted her donkey and rode along the caravan, giving instructions to her servants for unpacking the provisions. The soldiers advanced to accept the gifts of food and wine.

David shielded his eyes with his hand and watched Abigail, seated on her donkey, as she began her journey back to Carmel. The sun glared off the land mercilessly that day. It was difficult to see—but did she just look back at him and smile?

It was about two weeks later that the news came to David. He was riding out from the encampment to accompany several young men on a hunting expedition. His brother, Nate, rode up to join him.

"Hey, Dave, hold up," he called out.

David brought his mount to a stop.

"I just heard some news from Carmel," Nate said. "You remember Nabal, and his wife Abigail?"

How could he forget? He found himself dreaming of the shapely, gentle woman with the lovely face. It made him moody, wanting her, not being able to have her.

"Nabal's dead."

"Dead?"

"Yes. They found him yesterday morning. He died through the night."

"Hmph. He must have angered someone else. It was bound to happen."

"No, it wasn't that at all, Dave. He died of natural causes."

"God's will then." David urged his horse into a slow walk. Nate kept up. "What really happened?"

"It was the day after Abigail was here that he took sick. They say after she told him what she did, bringing us the food and wine, that he got so mad he had a *stroke*."

"Mad? She saved them from annihilation!"

"You know how he is—proud, cocky. All he cared was that his wife went against him. He didn't care that her actions saved them. Anyway, he took sick that day and never left his bed. He died ten days later."

David thought for a moment. "So that was yesterday, right? I'm sure the widow Abigail has had enough time to mourn for a dog like him. Send word to her—I would like her to join me here, so I can…you know…comfort her in her loss."

Nate raised his chin and chuckled. "You cunning fox! You were hoping for that all along, weren't you?"

David's grin answered for him.

"I don't blame you. It's a good thing Deborah joined me back in Adullam, or I'd be tempted, too. Then you'd have to fight me for her. I'll send the message to Carmel today."

31

Abigail

Abigail had been waiting by her tent in the afternoon sunshine for the group of men coming to accompany her to David's encampment. She was surprised to get an invitation to supper so soon after her husband's death. But life is short, and she was ready to move ahead. There was no mourning him anyway, the jackal. And the supper invitation piqued her interest.

David, the former captain of King Saul's army, was handsome and rugged. She felt if she had no further desire to get to know him after supper, she could leave the next morning and have nothing more to do with him. However, if his company was pleasant, as pleasant as he was on the eyes…who knows?

Abigail chose Timnah, one of her servant girls, to go with her. Her two other servant girls—sisters who belonged to her clan, but whose parents owed a large amount of money to Nabal—remained home. She dressed in her indigo ensemble and wore dainty leather sandals decorated with embroidery.

They arrived at the tent of David's sister-in-law, Deborah, feet dragging and dusty. Abigail graciously accepted the basin of water David's brother, Rad brought them to freshen up.

"I appreciate your wife letting us rest in her tent," She said to Rad.

"My wife? Oh—Deborah? She's my brother, Nate's wife. I'm not married."

Timnah giggled. Abigail murmured an apology. All these relatives already!

After Rad left, Abigail sat on the rug and removed her sandals. "I'm afraid I ruined these," she said, holding them out to Timnah.

Timnah peered at the sandals and rubbed at them with a damp cloth. The colored needlework design began to look a little cleaner. She worked on them for a few more minutes. "If we put them out to dry, the sunshine will fade the rest of the dirt, and the colors will show through." She set them aside. "Now, your feet."

Timnah dipped a cloth into the cool water and wiped her mistress' slender feet.

"That feels good," Abigail said. "I didn't think walking here from Carmel would be such a long trip."

"It was nice those men came to escort us here," Timnah said. She twisted the cloth in her hands, wringing it dry. "I just wish we had horses. Why do you think they didn't bring us horses? I know how to ride. And so do you. Then we wouldn't have sore feet. My feet are so sore. Are your feet still sore? Do you want me to wash them again?"

Abigail thought for a moment. "Yes. Yes, I would."

"Okay. Here, why don't you dip them into the water… Oops!" The basin of water tipped and emptied onto the rug. The women sprang up quickly and stepped onto a dry rug.

At that moment Deborah entered the tent with two small boys.

"Oh, sorry!" Deborah said. "I thought you were coming later." She turned Caleb and Obed an about-face and pushed them out of the tent.

"What happened?" Deborah snatched a few cloths drying on a rope overhead. Leaning over her rotund abdomen she began dabbing at the rug.

Timnah lent a hand. She knelt before the spill and rubbed the wet spot vigorously. She took a deep breath and said, "It was my fault. I was soaking her feet, and I spilled the basin. I didn't mean to. It's just her feet are so hot. Mine are hot too. It's so hot today. And the walk was long. So I—"

Abigail held up a hand.

Timnah closed her mouth and slunk back on the rug.

Deborah looked at Timnah, wide-eyed. "Um…It's okay. Just water. And you're right. It is hot. It will dry in no time."

She gathered the damp cloths and hung them on the overhead rope again. "So you're here to have dinner with David," she said to Abigail. "That's nice. He's nice. He comes from a good family. Hard working family."

She poured some fresh water into the basin, moistened a clean rag, and handed it to Abigail. "Here, wipe your face. A sweaty face isn't a good way to attract a man."

As Abigail freshened up, David fidgeted in moody silence. He combed his hair and beard and washed his face and feet. He donned a linen tunic, and a striped robe that had recently been washed. Then he changed his mind and put on a black robe. Thinking it too dark and unfriendly, he tossed it down and changed back into the other one. He couldn't decide on wearing a turban or head scarf, and finally chose to go bare-headed. His auburn hair was one of his best features.

While waiting for Rad to bring Abigail to his campfire, David's mind wandered back to another time, another place, another woman. Mical.

He second-guessed his motivation at wanting to get to know Abigail. Was it just a way to replace Mical? He missed the attention and companionship of a woman. He longed to hold the soft, warm body. Now that Mical was no longer his, he was justified in seeking another wife—right?

He paced the length of the tent. Distracted, he picked up the sword of the giant, and put it back down again, making sure it was securely sheathed. Soon, he heard the scuffing of sandals coming near his tent. Taking a minute to brush his hands down his robe to straighten it, he went out to greet his guest.

Rad, Abigail, and a maidservant all approached David's tent. Looking past his visitors, David noticed Nate's wife, Deborah, standing a distance away, hands clasped, beaming. Such a *matchmaker*.

Abigail drew near to David, head slightly bowed. She wore a little grin and peered up at him playfully from beneath her indigo headscarf. Her almond shaped eyes sparkled against skin the color of honey.

"Won't you…. Here. Sit down here," he said, indicating a crude wooden bench before his campfire. He had covered it with a wool rug earlier that day. Looking at it now, it still looked too coarse for women to sit upon.

David's actions were stilted, awkward. *I act like I was never alone with a woman before.*

Rad made as if to leave, but David, feeling suddenly outnumbered by *two* females at his fire, bid him stay.

Abigail sat demurely on the bench, hands folded in her lap. She tucked one foot neatly behind the other. After being set out in the sun for an hour, her sandals were dry again, and looked cleaner. "I hope you don't mind me bringing my maidservant. This is Timnah," she said to David.

Timnah smiled broadly and twirled a spiral of her blue-black hair in her fingers. She took a deep breath. "Nice to meet you, I'm sure. It was such a long journey. I'm glad we had time to wash up. That Deborah is so nice. We were so—"

Abigail raised an eyebrow at Timnah to stop the onslaught of comments.

David listened in silence, a little overwhelmed. Bowing, he said, "Timnah is welcome, as are you. We have roast venison and wine coming." He sat on a bench next to Rad, across from the women. "You already met my brother, Rad."

Rad smiled at the two women. Abigail smiled back. Timnah giggled.

David searched for something to say. "I…that is…we really enjoyed, I mean, *appreciated* the food you brought last week."

Abigail nodded.

"I…I heard about your husband—"

She shook her head. "It's alright. He got what was coming to him. Why talk about it?"

He looked down. "Of course…I'm sorry."

She laughed gently.

At that moment the women who cooked supper were bringing portions of food to all those around campfires. They left a bowl of roast venison and barley in sauce, and loaves of flatbread. They also poured cups of wine for David and his three guests before moving on to another group of diners.

The four ate in silence for a few minutes. David ate quickly and efficiently, a habit he picked up during his army days. Rad nibbled at his meal left-handed. As usual, he hid his right hand in the folds of his robe. He kept glancing at Timnah. She was a lovely young girl with dark skin and laughing eyes. Her simple garment shifted over her willowy figure when she moved.

Abigail savored the bread dipped in brown sauce. She finished her portion and dabbed at her lips with the remainder of the bread. Finally, she broke the uncomfortable silence. "I want to thank you for this meal, and for inviting us here." She folded her hands in her lap. "It was very kind of you."

David, after his false start, was eager to impress. "We—that is, some of the men and I—were successful in our hunt this week. God led us to a large herd of deer, and we killed several of them."

She considered this and looked around the orderly campsite. "I can see you have a very well-run encampment here."

He nodded eagerly. "I have a lot of help from my brothers. Nate heads my army. Rad, here, is in charge of all food distribution and supplies. We always have what we need, mainly due to his hard work."

Rad ducked his head, self-conscious. He peered up to see Timnah grinning at him.

Abigail took a sip of wine. She set her cup down on the bench next to her. "It's good to have people you can count on. Timnah has been with me for almost ten years now. Since I was about nineteen. I don't know what I would do without her."

Timnah took a deep breath, about to make a remark. Abigail touched her hand, and she kept silent, for now.

David and Abigail were finally engaged in conversation. As briefly as possible, he explained his purpose for settling in Maon with his brothers and the volunteer army—trying to keep his distance from King Saul. His falling-out with the

King was already known in these parts. Despite being part of Judah, Maon was several days' journey south from the royal city of Gibeah, and the clans in this region enjoyed some measure of independence from King Saul's influence. It was easy to understand why David would want to settle here.

David was beginning to enjoy himself and feeling a little less awkward. He was also glad to have Rad present, as his second, and was amused to see the interchange between his brother and the maidservant, Timnah.

As evening drew late, the group noticed Deborah approaching. "Excuse me…I made sleeping arrangements for the two women in my tent."

David stood and bid goodnight to his guests. He bowed and took Abigail's hand in his, saying, "I hope you will stay with us for a while."

"Hm. I planned to," Abigail said. She glanced up at him, then down again, her lips pressed together in a pleased smile. She rose to her feet and stepped away with Deborah, taking one last glimpse of him as she went.

David sat by the fire next to Rad and watched the women walk away. In the light of other campfires, he could see Abigail conversing with Deborah. Timnah peeked back, and David noticed his brother give her a shy answering smile.

"What was that?" David said to Rad, laughing.

"What? Nothing!" Rad frowned, rose quickly, and disappeared into the darkness. David shook his head and retired into his tent.

DAVID AND ABIGAIL SPENT MANY OF THE FOLLOWING evenings together. After supper, he played the lyre for her while she enjoyed a cup of mint tea. Sometimes they walked out, alone, to the perimeter of the encampment, as the breezes returned to the valleys. They had a lot to talk about: David's childhood and family, growing up on a sheep farm, the time he spent in King Saul's army.

When he mentioned "sheep", she got excited. She told him about the system she had in Carmel for breeding sheep to make the softest wool. She also had the sheep handled daily, either to examine their hooves for rot, check their teeth, or make sure their behinds weren't soiled. Or sometimes just for a cuddle. The frequent handling made the sheep quite tame and shearing was an easier time for all involved. David was impressed with her husbandry skills.

As the dry season was nearing an end, the two rambled over the gentle hills of Maon, seeking shelter from the hot sun in groves of olive trees. David enjoyed pointing out various birds in the trees to her—doves, sparrows, ravens. His mother taught him about birds when he was a boy, and he loved recognizing the different varieties. Abigail repeated their names after he identified them, to learn for herself.

Coming upon a trickling spring in a rocky crag of the hillside, they stopped to refresh themselves with a drink of water. They had been talking about his time living in Gibeah. He filled a small earthenware jug with water from the spring and handed it to her. She drank her fill.

He continued his story. "So, as I was saying, the King finally agreed to allow me to marry his daughter, Mical."

She laughed. "—*After* you gave him the two hundred sandals."

He nodded and took a sip of water. "She is no longer in my life, as you know. I received word about two years ago that she married someone else."

Abigail bowed her head. "It hurt, I'm sure." She sat down on a rock by the hillside. "When I was with Nabal, I kept my distance as much as I could. He was bad-tempered, especially when full with wine." Her voice became quiet. "I learned how to appease him during those times, and also to dodge his fists when he turned on me."

David reached for her smooth hand and held it in his rough, calloused one. He gazed down at her, his eyes full of longing. "You should never have been treated that way. If you were my wife I would never hit you or mistreat you. I would always show you respect. I would—"

She shot him a look of surprise and amusement, one eyebrow raised.

He smiled gently and scuffed a sandal in the dirt. "I mean…I was going to ask you tonight. I don't have much to offer you. We live as nomads, sometimes settled, sometimes on the move. But I know you would make me happy. And I would do everything to please you."

He took both Abigail's hands in his and she stood up, facing him. "Would you agree to be my wife?"

She leaned in toward him, and he clasped his hands around her curvy body, drawing her against him. She clutched at his back. The desire she had for him was evident in their kiss, long and deep. He had his answer.

32

Wedding In Maon

———◆———

Over the next week, a select number from the clan attended David's marriage to Abigail: Josh, Rad, Nate and his family, and The Thirty. Timnah and the other maidservants, and, of course, Abiathar, were also in attendance.

It was a simple ceremony. Living in the wilderness, most religious customs had been pared down to their most basic aspects. The few weddings, bar mitzvahs, and even one circumcision the clan observed were devoid of most finery and ritual. Abiathar did a good job of organizing these traditions into a simple time of celebration for one of their own.

Deborah joyfully helped Abigail get ready for her wedding day. She dressed her in a white linen gown and veil, the borders decorated with embroidered flowers in red and yellow. Timnah enjoyed her job as Abigail's attendant. "I still think we should have doves. We could release them as you walk to David. And maybe one will land on you. Or David. They would be so pretty. So white and—"

Both Abigail and Deborah held up a warning finger. Timnah closed her mouth. She busied herself braiding Abigail's hair into a coil on her head, to be crowned with a wreath of flowers.

David, clothed in a freshly washed robe, stood before Abiathar, his brothers at one side.

Even Abiathar was specially dressed for the occasion. He wore a new fringed shawl, one that Deborah had woven on her loom. It replaced the one he wore to Adullam which, by now, had no fringe left.

David took his bride's hand when she approached, and the two faced the priest, their attendants at their sides.

"May you…may you be as Jacob and Rachel," Abiathar started. He stroked the fringe of his new shawl. "Love one another. Always forgive each other. And keep God the center of your marriage."

David raised the veil and kissed his new wife gently.

Timnah had been craning her neck from her place next to Abigail, looking behind the couple. She was hoping that Rad, standing next to David, would notice her in her wedding best. She leaned back too far and stumbled against Abigail just during the wedding kiss, pushing Abigail into David's arms. David, impressed by Abigail's amorous response, reached around her into an even tighter embrace and yet another kiss, this one not so chaste.

They broke their embrace to cheers of happy wishes from the whole company. David's brothers gave him congratulatory back slaps. Abigail hugged Timnah and the two had a good laugh together.

At the wedding feast, Nate lifted a cup of wine. Never good with speeches, he made an attempt at a sage saying he heard once.

"Marriage is a way to come together to solve the problems you never had before you got married." Nate said, his chin raised. He took a sip. "Here's to David and Abigail."

"Here, here!" said the group, touching cups of wine one to another.

David watched Deborah leave the table in a huff. Nate glanced around, his eyes drawn together. He took off after his wife.

"Did you see that?" David asked Abigail.

She balanced her elbow on the table and leaned her chin lightly on her fingertips. She thought for a moment. "I'm not surprised."

He raised an eyebrow, still not understanding.

"What your brother said. I know he meant well. But really? '—problems you *never* had before you got married'?"

Enlightenment dawned on David. "Oops."

"Right. Oops."

———✦———

DURING THE REST OF THE RAINY SEASON, ABIGAIL FELL into her role as David's partner with grace and competence. And he felt fulfilled, finally, after all that time without a wife. She was a sympathetic listener. At the end of the day he aired his frustrations in heated language, and she listened, patient, sometimes gently chiding, until whatever was bothering him melted away. And she was genuinely interested in supporting his role as leader. Many times she was a diplomatic force, helping David find a way to soothe unrest in the clan.

David knew he should tell Abigail his secret—his commission by God to be the next king of Israel—the *real* reason they had to travel to Maon, and why he was in hiding from King Saul.

He was inclined to tell her one night when they were talking in bed. It was another wet night, and rain was sprinkling on the roof of his tent, dripping across the opening.

"Oh! I am ready for these rains to be over," he said, wiping his forehead. "Water keeps dripping on my head."

Abigail laughed gently. "Here, lets both slide over. And put that basin under the drip." She indicated the earthenware basin they used to wash up.

They did as she suggested, and covered up again with a woven wool blanket—a wedding gift from Deborah crafted in shades of green and white. She leaned her head into his shoulder.

"I love this blanket Deborah made," she said, stroking her face with it. "What a nice way to use up that soft wool I brought from Carmel. She's becoming quite skilled at weaving."

"It keeps her busy," he said. "After that remark Nate made at our wedding, she's been keeping her distance. He told me she is usually at the weaving loom till late at night. Even though he told her he meant to make the toast *without* the word 'never', she's still mad. Really, either way you say it, it doesn't sound right."

Abigail chuckled. "It's funny."

"What?"

"Nate. He always acts like he knows it all. I think *he* would like to be in charge around here…"

"…but we both know who rules his house!" David said, finishing her thought.

"Right! And she sure knows how to hold a grudge. It's been, what? Three months now?"

"Mm-hm. It's hard to believe you came to me, here, just *four* months ago. Seems you've been with me for years."

"I've loved every minute of it."

"It's so peaceful here, in Maon."

She nuzzled into his neck. "We can stay here forever."

David thought a moment. He peered up at the drip falling from the ceiling into the basin. Drip…drip…drip…. He knew he should tell her. It's been long enough. He could trust her, and it was important she knew. "That's just the thing. We can't."

She propped herself on an elbow and looked at him. "Why not?"

"Well…the reason I'm here, down here in Maon. The main reason is…I'm hiding from King Saul."

"You told me that." She sat up and reached for the tiny pot of lanolin she kept by the bed. "And fortunately, he hasn't bothered us here."

He closed his eyes. He wasn't saying it right. His head eased into the pillow a few moments as he thought of how he should say it. The rhythmic movement of his wife rubbing her hands with the lanolin lulled him. Drowsily, he said, "I have to return to Gibeah some day."

"Gibeah?"

"Yes…I have to go back. Jonathan said…Jonathan said he would be my right hand man." David's words were slurred. He had a fleeting vision of Jonathan riding away. He was holding onto the reins of David's horse, leading it. Soon, David was riding away with him, too.

The next morning they sat before their cooking fire at breakfast. The rain from overnight had ceased, leaving everything damp. It had been an effort to get a fire started.

"More tea?" David asked.

"Yes, please." Abigail held up her cup for him to pour.

The abundance of mint that grew along the streams in that region was a good source of the tea David enjoyed. Soon after she arrived at Maon, Abigail had her maidservants pick several large baskets full of the herb. After drying in the sun, it was crushed and stored in small tightly woven sacks.

She drank a sip of tea and set the cup down on the bench. "Last night…what were you trying to tell me?"

"About?"

"You said something about returning to Gibeah. And you talked about King Saul, and Jonathan."

David narrowed his eyes, trying to recall. He had a dream about Jonathan. They were riding in the training field together. Then he remembered trying to tell her about becoming the next king of Israel, but he wasn't able to get it out. And right now, he just wasn't mentally prepared to tackle explaining it all to her. He would tell her some other time. Soon.

"Never mind. I was falling asleep. I had a dream about being in the army with Jonathan. Maybe that's why I was thinking about Gibeah."

Abigail shrugged a shoulder. She gathered the breakfast things and took them into the tent.

33

Timnah

Timnah heard Abigail call to her early one morning. She was already awake and had folded her blanket neatly, placing it in a corner of her tent. The other two maidservants were in the encampment somewhere fetching breakfast.

Timnah had been willing, and even excited, about moving to David's settlement. She was tired of living on eggshells, never knowing when Nabal would show up and abuse her mistress or her. It was mainly a lot of yelling, but occasionally he would swing at her or throw something. Those times brought her back to her childhood in Egypt, living in slavery before coming to Carmel. She was glad to leave it behind.

"Hello, Timnah," Abigail said, entering the tent.

"Oh! Good morning," she said to her mistress, bouncing up from her mat. "I had the strangest dream last night. I dreamt my sister was living with us, and we were getting ready for her wedding day. She was wearing a lacy white gown, with silver jewelry, and a tiara, And there were these doves—"

"Mm-hm," Abigail murmured.

"—and they landed on our shoulders, and the one was trying to pull off her tiara, so we put them back in their cage, and then…and then…hmm, I forget the rest."

Abigail smiled at her. She twisted her dark brown hair into a long braid. "I thought I might wash my hair this morning. We could go to the stream you drew water from yesterday." Since the wet season was coming to an end, springs and creeks were filled with water from rain that occurred about every other day.

As Timnah began collecting the things needed for the hair washing outing, she heard David call to his wife from outside. Abigail's face lit up and she exited the tent.

"David! So glad to see you," Timnah heard her say. She heard the squeak of a kiss. "I was just going to take Timnah to the stream to help me wash my hair. Why don't you come with us?"

"I can't right now. I have a meeting planned with Josh and Nate this morning. But I have to say I don't like the idea of you going by yourselves."

"Hm. The girls go there every day to draw water."

"That's different. Sounds like you will be there all morning. I can have Rad accompany you. He can bring some men to stand guard."

Timnah smiled when she heard David mention Rad's name.

Abigail said, "We don't need a guard. It's really okay…"

"You don't understand. There are groups of Edomites and Amalekites from the south that raid settlements all over these hills. I'll see if Rad is free."

Yes! Timnah peeked outside the tent opening.

He was still talking. "You were, er, just, you know… going to wash your *hair*, right?"

Abigail ran a hand up his arm, so strong and warm. "Yes. That's all. Timnah makes a special scented soap that works really good on hair. You should try it."

"And have my men laugh at me for smelling like a woman? Ha ha! No thanks." He stepped away and headed toward the men's tents, looking for Rad.

Timnah moved aside to allow Abigail to come in. She took a deep breath. "I have all the things we need to wash our hair, my special soap, a small basket for rinsing, combs, towels. It's all here in this big basket. And there are extra towels in this sack, here. Although it's so hot and sunny out, we probably don't need all those towels. And we can bring some snacks along, too, in case we get—"

Abigail held up a finger. "Why don't you go find the other girls. Ask them if they would like to wash their hair too."

In the end, Abigail, Timnah, and the two other maidservants all decided it was a good day for hair washing. After breakfast, Rad and a few young men arrived at their tent, armed with swords. Together, they headed toward the stream.

As the women arranged their supplies, Rad busied himself with setting a guard in a perimeter among the hillocks and trees around the water.

Reserved around women, Rad was a challenge for even the skilled matchmaker, Deborah. He felt self-conscious about his deformed hand, and that stole his confidence. Keeping occupied with work kept his mind off not having a wife. He just couldn't picture himself being desirable to a woman, and tried not to think about it.

During the outing, he stole glimpses at the women. Timnah stood in the creek and poured water on Abigail's hair using a tightly woven basket. Her neat, sinewy arms shone with perspiration in the late morning sun. Droplets of water glistened on her dark skin. She balanced skillfully in the middle of the creek, toes gripping flat rocks just below the water level.

When finished with her task, Timnah stepped gingerly back to the creek bank, arms held out for balance. Nearly there, she lost her footing and took a step back to brace herself. Slipping on a mossy rock, she tumbled into the creek.

Rad dashed to the water as soon as he saw her fall. He reached out with both hands and helped her stand on the slippery stones. Her hands in his, he tugged her toward the soft earth of the creek bank, where he lost his footing and fell backwards, pulling her on top of him.

Abigail and the other maidservants watched this stunt with much amusement and broke out into laughter at the sight of the two struggling to right themselves.

Stepping back, Rad quickly hid his right hand in the folds of his robe. He said, "Sorry…I mean, I wasn't trying to make you fall again…"

Timnah flashed a bright, toothy smile. "What are you saying? You saved me! Thank you."

Rad flushed and muttered something about just doing his job. He quickly returned to his post.

The women towel-dried their hair and combed it in the sunshine, spending all morning at the task. By then, Timnah's clothes were dry, and the group made their way back to camp, the young men following behind. Rad grinned at the way Timnah skipped along the path, swinging her basket of supplies in her hand.

That night, he lay in bed, restless. His mind was filled with thoughts of Timnah. He could hear the peal of her laughter as she played in the water with the other girls. He recalled the fleeting looks he took of her—the bright smile, smooth and shapely arms, and eyes that glanced back at him, the color of burnished bronze.

The incident on the creek bank played over and over in his mind. He could once again feel the grasp of her hands in his. She did not recoil when he touched her with his maimed right hand. He felt her tumbling on top of him, and the instantaneous response his body made. He recalled how she looked with laughing eyes into his. He had it bad.

Abigail joined David for an early supper upon returning from the hair washing outing. After eating, she removed her headscarf and shook out her still damp hair. Tilting her head to the side, she ran a comb through a few times, separating the locks and combing them dry before the fire.

She paused in her task and glanced up at David, who was watching her. She blinked and smiled at him, lips pursed playfully, and handed him the comb. Lifting an eyebrow, he caught her meaning. He took her hand and guided her into their tent.

He led her to the low stool covered with fleece. Standing behind, he started at the crown of her head and drew the comb through her hair. She leaned back and a pleased "hmm" escaped her lips.

He smiled and continued to comb her hair, taking his time to carefully detangle the strands. This was a novel sensation. His own hair, lately worn short and choppy, received cursory attention every few days. His wife's was lustrous and thick as the tail of a king's war horse, a pleasure to comb. It hung down to her waist, and he stroked large sections, creating a fall of glossy dark brown which draped over her shoulders.

He leaned in, nuzzled his face into her hair, and nibbled at her neck. Laughing, Abigail tumbled off the stool, pulling him onto the fleece mattress with her.

34

A Spear and a Jug

Two years passed since David and his followers moved from the oasis of En Gedi, where he had spared King Saul's life, to the gentle hills of Maon. Some would have David relax his rigid stance of watchfulness against his enemy. He knew what King Saul was capable of, however. Since the volunteer army was still acting as a protective force in nearby sheep pastures and shearing tents around Maon and Carmel, they also kept vigilant lookout for any trouble brewing from King Saul.

One evening after supper, as David reclined in his tent, he played the lyre for Abigail, perfecting a new song he had written. As he strummed through the final verse they were startled by the sound of a horse neighing and sliding to a stop outside the tent.

David rushed out to catch Josh dismounting, the horse lathered and winded. "Nice way to disrupt my evening," he scolded. "You frightened my wife."

Josh leaned over, hands on knees, to catch his breath. "I'm sorry," he said to Abigail as she joined them.

"It's okay," she said, smiling in her friendly manner. "But how about you? Are *you* okay?"

He straightened up and gave her a nod. Then he turned to David and reported that army troops were arriving at Hakilah Hill, east of them. Israelite soldiers, prepared for battle.

David grilled him as a groom led the horse away. "Was King Saul there? Did you see the King?"

"The King? I didn't see him," Josh said. "We were up on the northern crest of the hill, hidden behind some boulders. Could see thousands of soldiers setting up camp."

David gnawed his lower lip. "Oh—he's there. *I know it.*" He looked directly at Josh. "I want frequent reports from The Thirty. Find out what their intentions are." He didn't want the Israeli army to have the advantage, but actually, they already did, just by being so close by.

Abigail watched her husband with concern. The appearance of his old enemy disrupted their serene existence. David had the look of the hunted—wide eyed and jumpy. That night he slept fitfully, arising long before dawn.

All the next day David received information from The Thirty. Their reports were disheartening. King Saul was spotted among the soldiers, and so was General Abner. Some thought perhaps it was just coincidental, King Saul's being there with his army. Perhaps they were on their way further east to fight the Moabites, or take care of unrest in southwest Judah, so often caused by the neighboring Amalekites.

But Josh settled the question handily. He appeared before David's tent in the evening to find him seated, silent, simply staring into the embers.

David glanced up and bid Josh sit beside the fire. He lifted a basket of dried fruit from the bench. "There's a few figs in there," he said.

Josh's eyes brightened. He picked one out and popped it into his mouth.

David waved a hand halfheartedly for Josh to begin his report. He was drained from feeling anxious all day, and was ready for some encouraging news.

"There is a small settlement of Ziphites near us. On the way to Hakilah," Josh said, chewing noisily. "I went there, as a 'lone traveler', looking for a place to water my mule. Struck up a conversation with the women there, at the well—great gossips they were. I asked them about the King's armies, if they were worried about them being encamped nearby. 'No,' they said. 'His Highness, King Saul is looking for that outlaw, David.'—um, pardon me."

"No," said David, holding out a hand, "It's okay. I want the truth."

"The Ziphite clan leaders notified King Saul where you are. Told him you are living in a settlement in Maon, near Hakilah Hill."

"They turned me in?"

"It's…something they do. Keeping the King informed of goings-on in this part of Judah…"

"Hm. They informed on us almost three years ago, when Jonathan visited." He pressed his lips together and looked sharply at Josh. "We shouldn't have stayed here so long. Why didn't we relocate?"

Josh shrugged a shoulder. Was he expected to have the answer? David knew why, however. It was Abigail. Living in domestic happiness this past year kept him from focusing on his mission, his aim—that of becoming the next king of Israel. Fact was, he was tired of running, and enjoyed the feeling of being settled down with his new wife. And now, the thought of moving was overwhelming. The entire clan was established here, it would take days before they were ready to leave.

"Just make sure I keep getting regular reports. Keep me informed of any movements of the Israeli army." He then dismissed Josh, who snatched up a few more figs from the basket before leaving.

David thought about Josh's story. About the Ziphites informing on them. It had a ring of truth, but should he believe it? Could it have been *Josh* all along—giving away their position to King Saul? His exhausted mind was not thinking logically. And there was nothing he could do tonight, anyway. He had to talk to Nate, and determined to bring it up the next day.

After a good night's sleep and a first cup of mint tea, David felt better able to decide what to do. Nate arrived for the morning meeting as he was inspecting the sword of the giant, polishing it with a soft dry cloth. It still shone beautifully as the day the metalworker restored it.

He sheathed the sword and said, "Nate, I need you to go to Hakilah Hill with me tonight. To that crest overlooking the Israelite camp. I need to see for myself what's happening."

"What's happening?" Nate repeated.

David shook his head. "I don't know—that's why I need to go. To the Israelite camp. Tonight. You can come with me."

"No," said Nate. He threw back his head. "You should ask one of The Thirty. What you really need is a spy."

David considered this. "Yes…that would be better. Have one of The Thirty meet me here tonight. Not Josh. I'm still not sure about him. He told me some story about the Ziphite people themselves informing on us. Perhaps so. But

it just seems Josh always knows when King Saul shows up."
He peered at Nate. "What do you think?"

"I know you have your suspicions, but he *is* a spy. It's
his job to know those things. I haven't found any reason
to distrust him."

"Mm. Yes…possibly. But for now just chose someone
else. I'll go with him and see what kind of military operation
King Saul has going on. Come back at sunset."

At supper that evening, David picked at his barley and
onion stew. He nibbled a small bite of mutton. He had no
appetite. He startled with every noise he heard as he sat by
the fire. His heart raced, and so did his mind.

"Are you sure you should go near the Israelite camp?"
Abigail said. She picked up a stray twig, broke it in pieces,
and tossed them into the fire. "Maybe you should ask Abiathar to seek God's will ."

"Abiathar is busy across camp. There is a sick boy. He is
spending all night praying."

"What if you're seen?"

"I'll keep hidden high up on the hill. I want to see how
prepared they are, maybe get a glimpse of King Saul. Try
to determine his frame of mind. We might have to move
again, and if they are just getting settled in their camp it
would give us more time."

He entered his tent and buckled the sword of the giant
around his waist as he waited for Nate to return. He paced
the length of the tent and kept looking out to see if his
brother was back yet.

He thought how it would be to see King Saul again, and
about his deadly spear, and the time, back in the palace, that
he was almost impaled with it. He couldn't afford a battle

injury. A sudden thought of Ozzy came to him. No—he wasn't going to suffer the same fate. He was sure that wasn't God's plan for his life.

He hoped it wouldn't come down to warfare. Despite the extensive training they accomplished, the army of volunteer renegades could never be successful against the mighty army of King Saul. They were far too outnumbered. How foolish and shortsighted he was, thinking that with a few hundred soldiers he could defend against the great Israeli army.

The best they could hope for was to remain hidden in the countryside. But now even that wasn't an option. King Saul was just too close. They could be overrun within an hour. Then what of his army, and his mission? He didn't want to believe that, after all this time, King Saul was still hunting him, especially after vowing to leave him alone the last time they had a personal encounter. He confronted him once, he would have to do it again.

Abigail entered the tent and remained with him. Self-doubt plagued David as he looked at his wife and realized he had much more at stake this time. Back then, in En Gedi, it was just him, but this time…He clutched Abigail's hand and they passed the time in prayer.

I look up to the mountains.
From where does my help come?
My help comes from the Lord,
Who made the heavens and the earth.
He will not let me stumble or fall.
As he watches over me,
He will not tire or sleep.

Psalm 121

Nate returned in near total darkness. Dense cloud cover hid the moon; the dying campfires lent little light. He brought with him one of The Thirty, a spy dressed in a dark robe, face concealed beneath a hood. David and Abigail met them outside.

"That robe you're wearing—it's too light. You'll be seen." Nate said to David. "You should wear something dark."

Abigail went back into the tent, and returned with a dark brown cloak. It hid his light colored tunic well. He and the spy set out into the night.

Stepping lightly toward the enemy camp, David could feel his pulse quicken and his breaths come shallow. His eyes darted about, and he imagined an enemy soldier behind every bush. After treading silently for an hour, they approached the crest of the hill overlooking the camp. Well hidden among rocks and scrub, they peered over a large boulder and observed the goings-on below.

The enemy filled the valley. Most of the soldiers were settling down in groups around dozens of campfires. The estimate of thousands of soldiers that was reported wasn't far off. Even as David gazed across the army camp, he wasn't able to see the periphery of it in the dying firelight.

He waited until all were sleeping deeply. Even the horses tethered nearby were asleep, every so often shifting position to rest a different leg. Cooking fires smoldered and the pungent scent of burning embers drifted upward. The air became cool and damp as night set in.

As David focused on the scene below, a coney nibbling at something near him brushed against his leg. He startled, sending the animal darting away. He sat back, took a deep breath to calm himself, and whispered, "Let's go down. I have to find King Saul." He rose up and began striding down the hill. The clouds having cleared, he was able to see his way in the moonlight. The spy followed behind, stepping carefully among the foliage and stones.

David glanced back at the hooded figure. "I get a little nervous with things like this…" he murmured.

"Good thing you're not a spy for a living," the spy whispered back.

Hearing his voice, David felt a cold shudder of warning go through him. As he continued down the hill, something nagged at him. Something wasn't right. He shook his head and re-focused on the task at hand.

Entering the encampment, the two worked their way past numerous tents and campfires surrounded by clusters of sleeping soldiers. Nearby mules and horses snuffled at the strangers, tossing their heads nervously.

He motioned for the spy to move ahead with him, to the next campfire, near the center of camp. His glance fell on the one sleeping nearest that fire, surrounded by troops bearing arms, even in sleep. He saw the thick black hair with the conspicuous white streak, and the ivory-shafted spear stuck into the ground beside him.

The spy turned his head toward King Saul as well.

The next moment, he was pulling David back, away from the slumbering men, and into the shadows of a tent. He clutched David's arm fiercely and whispered in his ear, his breath hot, "Let me kill him with his own spear. I won't have to strike twice!"

David jerked free of his hold on his sleeve, and in the moonlight was able to see the face clearly beneath the black hood. He now realized why he felt guarded earlier. Reaching behind the spy's head, he grasped the hood and yanked it back with one quick motion. "Josh?"

"What?"

"Why are you here?" David whispered harshly.

Josh shook his head, his eyebrows drawn together.

"I thought Nate brought someone else tonight…"

"No. Nate said you needed one of us. Told us what you had in mind. One of my men volunteered, but I wanted to do this with you. So I came instead."

David thought fast. Being here, among the enemy, this would be an opportune time for Josh to turn him over to King Saul. *If* Josh was going to two-time him, this would be the perfect chance.

He *did*, however, just offer to kill the King with his own spear.

The best thing to do would be to go forward with his plan. It felt right. God would shield him. God would help him succeed.

With voice lowered, David said, "Look—I won't let you, or anyone else, harm the Lord's anointed one. Do you think that's why we came here? I have a different reason. I'm going to break him yet. You'll see." He moved forward again.

"You want to help?" He murmured to Josh, behind him. "Pull that spear out of the ground. Bring it back with us. And here," he reached down and picked up a water jug "we'll bring this along, too."

Josh collected the spear. The force of pulling the spear out of the ground caused him to lose his balance and stumble against a nearby soldier. Incredibly, he did not wake up.

David moved on, heading toward the outer perimeter of camp. He tripped over a tent spike and spilled some of the contents of the jug, splashing a sleeping soldier on the face. He turned over and continued sleeping. David exhaled deeply. *Something's keeping these soldiers asleep.*

Josh caught up to David and the two mounted the hill, returning to the ridge where they started.

"I still think you should have let me strike him down," Josh said, leaning back against the boulder.

David pressed his lips into a sad smile. "The Lord Himself will strike him down one day. Or he will die in battle, or of old age. Whatever happens, I will not have his blood on my hands."

He set the jug down on the stony ground, and was about to lay the spear next to it when he realized the opportunity he had to get a really good look at it. This was the weapon that nearly struck him down just a few years ago in the palace.

In the moonlight David examined the ivory shaft, discolored brownish from handling. It was skillfully made of several sections of ivory fused together to form a pole that narrowed into a bronze spearhead. Into the ivory shaft was carved a basket-weave pattern to provide traction. The spearhead was tapered to a lethal point. It was a stunning weapon.

Josh said, "What do you plan to do with it?"

David balanced the spear in one hand, feeling the weight of it. "I think…I think I'll just return it. You'll see. I have a plan."

The two men settled down in the brush and waited for dawn.

David dozed intermittently. He woke to sounds of the army beginning to stir, to impatient animals waiting to be fed, and General Abner giving orders. Josh, ever vigilant, was wide awake and watching the activity below.

"The spear. Where's the spear?" David said.

Josh reached back and gave it to him. He drank deeply from the water in the jug and handed it to Josh. When he finished, David took the jug and spear and stepped in front of the boulder.

"What are you doing?" Josh rolled his eyes and rose to follow him.

"Stay here," David said. He tread down from the boulder several paces.

Josh remained concealed and watched him through narrowed eyes.

Standing on the hillside, David already had the attention of several of King Saul's soldiers. They quickly armed themselves. Someone went to notify General Abner.

Seeing General Abner approach, David called out, "General Abner! What kind of a man are you? Is this how you protect your King? See here." He held up the spear and the jug.

"Here is your master's spear, and a jug from beside his campfire. There is no one in all Israel as mighty as General Abner, and yet I came in the night and took these things from right under your nose. And why? To prove that *I mean you no harm*."

A voice boomed from behind General Abner. "Is that you, my son David?"

"Yes, your Highness. Why must you continue to hunt me down? It's been a long time since last we met, and I thought we had an understanding. And yet here you are—harassing me again. Threatening me by your very presence.

"I am nothing but a sparrow, just a poor little bird on the mountain. Why waste your time and your armies trying to capture me?"

King Saul trudged to the base of the hill and looked up. He was quickly surrounded by archers taking aim. "I'm sorry," he called out. "You can come home now, David, my son. Come back to Gibeah." He eyed the spear in David's hand, flashing in the morning light. "I see you have spared my life yet again. You have considered my life precious, even while I have been chasing you in the wilderness." He got down on both knees. "I am a fool, and have been very, very wrong to try to hurt you."

David didn't know if he could trust him. Dare he? Was this a true, heartfelt apology, or just an emotional moment, like at En Gedi? Could this be the end of his time running from King Saul?

He raised the spear in both hands, suspending it between heaven and earth. "Here is your spear, oh King. Have your men lay down their arms, and I will return it to you. As for me, may the Lord value my life as I have valued yours. May He rescue me from all my enemies."

David looked up at the spear he held high and observed it vibrating. His hands were tingling. He could feel a rush of power coursing through him from his upraised hands to the soles of his feet. Power from God. Power that helped him once again vanquish his enemy without the shedding of blood. He stumbled backwards as the feeling overwhelmed him. Then, just as quickly, it was gone.

"God will indeed bless you, my son," King Saul said. He struggled to get up from the ground. General Abner rushed to help him up. "You will continue to do heroic deeds and be a great conqueror."

A young soldier came up the hill and held out an unsteady hand. David handed the spear and the jug to him and glanced down to General Abner. The General gave him a nod and turned, shouting out orders for their departure. David stepped back up to the boulder where Josh was waiting.

His heart soared at the victory, not only for triumphing over his enemy, but also for overcoming self-doubt and keeping true to his purpose, to not harm the anointed King of Israel. With renewed determination, he and Josh returned to the encampment, and David to Abigail.

"How did it go?" Abigail asked, her voice weary. Her face was drawn—she had slept very little, and was up since before daybreak, waiting for David on the bench by the cooking fire. Tea was already brewing.

"Good…I think," David said. He tossed his cloak on the bench and sat on it, reaching for the tea. "Once again, the King professed remorse for mistreating me. And once again, I find it hard to believe him. I know God was on our side, however. He put a deep sleep over the soldiers. Not one of them woke up the whole time we were in the camp."

Abigail caught her breath. "You were in the enemy camp?"

"Yes, my dove." He cupped her face in his hand and looked into her eyes. "It was all in God's plan. We trusted in Him and He kept us safe. They are retreating at this moment." He kissed her and said, "We shall have a long life together. You'll see. The enemy can't separate us that easily."

35

A New Plan

Now that his location in Maon was known to King Saul, David knew it was time to move. Again. He longed to travel north, back into central Judah, into the Forest of Hereth again, so he could be closer to Gibeah and available to assume the role of Israel's next king, whenever it was time. Furthermore, he was thinking of seeing his old friend, Samuel, in Ramah, and introduce his new wife to him. He was sure Samuel would approve. Maybe traveling north with a small group would be a better choice. He could see the prophet and gain some guidance from him, advice on how he should proceed.

Still weighing his options, David was having tea with Abiathar, the priest, one evening after supper. They were making plans for the upcoming Feast of Tabernacles, the week-long holiday commemorating Moses and the Israelites' escape from Egypt and sojourn in the Sinai desert. Ordinarily, families took their meals in temporary structures erected in remembrance of that time. Since they already lived in tents, Abiathar had some other ideas to mark the celebration.

While they discussed plans for the Feast, Josh approached, his face grim. "I know you were still thinking about going north, to Ramah. But the information I heard today from The Thirty might change your mind."

David sighed deeply, "Don't tell me. King Saul is there. I wondered where he was headed when he moved his army from Hakilah Hill."

"No. No. Nothing like that. What I wanted to tell you is…." Josh cleared his throat. He looked down at his feet, then back at David again. "Samuel is dead. Went to God this past year. Died in his sleep." The news was disclosed suddenly, like a dropped rock.

David's heart tore within him. He gazed at Josh, open-mouthed. He set down his cup of tea and rested his forehead in his hand. The prophet, Samuel, the one who appointed him the next king of Israel, was dead. He was all alone now. All alone in his mission.

Abiathar waved Josh away and placed a comforting hand on David's shoulder, murmuring soothing phrases to him.

He looked at the priest, "That man had been my spiritual adviser for many years."

"I know…"

He felt lost. Empty. Small.

Thinking of Samuel from time to time when his faith was weak kept David encouraged. It kept him strong, just knowing there was someone, a friend in Ramah, who believed in him and who understood the daunting responsibility he faced.

And now…who could he talk to about it? His brothers, maybe. But not the way he could talk to Samuel. Samuel had God's viewpoint. Even when David had doubts, Samuel had faith that he would succeed. Samuel grasped the steadfast knowledge that God himself appointed him the next king of Israel, and that God would bring him all the way.

David wished he could confide in Abiathar, who seemed to have the same connection with God. But right now? The sorrow was too fresh.

He said, quietly, "I stayed with him for a month before King Saul chased me into the wilderness. He encouraged me when my faith was weak."

"He…he deserves to go to his final resting place. To the glories of Heaven," Abiathar said. "He lived a full and…and productive life."

David nodded. "He was getting sickly, having a hard time getting around. I'll miss him greatly."

DAVID NO LONGER HAD A GOOD REASON TO TRAVEL north. Additionally, Josh and his brothers advised him to keep as much distance between themselves and the Israeli army for now. It was important they move away from Maon, so David came up with a new plan. Something unexpected. He decided they should travel west, to the country of the Philistines.

The time to assume the throne of Israel had not come yet, so he felt the best place to hide and wait out his time was in the country of Israel's enemy. His reputation as an outlaw and expatriate had kept him from being a target of the Philistines over the past few years, even during their raids of Judean towns. Strangely, it would be safer there than in Judah. King Saul would not dare look for him there. And it would provide security for the clan—his numerous followers who depended on him for protection—and Abigail.

David knew he did not have the resources or enough soldiers to defend against King Saul if attacked by him. He knew that now. In addition, he was unwavering in his conviction—he would not gain the throne by killing the presently anointed King. The best thing he could do is go into hiding. Disappear for awhile. And wait.

He was certain that eventually God would work out His plan in his life. He was no longer the impatient young man of years ago. And even now, having experienced life running from King Saul, he learned his destiny will be fulfilled only in *God's* time. As the prophet Samuel had said, it was in God's hands. God was in control.

After discussion with his faithful advisors, his brothers and Josh, David decided to see an old acquaintance of his in the royal city of Gath—the Philistine ruler, King Akish. Accompanied by Abigail and Nate, he left early in the morning, to seek an audience with the King

On the journey, David relayed the story of how he escaped King Akish's grasp several years ago.

"So there I was, trapped in his entrance hall. His guards were coming for me with chains."

Abigail rode astride her own horse, next to David. "How did you get away?"

He laughed. "I…I…." He laughed some more. He couldn't stop laughing. He laughed so hard he began hiccuping.

Nate looked at Abigail across David's horse and raised an eyebrow. "Gonna share the joke with us?"

David reined in his horse. The others stopped next to him. He drew in a deep breath and blew it out through pursed lips. He said, with effort, "I…I pretended…I pretended I was a lion!"

"A lion?" Abigail said.

"Yes. A lion."

"I don't see how that would help," Nate said.

"Well…I got down on the floor and ran around on all fours. I roared! When the guards came near, I scratched them and tried to bite them. Finally, they threw me out into the street." David picked up the reins and urged his horse into a walk. "I could hear King Akish yelling something about me being insane."

He glanced to his side where Abigail was riding. Now she was laughing, a tear streaming down her face. "I can't believe it. What made you think of doing that?"

"I don't really know," he said, his face thoughtful. "I didn't think. I just did it. It just felt right."

The three rode in silence. Abigail let out a stifled giggle from time to time. Nate rolled his eyes.

David thought back to that incident. He had been a different person back then—scruffy, unkempt. He was running for his life and really did look the part of a madman. How far God had brought him since then.

"So," Nate began. "What makes you think King Akish won't recognize you as being the insane lion of those years ago?"

"I'm not worried about that. I look much different. Different clothes, different haircut. Besides, he won't even be looking at me. Why do you think I wanted Abigail to come along—he will be blinded by her beauty." He smiled in his wife's direction.

"Ugh!" Nate said.

"Aww!" Abigail said. She leaned her head in toward her husband.

David reached across and took her hand. He looked into her eyes. "As I am."

King Akish greeted David, Nate, and Abigail warmly when they were presented to him. Nate and David were dressed in finely woven brown robes and matching turbans. They wore new sandals with straps that wound up to the knees. Abigail wore her favorite floor-length indigo gown and matching head covering. The three presented an elegant picture to the King. He smiled at them and bid them approach the throne.

"Welcome, welcome." He held out a hand and David grasped it, bowing deeply. "When my gatekeeper announced your name, a thought of something that happened years ago came to mind. A madman broke into the palace. 'Captain David' he was claiming to be. Ha, ha! Chased him away we did. Never saw him again."

David shot a glance at Abigail, who had let out a snicker. She quickly regained her composure. He focused his attention on King Akish and waved a hand elegantly, "Back then there were some people seeking fame and attention by imitating me, because of how successful I was. But as you know I am seeking a new allegiance now."

King Akish nodded. "Of your recent activities we are greatly interested. A favorable impression on my troops you have made. Eluding King Saul isn't easy, and yet managed you have. With just a handful of soldiers."

David smiled to himself. He knew King Akish had a fair command of the Hebrew language. Still, his sentence structure was awkward. David hoped neither he nor his companions would mistakenly chuckle at, or even worse, correct the King's speech.

He bowed to the King. "We are grateful for your willingness to let us reside in your country for now. It *has* been an effort to keep avoiding the Israeli army, and I am no longer loyal to Saul, their King. I'm just trying to stay out of his way."

"Of course. And it is our hope, in return for letting you live here, join our cause you will—your army of skillfully trained soldiers we could use."

The next day the three made the long trip back to Maon. Abigail and Deborah began organizing the evacuation of the campsites, while Rad helped Nate arrange and pack all weaponry. They were moving to Gath. Timnah and the other maidservants packed Abigail's things, and then lent a hand among the other families.

As Rad was busy securing baskets to pack animals, he was suddenly knocked to the ground by someone carrying a large bundle. It was Timnah.

The two hadn't much opportunity to talk to one another since that day by the creek. Timnah usually had a ready smile for Rad whenever she caught sight of him. Encouraged thus, he began watching for her around the settlement. He tried thinking of witty or intelligent things to say to her at those times, but usually reverted back to a bashful answering smile.

This morning she was carrying a towering load of folded bedding to place in a basket on one of the donkeys. He was securing the donkeys together so one of his nephews, Obed or Caleb, could lead them. Timnah collided with him as he bent over to tighten a cinch strap. They both went down, the bundle spilling out around them. He was quick to apologize for being in the way.

She laughed. "Seems I'm always having some kind of accident when I get around you!"

Smiling to himself, he reached down to help collect the dropped items. From within the folds of a thick blanket several small objects spilled out: a clay figurine in the shape of a cat, a bracelet of hammered brass, and a few coins.

Quickly, Timnah said, "Here—those are mine," as she snatched them from him. She looked furtively around and placed them back in the folds of the blanket.

"Hey…where did you get this stuff?" Rad said, wary. These were not the usual things found in the region. And from what he knew, small amulets in the shape of animals usually symbolized gods and goddesses.

Quickly, she said, "I…I got it from my former mistress. Right. She was so pleased with me that when she had to send me away she gave me these gifts, and money. Soon after that I met Abigail, so I have just been keeping this, you know, for a rainy day."

"Ha ha! The way you're acting I thought maybe you stole them, " he said playfully.

She took a quick look behind herself, then turned back to Rad. "Shh! Of course not. But I don't want Abigail hearing you say such things."

"No…I…I didn't mean it. I was just joking. Besides, you're allowed to have a few of your own things. I'm sure Abigail wouldn't mind."

"I don't think she would. All the same, I'd rather she didn't know I had it." She reached for a strand of her hair and tilted her head. "Sometimes you just want to have something for yourself, you know?"

This was true. Being one of six brothers, he recalled how hard it was to have any possessions that were truly his own when he was growing up. He gave her an understanding nod and helped her place the rest of the items in the basket on the donkey. He fastened the top of the basket and finished tying the donkeys together.

Timnah lingered and watched him perform the simple task. Aged twenty-eight, Rad could pass for one much younger. Keeping out of battle and drills, he avoided injuries common with warfare. He also paid more attention to his appearance than many of the soldiers—bathing regularly, and kept his clothing in good repair. He found it helped his negotiations with neighboring communities if he was presentable and clean.

Rad could feel her looking at him as he leaned over the cinch strap, admiring his tanned, muscular arms and sun-bleached hair. He glanced up and met her eyes. He wanted to tell her how he felt, how he thought about her all the time, how he couldn't wait to see her when she left her tent early in the morning to fetch water, and that he looked for her at other times during the day. His mouth felt dry, and his pulse quickened. He *had* to tell her.

After finishing with the donkeys, he reached out and grasped her hand in his. He opened his mouth to say—

"Rad, get busy! We have to move out before the sun gets too high!" shouted David, riding past the entire company, urging all to look sharp and get moving. They had a long way to go and Nate and Josh had already left with their groups. David and Rad were to lead the two remaining groups on the journey to Philistine country.

Timnah giggled. Rad released her hand and watched her scamper bare-footed back to Abigail. She picked up a basket and took her place among the company.

Frustrated, it took considerable effort for Rad to once again focus on the business at hand. He mounted his mule and rode to the front of the group he was to lead. Before long his mind was taken over by the business of moving. He had to focus, guiding those behind him along the road to Gath. David took up the rear group. Soon they caught up with the other groups and all journeyed west together.

36

Among the Enemy

―――――◆―――――

If the ruse of alliance with the Philistines was to be complete, David felt his army and their families (a group of people numbering about a thousand now) should settle down in more permanent dwellings in that country. King Akish agreed to allow them to inhabit the town of Ziklag, bordering Judah, which they took over as their own. The former inhabitants were given until after the annual olive pressing to move, and were sent away with jars of oil as compensation for having to move.

David was pleased to finally share permanent lodgings with his wife. The house they occupied, a sturdy structure of clay and brick, was secure and spacious. The airy courtyard offered pleasant seating at mealtimes, and the surrounding rooms provided them a private space separate from the maidservants. The little things that make a house a home: a vessel of honey for the table, chairs padded with colorful woven mats, curtains over the windows, were arranged by Abigail. She also located a source of the mint David loved for tea and, uprooting a few bunches of it, planted it in a small bed in the courtyard, surrounded by a border of rocks.

As he settled into his new house, David began to formulate strategy that would use their stay in Philistine country for his own agenda. He allowed a few days for the clan to set up housekeeping, then called a meeting with his advisors—his brothers and Josh.

The four stepped onto the roof of the house, a more private space than the courtyard and surrounding rooms of the main floor. The men sat on reed mats and partook of refreshments. Timnah brought up a cheese and fruit platter, then walked around and poured water for all.

Rad turned and lifted his cup when Timnah drew near. She leaned in and filled his cup, allowing her leg to brush against his back.

"We have all had enough, Timnah. You may go back to your mistress," David said. He had noticed the exchange between his brother and the maidservant, and didn't want Rad distracted during their meeting.

Timnah climbed down the ladder that led to the lower courtyard. Before disappearing, David saw her give Rad an intimate smile.

David began the meeting by looking at each of his men in turn and saying, "Just so we are all in one accord, I expect anything discussed here to be kept in strictest confidence." He waited for the three men to nod in agreement, and continued. "I'm sure many of the clan are wondering why I brought us here. To the land of our enemies."

Rad raised a finger. "I have a question—"

David held out his palm to Rad. "Hang on. I just have a few things, and then we can all talk." He took a sip of water. "I want you to know, I am still a loyal Israelite. I honor King Saul. I am not interested in engaging him in a battle, and hope he will just leave us alone here. And I am not, I repeat, *am not* defecting to the Philistines."

"Of course," Nate said. "I would just like to know what we hope to accomplish here. What am I to tell my men?"

"I'm getting to that. The plan…" David paused until the men gave him their complete attention. "The plan is to attack and defeat *Philistine* cities."

"Philistine cities? But King Akish—" said Nate.

"King Akish won't know. In fact, when he asks, we will tell him that we are striking against *Judean* cities." David let this sink in for a moment as he handed around the platter of food. Josh snatched up several figs.

He continued. "In this way we will gain more and more of his trust. We will infiltrate his cities and work at defeating the Philistines from within."

Nate lifted his chin in a confident gesture. "That may work. My troops would be ready for that."

Josh split a fig. "There's a problem. Someone will warn Akish. He has spies, too. It won't be long. He'll find out."

"Can I say something?" Rad said.

"He won't know," David said, addressing Josh. "Not one citizen shall be allowed to escape. That is imperative. Additionally, all plunder—cattle, sheep, wealth—shall be brought to Ziklag, which will ensure our prosperity here, since we have grown so large in number."

"Excuse me," Rad said.

David looked pointedly at his brother. "What?"

Rad suddenly felt self-conscious, since all three men were looking at him now. He slunk down a little. "It's nothing."

"Rad," said David. "What's wrong?"

"It's just…since we moved here, to Ziklag…. Do you still want me to be in charge of food distribution and supplies?"

David nodded. "Of course. Why?"

Rad looked at Nate, next to him. "I'm sorry, Nate, but your wife…*Deborah*…she's taking over. And she was selling her woven goods in front of your house yesterday."

"I know. So what?" Nate's eyes flashed.

"It's *my job*, and she—"

David interrupted. "Rad, are we still bartering for food and supplies?"

"Yes, we have a good system. I have already met with officials from nearby cities. We will help with the harvests, and they have agreed to pay us in barley, wheat, and olive oil."

David stood up. He rubbed the back of his neck. He stepped to the low wall surrounding the roof and sat on it. "I think we should continue with that. None of us are farmers. And we need grain. And oil. At least here we have our own ovens and don't have to depend on heated stones to make bread. As far as—"

"I don't mean to interrupt," Nate said. He strode to the rooftop wall and sat next to David. "But my wife selling her blankets shouldn't be a problem for you, *Rad*."

"I have spent a lot of time making arrangements with other villages and towns," Rad said. He stood up and faced Nate. "Your wife said we should be selling our own stuff to each other. She's *interfering*."

Nate's nostrils flared. He made a sudden move toward Rad.

David reached out and snatched Nate's cloak, drawing him back. "Nate, Rad has a point. But so do you. I think, Rad, that whatever we can't grow, or make, we need to keep getting from outside sources. For now. Hopefully we will be more self-sustaining in the future."

He turned to Nate. "I think Deborah has a good idea, too. She should keep selling the things she makes. And she can collaborate with others who want to sell things. Organize a market. We have plenty of talented craftsmen, and women. Okay?"

Rad nodded. Nate opened his mouth to respond.

"*I don't* want to have to bother with that again. Since Ozzy died—" David's throat tightened. He looked down at his feet for a moment.

He got up from the wall and stepped to the small table where the water was set out. He poured a cup for himself and took a sip. He turned back. "I just have a lot more responsibility with the army now, Rad. Work it out with Deborah. There's plenty to do, and we have to be flexible, and cooperate with each other." He looked directly at him. "Really. Don't bother me with this again."

Rad stomped across the rooftop. He descended the ladder in a hurry and headed for his place across town. Nate smirked at David's admonishment of Rad.

David addressed Josh and Nate. "We'll talk more about these plans at tomorrow's meeting. I want your take on it, as well." He shook hands with Nate, who departed for his house next door.

As Josh strode across the rooftop, David delayed him. "Sit down for a moment longer, brother."

Josh sat on the rooftop wall and looked at David, eyebrows raised.

David paced the length of the rooftop slowly, arms crossed, and came back to Josh. "The thing is, I have something to confess."

"Okay …?"

He laughed nervously. "You'll think it's funny. I hope. Anyway…for a while now I was afraid you were…you were… working for King Saul. I thought you were informing on us."

"You thought I was a traitor?"

"Yes. I hate to admit it."

Josh remained silent.

"And I think I've been a little hard on you because of that," David said quietly.

Josh lowered his eyes. "You don't…you don't still think that—"

"No!…No. Since that day at Hakilah Hill I realized I could trust you. You've proven yourself."

"But, *why?* Why did you feel that way?"

David lifted both hands in a gesture of resignation. "Well, *someone* was betraying us. Or else how could King Saul know where we were? Seems he always has the advantage of us."

"I know how it's happening," Josh said quietly.

David placed his foot on the wall and leaned into his leg. He nodded, his face eager.

"General Abner has spies, too. All over Judah. And also clansmen, like the Ziphites, who report to him. They are coerced into telling what they know."

"Coerced?"

Josh nodded. He thought for a moment, then said, "The Ziphites…they have been known to collaborate with enemy tribes in the region, mainly the Philistines. To keep peace. Keep themselves from being a target. They give a portion of their harvest, or wool, whatever is required, and they are left alone. King Saul, he…he thought there was more to it, and feared the Ziphites were allying with the enemy against him. So he has…he has their children taken in the night if he thinks they are hiding something. It's how he controls them. Once he gets them to talk—and sometimes I'm sure they just make things up—their children appear, wandering back from the desert, sunburnt and hungry." His voice got quiet. "Sometimes they don't come back." He paused, swallowed, and continued. "Sometimes they're found half eaten out in the wild. That's why they were so willing to inform on us."

David was silent for a moment, then said, "How do you know this?"

"Because…because," Josh's voice caught and he stopped talking. He glanced down at the stone wall he was sitting on and traced a pattern in the stones with his finger. David watched, trying to be patient, waiting for him to be ready to talk.

Josh looked up with misty eyes and said, "Once it was me. King Saul thought I was withholding information. You know how paranoid he gets." He sniffled. "It was during our war with the Amalakites, back when I was just a young soldier. My wife had recently given birth to our daughter. She had bushy black hair, like me…" He smiled sadly, remembering.

David sat down on the stone wall next to him.

Josh continued. "At that time the Israelite army was commissioned by God to completely annihilate the Amalakite tribes. The prophet Samuel made that clear. But, as you probably know, King Saul saved some of the women for his harem, and several of their finest cattle and sheep. When Samuel found out the King didn't obey God's command completely, he cursed his dynasty. Then King Saul blamed *me*. Said *I* should have reported to him the prophet's whereabouts, since I was his spy. Then he could have had the women and livestock moved so Samuel wouldn't find out."

Josh shifted his position on the wall, and gazed into the brightening sky. "During his raving at me, I knew he would take out his anger on my wife and new baby. But if I went to them I would be considered a deserter. So I had a friend race home on a swift horse to warn my wife. Told her to take the baby and travel to her family in Bethel. They would be safe there, and have others around to protect them. My friend traveled with them, too. Before long, they were being chased by King Saul's men, searching for my wife and child." Josh focused his eyes on David. "My friend fought bravely, but as my wife was running from them she fell from a cliff. Both she and our baby daughter died."

David shook his head, saddened. He reached out a hand and pressed Josh's arm. "Is that why you came to me? Why you were so eager to kill him? To have your revenge?"

Josh nodded.

David sighed. "I understand now. And one day you will have your desire. King Saul will get his due, and then—who knows? The next king will be…" he paused "…will be much wiser. And just."

Josh glanced at David and raised an eyebrow. "That is my hope."

The men sat silently as the late morning sun shone on them. David struggled to absorb the knowledge of this outrageous action by King Saul. How much worse could it get? Stealing children! He hoped it would please God to make him the new king soon. Soon enough to stop the intimidation, the *terror*, caused by the present king, and establish a prosperous and peaceful nation in the land he loved.

Josh rubbed his sleeve across this brow. "Hot!" he said, with a smile, and rose from the stone wall.

"There's cool water to drink in the courtyard," David said as he descended the ladder, followed by Josh.

<hr>

As discussed during their meeting, over the next year, the volunteer army attacked several Philistine towns just west of Judah. Each conquest was so complete that no word reached King Akish.

At that time David was summoned to attend the annual conference of the Five Cities. Nate and Josh accompanied him to the city of Gath and they dressed in their finest cloaks to appear before the King. During the conference, King Akish held confidential meetings with representatives from each region.

He welcomed the three men into his private chambers. It was an intimate setting, rich in luxuries. The King was seated on a cedar wood chair padded with a new sheepskin. It was replaced daily, to ensure his generous behind was always comfortable. A servant in a brilliant linen robe attended the King. The heat of the day had little chance to escape this enclosed, wood paneled room and King Akish survived by having his servant fan him with a large palm branch. The golden glow of several oil lamps shone on the King's bald cranium, damp with perspiration. From time to time, the servant used a rooster's tail feather to chase away flies that gathered there.

A young lady with a winning smile produced a tray of fresh figs and dates. She also passed around a basket of fruit pastries, sticky with honey. Wine was served in gold cups. David, Josh, and Nate sat on cushioned benches and sampled the treats placed before them. Josh's eyes lit up and he quickly ate three figs. David longed for a large jug of water to slake his thirst and cool him in this close room, but instead accepted the wine graciously, trying not to drink it too fast.

King Akish urged them to take more. "The pastries, are they not delicious?" He popped one into his mouth. The servant hurriedly brushed the crumbs from his beard and generous abdomen with a tiny horsehair whisk.

David stood up and bowed deeply. "We are honored to be invited here, your Highness."

The King waved a hand in a superior manner. "It pleases us to discuss our future together. But first, we require from you a report. Tell us of which cities you have been plundering."

David was prepared for this request. He knew it was important to make a believable case for his strategy of deception. He, Nate, and Josh rehearsed responses to questions they thought King Akish would ask on the journey to Gath.

David said, "I hope your Highness will be satisfied with what my army has accomplished over the past year. We raided several towns in Judah as far east as Jezreel. We have left not one person alive, and have gathered and transported all spoils to Gath." Nate and Josh nodded solemnly.

King Akish smiled. He leaned forward in his chair. "To us this is greatly pleasing."

He motioned to the young lady to bring more wine. She cheerfully poured for the King. David observed him eyeing her in her close-fitting tunic, watching as she exited the room.

He turned back to David. "Of your loyalty to us we are satisfied. We wish to extend to you an opportunity. A chance to prove to us your…your—" He motioned to the servant, who leaned close to him. The King whispered something in his ear. The servant whispered back to him.

The King continued, "—your *commitment*. A great military strike we are planning."

He took another sip of wine. The servant dabbed at his lips with a small cloth. The King waved him away impatiently. "Next year, against the army of King Saul we, and the other Five Cities, will be in battle. With us you will be marching."

David looked at Nate and Josh. He didn't anticipate this. This wasn't one of the situations they rehearsed, and it caught them by surprise.

Nate stood up and bowed quickly. He lifted his chin and said, "Forgive me, your Highness. Our army…our army is of a moderate capacity. What I mean is we…we are still growing. Still training. We didn't expect—"

King Akish looked at David. "What is this he is saying?"

David glanced at Nate, who looked like he bit into a sour grape.

He stepped forward and addressed the King. "My brother. He is too modest. Yes, it is true, we aren't a large army. But we are willing, *eager* even, to support you in this operation. It would give us great pleasure, right, Nate?"

Recovering, Nate gave an enthusiastic nod.

"It pleases us to hear this. We will discuss with you, at a later date, the particulars," King Akish said. He picked up a small mallet and rang a gong on the table next to him. David, Nate, and Josh were escorted past the separating curtain to an outer room.

Before leaving, David lingered a moment past the curtain, just long enough to hear King Akish say to the servant, in his own language, "After going to war with us, all Israel will despise their former hero. David will be locked in service to us forever."

37

Clandestine Meetings

During the first year of living in Ziklag, Rad and Timnah found ways to be together, usually meeting in secret. One evening, Timnah called out to Abigail, as she stepped to the door of the courtyard, "I'm going to get more bread from the ovens. We need some for breakfast tomorrow."

Abigail was seated at the table counting the coins she and David kept in a leather purse. "Okay. Tell her I'll pay her later."

Timnah skipped out the front door and caught up with Rad, who was concealed behind the chicken house. They went for a walk along the inside of the city wall.

"Do you think we still have to meet in secret like this?" he asked.

She shrugged a shoulder. "I don't know how Abigail would feel if she knew we were seeing each other. She always has something for me to do. She wouldn't want me taking time to go for walks with you."

"She shouldn't mind. After all I *am* David's brother. He knows I've been seeing you. Sometimes he teases me about it."

She took a deep breath. "Maybe she wouldn't care. But she's really attached to me. She wants me at home whenever she's there, and depends on me to get meals ready, and keep things clean, and organize the pantry, and buy stuff we need at the market. She got used to me doing all that when we were back in Carmel." She stopped talking abruptly. After a moment, she continued in a quiet voice, "Nabal used to yell at her a lot, and make her cry. I could always think of something to make her smile. I think that's why she's so fond of me."

Rad placed an arm around her shoulders as they walked, silently, for a few moments. "So…back then, in Carmel, how did you start working for Abigail?"

She leaned her head into his shoulder. "Well…let's just say she took me in when I was about ten, and I've been with her ever since." They stopped at the city gate and sat on one of the stone benches that lined the street into the city.

"How about before that?" he said. "Forgive me, but you don't look like your family is…um…from around here."

Timnah twirled a strand of hair around her finger and tucked it back beneath the headscarf. She tilted her head and looked at Rad. "No, we're not."

"Where then?"

"West of here."

"Canaan?"

She shook her head.

"Egypt?"

"Further west."

He laughed. "You're gonna make me guess?"

"*You're* the curious one," she said, grinning at him.

He clasped her hand. "I just want to know all about you."

"Well, If I tell you, you have to do something for me."

"Sure. What?"

She reached for his other hand. The one he kept tucked beneath his robe. She held fast as he resisted, and traced the ugly scar where the last two fingers used to be. "You have to tell me how this happened."

Rad jerked his hand away and stood up, crossing his arms, hiding his right hand again.

She stood and linked her arm into his, laughed lightly, and said, "Okay. Fair enough."

She began walking along the street, pulling him along with her. Soon, he had to run to keep up. She released his arm and sprinted, laughing, further up the street and into the town center, stopping at the ovens to collect two loaves of freshly baked flatbread.

"Abigail will pay you tomorrow," she said to the woman baking bread.

They walked the rest of the way in silence and stopped at the chicken shed. Timnah went in to retrieve eggs.

"See you tomorrow?" Rad said when she emerged.

"Hm. We'll see." She turned and skipped to the house.

He trudged moodily home. He couldn't understand why she was so reticent. Usually so talkative, for some reason she wasn't willing to divulge much information about herself. What was she hiding?

RAD KEPT BUSY DURING THE REMAINING WEEKS OF THE dry season, sending groups from the clan to help with threshing barley and wheat in nearby farms, and then amassing large amounts of the grain to store in tight brick buildings in the center of town. Soon after was the gathering of olives, and the pressing of oil. He was sent home with several large earthenware jars of oil. His staff of helpers ensured the fair distribution of these staples to all city dwellers. He also arranged a weekly market with Deborah, next to the grain buildings, with stalls of pottery, baskets, baked goods, woven items, and specialty food items.

On one market day Rad caught up with Timnah near the town center. It had been three weeks and four days since their last encounter, and he approached her circumspectly.

"Hey," he said to her in front of the dried fruit stand, keeping a couple paces away.

She stepped toward him and flashed a bright smile. Her headscarf fell back as she lifted her head to greet him. "Hey, yourself."

"Going shopping?" He was relieved she was being so friendly.

She took a deep breath. "Oh…Abigail needs a new washbasin. The old one was at the bottom of the ladder. I don't know who put it there. I don't think I did it. Anyway, when I stepped down the ladder—I was up on the roof putting some washing in the sun to dry. It was so hot yesterday. Everything dried so quickly. But I knew it looked like rain later on. So I had to gather it up after it dried. And I was carrying it down the ladder. And I didn't see the basin there. I stepped down on it, and it broke. And I twisted my ankle. But it feels better today. But then I dropped all the washing. And I had to fold it all over again—" she paused to take a breath.

Rad jumped in. "So that's why you need to buy a new basin?"

She tilted her head. "Yes, that's why I have to buy a new basin. Want to help me pick it out?"

He looked up to the sky. Dark clouds loomed close, threatening rain. "We'd better hurry if we're to beat the rain."

They perused the few stalls of the market. At the pottery stall Timnah found a nice deep washbasin to purchase, fired sky blue. She paid the merchant, and Rad carried it for her in a string bag. The two continued walking until they reached the city wall, where they sat down in the shade, the sun setting behind them.

Timnah reached for Rad's right hand. He tugged it away, but she didn't let go. "Tell me."

He relaxed and allowed her to hold it. What would it hurt? And he couldn't resist those pleading eyes, that cute smile.

He let out a sigh. "Okay. This is what happened."

There was a long silence as he gathered his thoughts.

"I was…I was in a fight with a wolf one day while watching the sheep." He looked sideways at her. "The wolf grabbed a lamb, and I went after it. It dropped the lamb from its mouth and turned on me. It didn't let go of my hand till I stabbed it with my knife a few times. Then it ran off."

He paused a moment, recalling the event. "Dave was with me that day, but had gone to the other side of the hill with some of the sheep, to look for better grazing. He came running when he heard me yell. He wrapped my hand in a strip of cloth to stop the bleeding, and took me to my father, who knew how to care for such wounds." His voice got quiet. "He still blames himself for it, since we were supposed to stay together that day."

Timnah looked at Rad with rounded eyes. "How long did it take to heal?"

"I don't know. I developed a fever, and passed out for a few days. My father kept a poultice on it until it formed a scab. I was only twelve years old."

"I'm glad you survived," she said, her voice somber.

The wound was ugly, and always made him feel disfigured. He tried to forget about it, but it was a constant reminder about his failed attack on the wolf. Sure, he chased it away, and kept it from harming any of the flock, but at what price? He was maimed for life, placing him on the fringe of usefulness and desirability, unable to join the army, relegated to tending sheep.

He smiled at Timnah. This was nice—having someone to talk to, to confide in, someone who was interested in him. Being with her made him feel like he meant something to someone, like he *mattered.*

"I'm glad I survived, too." His words came spilling out. "You know, all my brothers had the chance to do courageous things—the oldest ones were famous warriors in King Saul's army. And even David, ever since he killed that giant, everyone admired him so much. He was a hero. And I was…I was still just a shepherd—all I would ever be. And it was probably just luck, you know, that made him strike Goliath in just the right place on his forehead."

She looked at him with understanding. "It's always like that, some people are just lucky. Even if they don't work hard, it all just falls into place for them."

"Don't get me wrong," he said. "I respect my brother, and since he is going to be king of Israel someday, I'll always be loyal to him. I just know I have a lot to offer, too. If it wasn't for me, this clan would never have enough to eat, or building supplies. He depends on me to take care of all that."

"And I'm sure he appreciates all you do." Timnah became quiet. She got up and held out a hand. Rad picked up the washbasin and stood up, taking her hand and keeping pace with her along the city wall.

She glanced up at him. "What you said just now, about your brother becoming king of Israel. Is that true?"

His heart jumped. He slipped a sideways look at her. "Um…yeah. About that. It's not generally known. And I probably shouldn't have told you." He turned to face her. "You can't tell anyone. Not even Abigail."

"She doesn't know?"

"I don't think so."

"Why?"

"It's complicated."

"Come on…you can tell me."

"I shouldn't…."

"I won't say anything." She tilted her head and gave him one of those smiles he went crazy for. "Please?"

He was silent for a moment, conflicted. In the end, he knew he would have to explain it to her. He hadn't meant to blurt out the family secret, but there it was. "When Dave was a boy, about ten or eleven, a prophet came to our tents in Bethlehem. He said one of us, a son of Jesse, was to be the next king of Israel. After King Saul."

"Not one of the princes?"

"No. One of us. And, funny thing is, the prophet picked the youngest of us, my little brother, Dave."

"And you kept it a secret? Wait a minute…is that why he's running from King Saul?"

Rad hedged. "Yes…King Saul must have figured it out. But Dave doesn't want anyone else to know. He's afraid the clan will want to start a revolution against the King."

"Why not? That way he will become king sooner. It sounds like a good idea."

"It's not like that. Dave wants to wait till it's his time. Till it's *God's* time. That's why we are hiding out here in Philistine country." He squeezed her hand as they walked and said, "So you have to promise not to say anything. Please. Promise."

She let out a peal of laughter. "I'm good at keeping secrets. You can trust me." She released his hand and skipped along the city wall. Her headscarf came loose and locks of hair bounced about her shoulders. Rad trotted along with her.

They stopped near a closed city gate. A sprinkle of rain started to fall, cooling the air and refreshing them after the run.

Rad turned to her and looked at her in silence for a moment. "I've waited a long time to meet someone like you, Timnah." He brushed a damp wisp of hair from her forehead.

She lowered her eyes. "I'm not sure I am what your family would want for you. Especially Deborah. She probably has another girl in mind." Rain began pelting down, muddying the dirt around their feet. "And I hope that Abigail wouldn't—"

"This is *my* decision to make. *Our* decision," he said. He placed the wash basin on the ground and took both her hands in his. "In fact, I'm going to tell Dave I want to marry you."

"You want to marry me?"

Rad tilted her chin up so he could look down into her eyes, bright with expectation. Rain dripped from his forehead onto hers. "Yes. I want to make you my—"

He was interrupted as Timnah, on tiptoes, brushed his lips with hers.

His return kiss was clumsy and desperate, both hands clutching the curve of her jaw. He had desired her for so long. Ever since that evening by David's fire, at the first supper with Abigail. It was something he thought about every day, and usually in his dreams. Holding her now, he was satisfied with the warmth of her full lips, wet with rain, the taste of her mouth, and the feel of her body against his.

He didn't want to let her go, but finally released her. She sighed contentedly as he walked her home, arm draped around her shoulders. His step was light, exultant. He was glad she couldn't see him grinning so foolishly, and looked to his other side till he could tame his expression into something more restrained. At long last, he did it. He showed his feelings for her. And she accepted him. *She* felt that way, too.

It was a short shower, and now the earth smelled fresh and new. She leaned in for one more kiss behind the chicken house. He watched her go through the front door into the courtyard. It was only then that he remembered she didn't carry out her end of the agreement—she never told him where her family was from.

He smiled to himself at the way she bewitched him. He didn't think it possible after years spent watching women from afar. This woman, this flesh and blood woman, would be his life-long companion, helper, lover. At last he found someone who would bring meaning and joy to his life.

38

Attack On Ziklag

Several weeks after the meeting in Gath, the volunteer army was successful in another conquest. David rode in the forefront, the sword of the giant at his side, as he and Nate led the troops home. They had delivered much of the spoils to a small Judean village and were now riding back home through a barley field, freshly prepared for planting. They encountered a man lying on the furrowed ground. David's horse nearly trampled him.

He reined in his horse and called out to the man. He didn't move. David observed the tattered clothing, the emaciated body, the flies gathering around the mouth. Maybe he was dead? He motioned to Nate, riding next to him. Nate dismounted, approached the man, and lifted his shoulders.

His eyes sprang open upon being handled. He glanced from Nate's face, close to his, to David, and the army, and back to Nate. "Don't hurt me!" he said, shielding his face with his hands.

Nate looked up to David and raised an eyebrow.

"Bring him some food," David said to his aide. Water, and a handful of raisins were given to the man, who consumed them at once.

David dismounted and stepped closer to the man, who was now standing upright, supported by Nate.

"Tell me your name, and where you have come from," he said.

The man bowed at the waist. "I am S-sayed. I am from Egypt. A s-slave."

"And what are you doing here? Don't you know you shouldn't be here, this close to our city?"

The Egyptian began laughing hysterically. Nate struck him to the ground. He lay in the dirt and cowered in fear. Nate held his spear to the Egyptian's neck, which jolted him into a more rational state of mind.

The slave grasped the end of the spear with bony hands and begged, "P-please don't kill me."

David stretched out his arm for the spear, and propped it on the ground by the rounded end. The slave looked up at him. "I have n-news for you. About Ziklag…It's b-been destroyed."

"What do you mean?" David said through clenched teeth.

The slave knelt before him and clutched at his legs. "It's the Amalekites They w-were in Ziklag yesterday, when you were gone. They b-burned it to the ground! All is gone!"

The Amalekites. Enemies of the Israelites and Philistines alike. A menacing, pagan population. Still causing trouble.

David eyed the slave with suspicion. Thrusting an accusing finger in his face, he asked, "How do I know you are telling the truth? Are you a runaway?"

"No! I've been sick. S-see?" He spread his gaunt arms. "See? I'm losing weight. And I'm weak. I c-can't work anymore. The Amalekites…they left me behind."

"Mount up!" David commanded his soldiers. And to the slave, "You may follow behind as best as you can. No treachery, or your life will end" he snapped his fingers "like that."

The battalions of cavalry and foot soldiers traveled quickly to what was once their city. As the Egyptian slave reported, it was destroyed. Very little remained of any wooden structures or houses. Soldiers dismounted and stumbled around, dazed, to where their homes had been for two years. They looked for belongings, animals, and—Heaven help us!—remains of loved ones.

David and Nate strode rapidly through the ruins of Ziklag until they came to their own neighboring houses. The chicken shed had been burnt down and there were several corpses of the poor chickens among the cinders.

David stepped across the threshold of his courtyard, fearful of what he might find. He frantically checked all the rooms one by one. No sign of his wife anywhere. The furniture in the rooms and the ladder to the rooftop were burnt to blackened shards. The tangy scent of smoldering wood hung in the air. He clambered up to the roof on a section of broken-down wall and found the floor mats a mess of charred reeds, the corner table a pile of ash. He climbed down to the courtyard and stepped back out to the street.

He stood, unmoving, and gazed down streets which recently were sites of happy activity—people selling goods on market day, children playing. Now, in their place, were burnt out buildings, destroyed food stores, a battered city wall, and most of all—silence.

There was silence as the men absorbed what had happened to their city, to their families. No sound of babies crying or women gossiping with one another. No sound of merchants calling out their wares. Just silence.

And then, quietly at first, but building over the next few minutes, David heard the sound of mourning as reality sunk in. He joined with his companions in sending a cry of grief up to the heavens.

He dropped to his knees among the rubble and said, "Abigail, my little dove, what has happened? What have they done? Where are you?" He looked up to see his brother Nate approaching.

Nate grasped him by the shoulders and stood him up. He said, "Dave, don't you see? They must have carried off our women and children. There are no remains here. No bodies."

His mental fog clearing, David surveyed the area with new awareness. *There are no bodies. They've been carried off—*

Just as he turned back to Nate an arrow whizzed by his ear and a gruff voice called out, "You!"

David spun and spotted of one of his archers standing about twenty paces away, weapon drawn. "Me?"

"Yeah, you," the archer said, taking aim again. "This is *your* fault." He drew back on the bowstring.

A group of several more soldiers approached. There was menace in their eyes as they brandished their weapons. Several hefted large rocks.

Nate strode in front of David and drew his sword. "Put your weapons down!"

The group of angry soldiers continued advancing.

David stepped beside his brother and held his sword high. The blade gleamed in the sunlight and sent flashes across the scorched earth. "Is this how we trained you? Sure, you could run us through easily. Why not? If it wasn't for me you wouldn't be here in the land of the Philistines." He had their attention. The archer lowered his bow, but kept the bowstring taut.

David climbed onto the pile of stone ruins that used to be his house. "You wouldn't be here, wandering in the wilderness. On the run from King Saul. Living with your comrades in arms. Training to be very skilled warriors.

"You would be…where was it? That's right—*in prison.* Or on the run from the law. Or perhaps *executed*." There was silence as all absorbed David's words.

Nate looked up at David and nodded. He threw back his head and said. "As you can see, there are no remains here. Our women and children have been taken by the Amalekites. So you can stay here and argue about who's fault this is, or you can go with us and run down those pigs, and save our families."

The face-off lasted another minute before the archer stood down. "All right. We'll go after them with you. But our women, our children, had better be unharmed." He looked around at his supporters behind him, then back at David, pointing at him with his bow. "Or we come after *you*."

David climbed down from the ruins and pointed a thumb back toward where the soldiers were retreating. "I'll deal with him later," he said to Nate. His main goal now was to rescue his wife and the others. He would find a way to discipline the mutineers at another time. He looked around him. "The slave. Where's the slave? Bring him to me."

Nate immediately went to search for Sayed, and brought him to David. He fell to the ground and trembled before him.

With all the gentleness David could muster, he said, "Brother Sayed, stand up. Please, tell me where your master went. Where did he take our people?"

Sayed stood on weak legs and said, "P-please. P-promise me you will not hurt me. I will take you to them, b-but swear you will not hurt me, or turn me over to them."

David placed a hand on each of his bony shoulders and looked him square in the eyes. "I promise. You will not be harmed. We just want our wives and sons and daughters back. *We will protect you.*"

And with that, Sayed told David everything. About the Amalekites seeking revenge for a recently destroyed sister city. About how they shot fire-arrows over the city walls, and how they broke down the gate. How they stole all the women and children. And when he couldn't keep up, how his master left him in the barley field to die.

39

The Rescue

———

David turned to Abiathar at this time. The priest routinely traveled with them into battle, giving David easy access to the will of God. He needed to hear God's voice, *now*, concerning what to do about the Amalekites. They must succeed in the rescue, and bring back the women and children. He faced mutiny if they didn't, and he couldn't bear the thought of losing his wife. Again.

The priest walked to the edge of the broken and burnt city wall to confer with God. When he returned to David he said, "God says, 'Go. Chase after the Amalekites. You… you shall catch them and recover everything.'"

The men spent a restless night, sleeping rough on the ground in their ruined city. Nate roused them after a few hours. They left Ziklag and began traveling before daylight, David and the Egyptian slave on mounts in the forefront. They headed south, toward the camp of the Amalekites.

The army chanted as they traveled—a mantra David taught them:

> *"Clap your hands, all you nations,*
> *shout to God with cries of joy.*

For the Lord Most High is awesome,
He's the King of all the earth.

He will conquer all our enemies,
and place them all beneath our feet."

Psalm 47

They stopped chanting when they approached Besor Brook, just as night was beginning to yield to morning. The delicate pink light of early dawn shone over the flat landscape. After taking a few minutes to rest, a third of the company was still exhausted from the events of the previous day, along with little food and sleep. They couldn't go on. David agreed to let them stay and guard the provisions and pack animals. Abiathar, Rad, and the Egyptian, Sayed, were among those remaining.

As Nate re-organized the army into companies, David searched for Josh among the troops and supplies. He pulled him aside and led the way to the bank of Besor Brook. It was a wide, shallow body of water, which drained into the Great Sea many miles west.

"Josh, I have a mission for you."

He nodded at David.

David squatted down and splashed a hand in the water. Josh sat on the riverbank with him.

"We have to get the women and children out of the Amalekite camp before we attack, or some of them may be harmed," David said.

"I can't very well sneak into the camp," Josh said. "Don't look anything like them." His mop of curly dark hair was a distinct difference from the Amalekites' style— long strands of a nondescript color, allowed to form into ropes dangling across their shoulders. Beards were kept untrimmed, as well.

David gnawed his lower lip. "No…I know. And from what the Egyptian slave said, those brutes don't even have tents. They sleep on the ground, wrapped in the animal skins they call clothing. Fire arrows were probably their most sophisticated weapon; their swords and shields are rough cast-offs of tribes they got the better of. He also said they usually revel all night long after a conquest."

"Savages!"

David sighed deeply. "I don't want to think about it. But it means they probably sleep late, which may give us just enough time to get to our women, depending on where they are being kept."

"I'll take someone with me," said Josh. "We'll stake out the situation, and come back to you."

"Good man," David said, clapping the spy on the shoulder.

The volunteer army was given an hour's respite while Josh went on his assignment. David happened upon Rad, seated at a campfire, staring into the embers. He sat next to him.

"You probably regret going to that last battle with us."

"Hm. I should have stayed back. I could have protected…"

"—Timnah?"

Rad nodded. "I wish I could *do* something. I can't stand thinking what she's going through."

"We *will* recover all our women, be assured of that." He patted Rad's knee. "And when we do, spend some time with her."

Rad looked at David with raised eyebrows.

"Yes, spend time with her. Get to know her better."

"But the food stores and supplies. I'll have to arrange to restock everything, since it's all been burned…"

"I know. And I know you will. But there's other things that are important. As my friend, Jonathan once advised me—Follow your heart. It will lead you to the right woman. And maybe it's *her*."

Rad lowered his eyes and smiled to himself as David rose to await Josh's return.

When he arrived, he met with David and Nate by the riverbank, and reported that the Amalekite camp was set up as expected: supply wagons surrounded a central area of campfires and piles of sleeping soldiers, about three hundred in number. Camels and mules were tethered at one end of the encampment. Their women, children, and older men not part of the army were tied in clusters to the wagons at the other side.

"I saw Deborah, Abigail, the servant girls," Josh said.

"My boys? Did you see my boys?" Nate asked.

"They were with your wife. Tied to each other. They were safe."

"Were you able to communicate with any of them?" David asked.

Josh shook his head. He looked down and scuffed a sandal in the sand. "There was a man bringing a bucket of water to them. While I was watching, he watered the mules, and then took the same bucket to the women so they could drink." He glanced up. "He was laughing."

"The brute! Treating them like animals." Nate pounded his fist into his open palm. "I say we attack now!"

David placed a restraining hand on his brother's arm. "Wait. We have to get our women and children away before we rush into anything. We don't want them getting hurt."

"—then he untied them," said Josh.

David and Nate both turned to Josh. "Untied them?"

"Yes. He was yelling something about them cooking breakfast."

"That's it!" Nate stomped toward the waiting lines of army troops.

David caught up with his brother. "Wait! Don't you understand? That's the best news. If they're untied, they will be able to get away. We just have get to them before they are tied again, or taken away."

Josh approached with a plan. He kneeled on the ground and drew in the sand with a stick. Besor Brook ran west to east, with them, the volunteer army, stationed to the north, and the Amalekites' camp across the brook, south, about a half mile downstream. They could cross the water at that point, it was shallow enough, being the end of the dry season, and invade the enemy camp. At that point the ground rose to a high embankment along the brook, so they wouldn't be seen coming.

The men got up from the ground, each considering the plan. "We still need to get our people away before we charge in." David said. "That is my main concern." He walked away a few paces, and returned. "I say we have about a hundred women, and ten or so children. If I get a head start—I'll have you two lead the army—I can get some kind of signal to Abigail or Deborah. Get them to gather everyone in a group right before you strike."

"The signal. It has to be something covert. Something only our people would recognize," Josh said.

They were silent for a moment, thinking.

Nate looked up. "I know. The donkey—Caleb's donkey."

David raised an eyebrow at Nate.

"Consider it—the Amalekites wouldn't think anything of it. There are wild asses and other animals roaming all over the region. But my son would recognize it. So would my wife." He saw that David and Josh didn't comprehend. "It has a…a patch over one eye. A black patch. That's why Caleb calls it 'Patches.'"

David grinned at his brother. "Patches. Cute."

"Hmph," Nate said, crossing his arms.

"But it *is* a good signal. Subtle," Josh said. "They'll know we're nearby when they see the donkey."

David was skeptical. "You really think that's the best we can do? What if it wanders off?"

"If you untie the rope from it near the camp, it will walk right in. It loves people," said Nate. "I'll go get it. It's tied to a supply wagon."

Before setting out for the Amalekite army camp, David spoke to his men, grouped in battalions of foot soldiers and cavalry.

"My faithful men, we are embarking on a rescue mission. This is not like our strikes against Philistine towns, where we leave no survivors. We will do only what is needed to save our women and children. When we have recovered them all, and chased away those heathens, we'll come back here, to Besor Brook, and unite with our brothers guarding the equipment. Then we will make plans to return home."

"I say we kill them all!" a soldier cried out from the back. Several others shouted agreement.

David looked over the columns of troops. "No!" he called out. "If we start fighting, there will be collateral damage. We may lose some of our own. Our primary objective is the *rescue* of our loved ones. God is on our side. He will help us prevail."

He stepped aside and spoke with Nate privately. "Don't let them get carried away. I don't want unnecessary bloodshed."

"I don't agree," Nate said, his eyes challenging. "You should let us slaughter those savages. It would serve them right. They should be punished for what they did."

David's eyes flashed. "If we start an all-out battle with the Amalekites, we would just be asking for retaliation. And our women and children would be placed in harm's way." He looked directly into Nate's eyes. "I *won't* lose Abigail."

He took the reins from his aide and mounted his horse. "You have a wife, and children there, too. Let's not endanger any of them by being foolhardy. I'm counting on you to stay in control."

Nate paused and then gave a nod, his face grim.

David fingered the hilt of his sword as he sat in the saddle. The sword of the giant. He knew it would help him avenge their abducted family members. He knew God would grant them success. He grasped the rope tied around the donkey's neck and made for the brook.

"Give me a few minutes," David said. "And God be with us all."

A half mile downstream David located the embankment that hid the camp of the Amalekites. He rode his horse quietly across the water, leading the donkey, and dismounted on the other side. He placed a rock on the reins dangling on the ground to secure his horse at the riverbank.

"Come on, Patches," he whispered, and tugged on the rope. The donkey obediently followed him up to the ridge. Hidden behind a stand of tall rushes, David looked down the embankment and monitored the enemy camp.

Several of their women were bringing large loaves of freshly baked flatbread to the just-rising Amalekites. He could hear Timnah's voice ringing out cheerfully, and he thought he saw Abigail, bent over a group of animal-skin clad men, offering bread. Many of the captured family members were still seated in a huddled group on the ground, near a supply wagon.

David began to count them, the better to know how many had to get away. Patches started tugging at the rope, pulling toward camp. Before David could stop it, it brayed loudly. He saw one of Nate's boys glance up. The child shouted something.

David grasped the donkey's face, closing its mouth against further noise. It resisted, pulling against the rope, struggling to be free. He could see some of the women, as well as two or three Amalekite soldiers look up the embankment. Crouching down lower among the reeds, he maintained a firm grasp on the donkey. He looked behind him, to the brook, and listened for the sound of his army approaching. Where were they? He didn't want to release the donkey too soon.

While he waited, Patches continued struggling. The donkey finally gave a great lunge forward and ripped the rope from his hand. Free of restraint, it trotted joyfully down the embankment, right into the enemy camp, the rope dragging behind it.

A few of the children broke from the group of captives to greet the donkey, which obviously belonged to them. David knew the enemy would notice the rope trailing behind it, and the children gathering around their pet. Surely they would suspect his army was nearby. He couldn't wait any longer.

He stood up among the rushes and saw Abigail whirl around, searching the outer perimeter of the camp, and gazing up to the ridge. Two Amalekites were already striding up the embankment. When they drew near to where David was hidden, he dispatched them both quickly with his sword. He then ran back down the other side to his horse and mounted hastily.

At that moment, he heard splashing behind him. He spun around to see the cavalry, Nate in the forefront, charging through the shallow water.

David shouted to his horse and vaulted over the embankment. He reached the camp just as the volunteer army hurtled across the ridge.

"Abigail!" he called out.

"David!" Abigail grasped Timnah's hand and raced along the riverbank, following her husband on the horse. The rest of the captives were close behind.

David glanced back just once, long enough to see the volunteer army effectively taking on the Amalekites.

He slowed his horse to a walk, allowing the group to catch up. Some of the children looked up to him and shouted for joy. Abigail held up her skirt and rushed to him, calling his name. He reached down with his left arm and swept her up into the saddle in one fluid movement. The group continued fleeing until out of earshot of the fray.

David stopped within a grove of olive trees and dismounted. He helped Abigail down from the saddle and drew her in for a hasty kiss.

Deborah strode near, holding tightly onto Obed's hand. "David!" Deborah said. "Thank the God of Abraham you came to rescue us!" Several other women joined in giving thanks to God for helping David and his army be successful in their deliverance.

David stood guard as the men, women, and children settled in clusters among the olive trees. "Are we all here? Is anyone missing?" He searched their faces—tired, all, but still on the alert. Most of them were shaking their heads 'no'.

A voice came from within the group. "Caleb! Where's my Caleb?" Deborah rose and scanned the assembly frantically.

She turned to Obed and said, "Where's your brother?" Her voice rose with panic.

David approached. He placed a hand on Obed's shoulder. "Did you see Caleb?"

"He was leading Patches," said Obed. "I was running with Mother, and they were behind us."

David looked up and gazed back toward the camp of the Amalekites. Deborah was already wailing. "Be quiet!" he said to her. "Listen."

The braying of a donkey reached their ears. Presently, Caleb appeared, dragging the uncooperative Patches by the rope. Deborah rushed to her youngest son and began hugging and scolding him all at once. David let out a relieved sigh.

The group rested beneath the shady trees as the sun rose high in the sky, mothers rocking young children, others lying in the grass with eyes closed, listening to the soothing sounds of water washing over stones in the brook. They were waiting for Nate and the army to arrive.

At length, the rhythmic sound of marching soldiers and cavalry was heard, coming toward the olive grove, Nate and Josh in the lead. They dismounted and enjoyed a moment of triumph with David as they congratulated each other on a successful mission.

Deborah ran to her husband and, standing on tiptoes, covered his face with kisses. With effort, Nate broke from her embrace. He cleared his throat and quickly looked around.

David approached him with a wide grin. "She missed you."

"Well…she…that is—" Nate blustered. Spotting Obed standing near, he said, "Did you take good care of mother?"

"I wasn't worried," Obed said, and spat on the ground.

Caleb wandered by, gently leading Patches, humming a happy tune.

Nate rolled his eyes. "Sometimes I don't think this one even knows what's going on," he said to David.

David laughed. "So…so what happened to the Amalekites?"

"Ha ha! We caught them by surprise when we charged over the ridge. Some of them drew their swords, ready for a fight, and were taken on by our men on the ground. Others were unarmed. We let them escape on their camels. Despite their bravado in attacking our city, they were no match for our well-armed soldiers. Why do you think they attacked Ziklag when *we* weren't there?" Nate said. "Our cavalry chased them south, back to their country."

David grasped Nate by the upper arm. "Well done. I appreciate you following my plan for this rescue. All our women and children are safe because of you."

Nate tossed his head and murmured, "Hmph. I just thought…I knew it was the best way to get the job done."

David began walking away, and was called back by Nate. He placed a hand on David's shoulder. "You…you were right. And I was getting carried away. The important thing was to save our families." He glanced down for a moment and then back to David. "You will make an exceptional king. The prophet was right to choose you," he said.

The army went back and recovered plunder from the deserted Amalekite camp, and whatever was taken from Ziklag, including mules and donkeys. When they returned to the olive grove, the group had a meal of whatever food was brought back. Revived, they traveled back to the two hundred who remained on the other side of Besor Brook, and camped there, readying for their trip home. Back to a burned down city that was theirs. Back to Ziklag.

In the evening by Besor Brook, Nate approached David as he relaxed next to a campfire with Abigail.

"Nate, how goes it? Here, have some water."

Nate squatted before the fire and took the proffered cup. He held it without drinking and tossed a stray twig into the fire.

"Was there something you wanted to talk about?" David asked.

"It's just that some of the soldiers are talking…"

"Well? About what?"

"They're complaining. About the ones who stayed behind here, with the supplies."

David looked pointedly at Nate. "What's the problem?"

Nate shifted his weight on his haunches. He hesitated. David waved his hand impatiently.

"They say since they risked their lives in fighting the Amalekites, and saving the women and children, and the ones who were afraid stayed behind, that they shouldn't share in the plunder. They say to give them back their families, and send them away."

David considered this. He began, "First of all, they weren't afraid. They were simply exhausted. And secondly—"

"—We all share in the spoils of war." This from Abigail, seated next to him. The two men looked at her in surprise.

She nodded. "The ones who guard the equipment and animals should also be rewarded, and not treated any differently."

David grinned as he took her hand. "Well said, my dove. And just what I think, by the way."

And to Nate, "Who was it that complained? Was it that archer that threatened me back at Ziklag? Was it Uri?"

Nate pressed his lips together. "It was."

"I thought as much. Please tell him that those who guard the equipment shall be rewarded the same as those who fought the battle. No exception. If he has a problem with it, he can come here, to me, " he flashed Abigail a big smile, "and then he can deal with my wife."

Nate got up and turned to leave.

"And Nate," David said. Nate turned around. "Tell Uri that he is free to leave whenever he wants to. He has no contract here. He had no obligation to me. If he is dissatisfied with the way we run things here, he and his family can leave at any time."

Nate nodded and retreated into the firelight of another campfire.

David was alone with his wife once again. He rolled his eyes and shook his head. "You won't believe the problems…. But that's not what we should talk about now. You were telling me what happened…"

Abigail tucked her legs beneath her and covered them with her gown. "Well, I was saying, at first we women thought it was our husbands returning from battle. We heard horses running, and men shouting. We were glad they were coming back, and some of us ran home quickly to get a meal prepared. Then, when the fire-arrows began coming over the wall," her voice caught. She paused a moment. "When we saw the fire-arrows we realized it was an attack. We had to run out of the city, because fires began breaking out in all the homes and streets.

"We ran right into those jackals' arms! They tied us with ropes and made us walk all the way to where you found us. It took till nightfall. I was so worried, but Deborah walked with me and held my hand. She told me not to be fearful. I tried to be brave, but, to be honest, I was terrified. I was so afraid of what they would do to us—to Timnah and the other girls—" She brought her hand to her mouth and stifled a cry.

He encircled her waist with his arm and pulled her close.

She swallowed and wiped her eyes. "Deborah…Deborah kept praying quietly the whole time we were walking. She said God would save us. She knew this wasn't the end. And her words helped me stay calm. I'm just glad she wasn't hurt, considering her condition."

He shook his head, eyes puzzled.

"Her condition…you know…she's expecting."

"I didn't know that," he said, grinning.

"She's a traditionally built woman—you just can't tell."

"Mm-hm."

They remained silent a few moments, each reliving the extraordinary events of the past day.

Abigail looked up into David's face with a bemused grin. "I was surprised when Caleb's donkey came wandering into the camp after we made breakfast. Was that planned?"

"Sort of," David said. "There *was* a plan, anyway. Patches had his own plan, so it seems. But in the end it all worked out."

"*Yes.* I knew it could only mean one thing—that you were coming for us. I started telling the other women and getting them together. And before I knew it, there you were!"

"I don't think we would have found you so quickly if it wasn't for an Egyptian slave we stumbled upon," David said. "He guided us to Besor Brook and the Amalekite encampment."

"I hope you plan to reward him."

"Of course. But more importantly, we have to get you, and everyone else home. We have to start rebuilding the city immediately. And organize a guard, make it safer for you when we are gone. I was foolish to think the thick timber and stone walls of the city would be enough protection while I was away with the army."

Abigail was spent from a sleepless night and all the walking. She tried to tell David more of what happened, but her words came out slurred, and a few times she just stopped talking mid-sentence. She couldn't keep her eyes open. She leaned against David's arm, and soon he felt her body relax and her breathing come regular and slow. He helped her lay down in the grass and covered her with his cloak.

He sang quietly to her:

> *Praise the Lord, my soul;*
> *all my inmost being, praise His holy name.*
> *Praise the Lord, my soul,*
> *and forget not all His benefits.*
> *Praise the Lord, my soul.*
> *Praise His holy name.*

Psalm 103

He remained seated by the fire and his sleeping wife, on guard, during the rest of the night. As she slept, his thoughts kept him awake. He had to tell her. He had to be honest with her about becoming king of Israel. He hoped it would happen soon, too. Living in this land, the land of his enemy, the Philistines, so close to the savage Amalekites, just wouldn't do anymore. He longed to return to Gibeah and take his place on the throne. *He* was ready. But when would *God* be ready?

Rad eagerly scanned those returning to Besor Brook that afternoon, looking for Timnah. Finally, she scampered toward him, adrenaline and youthful energy propelling her to his side. He whirled her around in a tight embrace.

"I'm so glad you're okay!" he said.

She clutched around his back. "I *am* okay."

She continued talking as the two made their way through the camp. "We were awake all night. The boys and girls were all so afraid. They kept crying and complaining. But then I started telling them a story. I made up a story about a wicked king and a magic horse. I told them the magic horse would save them. They listened to the story and stopped crying. So I just told them stories all night, just to keep them happy. The mothers were so glad I was there. They all thanked me. And even Abigail said I did a good job. She said I would be a good mother some day—"

She hesitated and gave him a shy smile.

"You will make a lovely mother," he said, his eyes earnest.

They found a place beside a campfire to eat a meal and rest together.

In the firelight after supper, Timnah curled her hands around a cup of warm mint tea as she began relaying her story. Rad, exhausted, was barely able to listen. So he didn't hear about the Edomite she talked to that night. The young man by the campfire who was kind to her. The one whose wife was named Jadah. Jadah, who might be her long-lost sister.

Rad fell into a deep sleep and dreamed foggy, disjointed dreams about a magic horse, and babies, and Timnah.

40

Returning Home

———

Rad felt a hard thump on his shoulder. Rolling over in the dirt next to a spent campfire, he woke to find Nate looking at him expectantly.

"What?" Rad asked, shielding his eyes from the bright sunshine.

"Get up! We have to move out."

He looked around. Timnah was nowhere in sight, and all around him were pack animals and clusters of people milling around, ready to head for home.

Nate kicked some dirt over the remnants of the fire. Rad rose and stretched, and gazed across the gathering, catching Timnah's eye. She was at Abigail's side with the other servant girls. A glint of morning sun reflected in her eyes and smile.

Mobilizing, Rad jumped to his feet, "Yep, coming!" He mounted the mule which Nate had saddled, and made his way toward Abigail's group.

The young children ran around joyously, glad to be on their way home, already recovered from yesterday's experience. The women were chatting with one another as they walked, describing the terror they felt at being abducted, the worry of how they would be treated—or mistreated—

by the enemy soldiers, and the joy at being saved by their valiant men.

Deborah walked with Abigail. They talked to each other the whole trip home, making plans for rebuilding and redecorating their houses. Caleb lagged behind a little, strolling along with Patches. Obed rode in the saddle with his father. An air of relief and hope was felt among the entire company.

"Hey!" Rad said to Timnah when he caught up with her. She flashed him a wide grin and reached out for the mule's halter, stopping her.

"Want to ride with me?"

Timnah noticed Abigail was engrossed in conversation with Deborah, several paces ahead. She turned back to Rad. "Sure! I love to ride. I used to ride all the time in Carmel. Or at least whenever I could." Rad slid back a little and Timnah sprang into the saddle with ease.

He tapped the mule with his heels to urge her into a slow walk.

Timnah turned to look at him. "So…before you passed out last night, do you remember what I told you?"

He gazed up in the distance, trying to remember. "About telling stories to the children to calm them?"

"Nope," she said, shaking her head.

"Oh! You said…you said you weren't harmed, and, um…. I'm sorry, that's all I remember. I think I fell asleep."

"I told you about someone I met—someone who worked for the Amalekites. He was from Edom, and was skilled in training camels. We started talking. He was real friendly."

"How friendly?" Rad asked.

Timnah tilted her head. She giggled. "Not *that* way. Just nice. Like he didn't really want to be in on the attack on our city. He was young. Probably younger than you. And he was telling me about his wife named Jadah."

"Jadah? So, someone you think you know?"

She was silent for a moment. In a quiet voice she said, "I thought maybe my older sister."

"Your sister?" His ears pricked. So here was another hint at Timnah's past. He hoped she would tell him more. Maybe by now she trusts him enough not to hold back.

She nodded.

"Hm. Is that because she's from…. Where is it you're from again?" He looked sidelong at her.

She faced front again and sighed. "Cyrene. It's west of Egypt."

Of course. He knew Cyrene was in that great land that always saw the sun; the land where people were the color of shadows, to protect them from the unyielding heat. It made sense now.

The mule they rode stumbled into a coney burrow. Timnah grasped a handful of mane to keep herself steady in the saddle. Rad tightened his grip around her waist.

"So now you know," she said. "That's where I'm from. And that's where this man's wife is from. And she is called 'Jadah'. I really think it's my sister."

He shrugged a shoulder. "Possibly. It's something we can check out, if you want."

"Yes! I knew you would want to. So I thought we could go back to his village and see if it really is my sister. Let's go right now. It's not that far. Just across the brook and over a hill. We could be there before sunset. Won't that be great?"

He thought a moment, gazing toward the extended line of family and friends marching onward. He noted the backward twitching of the mule's long ears. He tugged on the reins, and she came to a stop. Timnah turned around and looked at him, her face bright.

He looked into her eyes. He took a deep breath and let it out in a sigh "I think it's something we can plan to do. After the wedding, and after we help rebuild our city. We can ask my brothers and some of the others to ride with us to find her. I don't want to go into Amalekite country alone."

Timnah pressed her lips together. "I really want to go today. Can't we just go back there now? The village is close by. Why wait?"

"Why the rush?" Rad asked, slightly annoyed.

"It's because…because…he said she is with child."

He wanted to, with all his heart, tell her 'Yes!'. He wanted to go look for her sister if it would make her happy. But he also knew he had responsibilities at home. The rebuilding of the city was going to take all his time. There would be innumerable supplies to be gathered, and food staples to stock up on. David and the people of the city depended on him, and he couldn't let them down.

"Look—David counts on me!" he said. "He'll need me to help rebuild. I'm in charge of all supplies and food. I have to make sure we have enough to eat and materials to rebuild our houses. I can't go chasing down long-lost relatives—"

His tirade was interrupted by a displeased Timnah dismounting hurriedly. She dashed to catch up with Abigail and Deborah and continued with them, never once looking back.

Rad spent the rest of the trip riding his mule behind everyone, keeping Timnah in sight, watching to see if she would turn around. He wanted to smile at her. He hoped she would come back to talk to him. But she didn't. She traveled with the other women until the sun climbed high in the sky and they reached Ziklag.

David remained mounted on his horse at the main entry to Ziklag while the inhabitants entered, stepping over burnt beams that was once the city gate. An owl among the ruins, disturbed by the clamor, took wing. A haze of smoke and ash hung over the entire area dimming the sunlight that usually poured in at this time of day.

When they finally arrived at the sad remains of their homes, they found mounds of rubble and piles of charred wood, still glowing with latent heat. They spent the day gathering what belongings weren't destroyed and preparing a meal together, first separating the burnt grain from what was usable, and salvaging any food items from their own houses. The simple act of cooking and eating with others who suffered similar loss was cathartic, giving all a sense of unity and friendship.

Josh scheduled The Thirty on watches throughout the night so family groups and companies of soldiers could rest peacefully. Subdued conversations could be heard—some planning the rebuild, others reliving the day's events, husbands and wives expressing their feelings for each other. Soon all that could be heard was the call of the owl and the regular breathing of those sleeping.

———◆———

OVER THE NEXT WEEKS EVERYONE PITCHED IN TO REBUILD. They were enthusiastic about constructing each others' homes and the city walls. It was a time for all to pull together.

Rad was busy gathering food staples, building supplies, and household goods, calling in favors from leaders of some of the villages near them, over the border in Judah. He obtained other items on credit, promising to work it off once their city was functional. He was gone every day—it kept his mind off not seeing Timnah, as she had lately made herself scarce.

One day during the second or third week of rebuilding, as Rad returned home from a meeting, his mule almost trampled the Egyptian slave, Sayed, who was stepping in front of the gate as he rode in. Sayed darted out of the way just in time.

"Hold up!" Both Rad's mule and Sayed responded to the command. Sayed looked up, eyes rounded and eyebrows raised.

"What are you doing here?"

"David s-said I could stay here as long as I remain near the wall. I have a small c-campsite over there," he pointed to the wall to one side of the gate. A tent and campfire were positioned there in a neat arrangement. "See? I don't cause any trouble."

Rad dismounted and handed the reins to him. "Well, here! Make yourself useful. You can stable my mule and then come to my tent. My house isn't finished yet, so I could use some help. You look like you're feeling better. You've gained weight."

Sayed took the reins and patted the mule's neck. "I am feeling b-better, and I would be happy help you."

"Good. After you take care of her, come immediately to my tent. You can get me some supper." Rad was glad to make use of the Egyptian. And he was glad to have some company—it had been lonely, living in a tent, having no one to talk to. Timnah's obvious avoidance of him stung.

Sayed turned out to be very useful indeed. He prepared a delicious supper for Rad, excited to have the right ingredients to make a proper stew. An experienced servant, he took care of Rad's needs wholeheartedly.

Having Sayed do the cleaning and cooking gave Rad some much needed free time at the end of the day. The two usually had a cup of tea together before turning in. Sayed continued to sleep outside, wrapped in a blanket near the doorway of the tent, despite Rad offering him space within the tent. It was just what he was accustomed to.

One evening as they sat together at the fire, while reaching for the pot of tea, Sayed's robe rode up on his arm, revealing a tattoo. It looked like a cat. Rad hadn't noticed it before, and asked him about it.

Sayed pulled the sleeve up all the way and said, "It's Bastet, the g-goddess of the home. She is Ra's daughter…"

Rad didn't hear the rest of the explanation. He just knew he saw that figure before. It was the small cat figurine among Timnah's secret possessions. She had some explaining to do.

41

Coming Clean

It took about a month for David and Abigail's house to be completed. They moved back in as soon as the bricks and mortar were dry. Timnah kept busy over the next few weeks setting up housekeeping. She purchased lengths of woven material at the market and set the two other maidservants on sewing tasks—curtains, sacks for storage, and covers for cushions to be stuffed with wool. She organized the inner courtyard and cooking area, as well as the new food pantry. Large clay jars with tight-fitting lids held wheat, barley, and lentils; they kept the mice out. Oil was stored in a special glazed earthenware vessel, and baskets hanging from pegs on the wall contained drying herbs.

She was glad to have work to do. She was still fuming about Rad being so dismissive to her. He hadn't talked to her since that day, when they were freed from the hand of the Amalekites. He just always seemed too busy. Maybe it was because she told him she was from Cyrene…. She had purposely avoided telling him the land of her birth, and now he knew her family wasn't part of the Hebrew tribes. She was aware of prejudiced people, like Nabal, who may not accept her, since she wasn't from the same background, and hoped it didn't change Rad's feelings toward her. Although, right now, *she* wasn't happy with him anyway. Her heart ached, remembering that she was *this close* to locating her sister, and Rad had refused to help look for her. His *work* was more important.

As she took her time arranging the food stores, Timnah's mind went back many years to when she and her older sister Jadah left their home country of Cyrene. They were just children then, nine and ten years old, and two of six offspring. Their parents were poor farmers, and daughters required a dowry to marry well. When they were old enough to work, their parents sold them to a caravan traveling to Egypt.

The four sons weren't sold. They could work the farm.

It was up at dawn and to bed long after sunset for the sisters. Their masters were a wealthy couple with babies who needed constant attention. Timnah and Jadah not only took care of the babies, they also did all the cooking, cleaning, and milking the goats. They lived in the goat shed and slept on straw next to the animals.

They lasted about a year. After the third baby was born, the master started coming to the goat shed at night, sometimes a few times a week. It was Jadah who most often was the victim of his attention. Soon, she began planning their escape, waiting for conditions to be just right. Timnah remembered it like it was yesterday—it was the night of the new moon, and the masters were sleeping deeply, being full of the strong wine Jadah kept serving at dinner.

"Timnah," Jadah said that night.

She felt her sister shake her by the arm and said, "What? I'm sleeping." She had a hard day, taking care of the children, the infant sick with colic, and the older ones teething. She was comfortable curled up in her straw bed.

"Well, you have to wake up. Look here." Jadah produced a covered basket she had hidden in the straw. She moved the cloth aside to reveal several loaves of flatbread, half a round of cheese, a cake of dried figs.

Timnah sat up quickly. She looked at Jadah, her eyes big. "What did you take that for? Don't you know they'll find out? We'll be thrashed for sure."

Jadah covered the food again. "Shhh. It's for our escape. We've talked about running away. Now is the time to do it. It's dark out. The master is asleep. We leave tonight." She rose from the straw and grasped the basket with a strong hand. "Come on!"

Timnah stood up and stretched. "Where?"

"Anywhere. I'm not staying here. We can travel north, to Judah, or Philistia. I heard they treat servants better there." Jadah reached for her sister's hand and tugged her along. The goats stirred, beginning to follow the girls to the door of the goat house. One of them bleated.

Timnah shushed it. She pulled out a few handfuls of hay and placed it in front of the goats. As they pulled at the hay, the sisters snuck out the door, being careful to close it securely at they left.

They traveled east for a few weeks, sleeping under the stars and scavenging for food when their basket was empty. Their journey took them along the shore of the Great Sea.

It was when they began traveling north, into the land of the Amalekites, that they became separated. One day Jadah went to a stream to fill the jug with water. She never came back. Timnah waited a few days, hiding in an unused sheepfold, subsisting on stray stalks of wheat and barley, and leeks she found growing near the water. Despite fearing to stray far from her shelter, she ventured out at night and explored two or three small, unwalled settlements in the region. When she was unable to find Jadah, she continued northeast, until reaching the gentle hills of the lower Judean country.

She remembered the sorrow and desperation she felt at losing her sister. At first she just wanted to give up. At age ten, she had already experienced much unhappiness at the hands of her masters. She barely had the emotional strength to go on. Her wanderings took her to Carmel, to the settlement of Abigail and Nabal. Abigail took her in as she would a stray lamb, and nurtured her until she regained her health and strength. That's why she felt such a commitment to Abigail, who treated her as a mother would, and why she would always be loyal to her.

Timnah was finishing her tasks in the food pantry when Abigail returned home. She had been to the market after spending the afternoon with David, surveying the progress the builders were making in the rest of the city. Several weeks of building revealed first-rate improvements to the city. Granaries repaired with sun-baked bricks and a rebuilt bread oven graced the center of town. There was a new wooden chicken house behind Abigail and Deborah's homes, complete with a flock of young hens. The city was looking better than ever.

When Abigail passed through the door of her courtyard she nearly tripped over a chair that was right in the doorway. "Timnah, what's this doing here? I almost fell over it."

Timnah leaned back and looked out of the pantry doorway into the courtyard. "I didn't put it there."

"I don't care who did. Put it with the other chairs, please." Abigail carried the basket of cheese, honey, and a few other items she purchased to the table and set it down.

Timnah huffed. She strode across the courtyard and picked up the chair, fairly tossing it into position by the table.

Abigail paused in unpacking the basket. "Wait! What's this? What's with the attitude?"

Timnah felt irritable. She was hurt, and angry at Rad, something she couldn't talk to Abigail about. Something that had been eating at her for weeks. And thinking about Jadah and their escape from Egypt made her even more determined to find her. Why couldn't Rad see how important it was? She needed his help, and he wasn't there for her. She wanted to do something to make him sorry for dismissing her so callously.

Like a telling a secret.

Timnah looked at the floor. "Oh…it's nothing."

"Nothing?"

Timnah nodded.

Abigail sat down on a chair, and motioned for Timnah to sit down, too. She sat across the table from her mistress and looked down at her hands folded in her lap.

"Timnah," Abigail began. "Look at me."

She obeyed, looking up with innocent eyes.

"Now, I know something's bothering you. You're never this quiet. What's on your mind?"

Timnah fiddled with a strand of hair that had come loose from her headscarf. "Hmm…I'm just worried about something I heard today. At the bread oven."

"And…."

"I shouldn't say." She was still conflicted. Should she tell? Maybe she shouldn't say anything. What would Rad think? But…what did she care? He wasn't concerned about *her*. Always too busy with his *projects*. Couldn't make time for her, for the one really important thing she needed him to do.

Besides, Abigail had a right to know. And since *she* knew, it was her duty to tell her, right?

Abigail sighed. She fixed Timnah with firm eyes. "Out with it."

Timnah met Abigail's look. She took a deep breath and said, "I heard…I heard…David is planning to be King of Israel." She quickly decided to embellish the story. "And that's why we are here, in Philistine country. So we can join the Philistine army in defeating King Saul, and he can be King."

Abigail was silent for a moment. She rubbed the knuckles of one hand with the other. "Who told you?"

"When Rad—I mean…*the person* told me, they said no one else knows."

"Why did he—they—tell you?"

"I don't know. It's probably not true…"

"Probably not. And I trust you aren't the kind to indulge in or spread gossip. I expect you not to let this go further. Understand?"

Timnah nodded. She understood. She had no desire to spread this news. She told the only person she was interested in telling.

See how Rad likes *that*.

Timnah began preparing supper as Abigail left the courtyard. She retired to the inner sleeping room she and David shared. The newly made sleeping mats and covers were all neatly arranged in rolls. The floor had been swept. The night pot was set next to the wall, scrubbed clean.

Abigail stepped to the window and was greeted by the turtledove that lived in the fig tree by their house. The dove was used to David leaving a few crumbs on the sill, and lighted there hoping to find some. "Sorry,"

Abigail said with a pout. "I don't have anything for you." She watched the bird fly to the roof of the house next door, Deborah and Nate's. Her attention then focused on Deborah, walking home, carrying a basket of fresh bread. She was large with child, and swayed as she walked. *Maybe they will have a daughter this time.*

As she stood gazing out the window the sounds of chickens making low clucking noises came from within the shed as they began roosting for the night. The young hens had been faithful in providing enough eggs for her household. There were so many, in fact, that Timnah took some to market to sell last week. Abigail thought about a few things she would have to purchase next time she went to market—David needed new sandals and a leather belt….

She turned away from the window. *He should be coming home soon.*

She crossed the room, sat on the low stool next to the washing stand, and reached for the lanolin based compound, rubbing a small amount onto her dry hands. She sniffed it—the light scent of lavender was pleasing and offered a tiny amount of calm to her anxious spirit.

Her thoughts were a jumble. *Her husband—King of Israel? Could this be true? Is this why they moved here—to ally with the Philistines against King Saul?* What Timnah told her tore at her heart. While her first marriage was more servitude than anything else, her relationship with David was a partnership, as God intended for married couples. Nabal had showed only disdain and anger toward her, but David respected her. He *depended* on her. And now this, if it was true, this *huge thing* was being kept from her. Was there anything else?

She leaned her head back against the wall, closed her eyes, and waited.

It was dark out when Abigail heard the courtyard door drag open across the hard dirt floor. She could hear Timnah greet David and offer water to wash his feet. She was a good servant—resourceful, inventive, and well-organized. She did the work of three, which made it possible to share the other two maidservants that came with them from Carmel with Deborah. They were there now, helping take care of her growing family.

Abigail heard heavy footsteps and looked up when David entered their sleeping room. The familiar scent of horses and sweat came with him.

"Come on out," he said. "Timnah has supper laid."

"We have to talk."

He turned back around in the doorway, stepped into the room, and looked down at his wife, seated on the stool in the darkness. She remained silent.

He squatted down before her. "What? What happened?" She turned her face from her husband. Bitter tears coursed down her cheeks, something that happened when she was feeling hurt or angry. She couldn't stop the flow of tears. And that made her even more frustrated. She wiped her face with her hand, catching a whiff of the lavender again. David reached her a felt drying towel from the wash stand.

"Please," he said, his voice tender. "Tell me."

Abigail dried her face and blew her nose. She sat quietly for a moment, twisting the towel in her hands. She looked at David, and could see his eyes, full of concern, in the little bit of light let in through the window.

"I heard…I heard," she started.

He nodded, eyebrows raised encouragingly.

"Okay. This is what I heard. You tell me if it's true."

"Anything, what did you—"

She stopped him with and an outstretched palm. She took a deep breath and let it out through pursed lips. "I heard you are to be the next king of Israel."

He opened his mouth to answer. Then closed it, wrestling with his response.

"And," Abigail continued, "And that's why we are here in Ziklag, to plan an attack on King Saul to overthrow his kingdom."

"Not so!" David said. He stood up. "I am not planning an uprising. Whoever told you that is wrong. I would never harm the present King of Israel."

She remained on the stool and looked at her hands as she rubbed them. "So…So it's not true?"

He sat down on the floor against the wall and thrust his legs out before him. "No…It *is* true. About me becoming the next king of Israel, that is."

"And you were going to tell me…when?"

"I'm sorry! I wanted to tell you. I tried to tell you."

"All those times riding out with you, all the nights in bed together, you couldn't find the time?"

David sighed. "I know. It was wrong of me. Why didn't I tell you?" He slumped his shoulders, defeated.

This wasn't helping. Abigail still didn't know anything. But berating her husband wasn't the way to find out. She would have to be strong. She would have to confer with him the way she always did. Discuss. Plan. That's how this needed to go down.

She dried her face with the towel and blew her nose a final time. She rose from the stool and reached out to him. "Let's have supper."

He allowed her to help him up from the floor and lead him to the table.

Timnah served the barley stew, flavored with garlic and rosemary. The flatbread, baked in the communal oven this afternoon, was still a little warm. There was herbed goat's cheese to spread on it.

"Thank you, Timnah," David said.

Abigail glanced up at her maidservant. Timnah avoided looking at her.

"My pleasure," She murmured to David and quickly retired to her own sleeping room. She would rise early in the morning to wash the dishes before preparing breakfast. This was their nightly routine. David and Abigail liked to linger over supper, discussing important events of the day and having a last cup of wine before bed.

David, always hungry, began slurping at the stew. After a few bites he put his bowl down and glanced up at Abigail.

She placed a spoonful of stew onto a wedge of flatbread and nibbled at it. She saw the regret in his eyes and thought she would give him time to explain himself.

"Look, I…" he began. "I know I should have told you. It happened so long ago, and I've gotten used to waiting, preparing. I don't really know when it will happen. The prophet just said it would be in 'God's time.'" He paused a moment, befuddled. How to explain it to her? "I'm not— we're not—here to fight King Saul. I'll not go against God's will and start a revolution. He has a plan, and it's up to me to wait for it."

Abigail could feel the tension across the table. It was almost vibrating. Then she saw David look at his hands, held open before him. When he looked back up, his face was the face of a child. Unconcerned and free.

"Feel," he said, smiling. He held his hands out.

She drew her eyebrows together, reached across the table, and grasped his hands. They were vibrating, and she felt energy shoot up her arms. She released them abruptly. "What was that?"

He laughed gently. "Whenever I talk about becoming the next king of Israel, or when God wants to remind me He is with me, I get this sign. My hands tremble and my body fills with the power of God's spirit. You felt it?"

"Yes…but why?"

"It all started when I was eleven years old. The prophet, Samuel, came to our tents. He came to anoint the next king of Israel. Me."

She was drawn in as he told the story. It sounded so impossible. Why would the prophet anoint a *child* to be king? She didn't understand.

David ended with, "So, when the anointing oil was dripping through my hair, I could feel power go through my whole body, and in my hands. They tingled. Just like now. It's God's way of letting me know His plan for my life."

Abigail was still confused. She shook her head. "But you were just a child. Why not Nate? Or one of your brothers already in the King's army?"

"Let me tell you what has been my precept all my life. Before he left, Samuel said, '*Man looks on the outward appearance, but God looks on the heart.*' It's what I've always believed."

She nodded. She liked that, and felt it was true. God *does* look on the heart. She took a sip of wine. But this thing about her husband becoming king? It was so much to absorb. It explained a lot—King Saul's dogged pursuit of David, David's opposition to move back north. It also changed everything, like her hope for a modest lifestyle, maybe moving back to Maon and raising children…Now she was to be *queen*. However, if she was anything, she was adaptable, something that has helped her cope in many situations.

"So we wait, until—?" Abigail shrugged her shoulders.

"Until it is *God's* time. Until I hear from Him."

She stood up and reached into the niche above the table where the wine was kept, poured for herself and David, and sat down.

Raising her cup, she pressed her lips together thoughtfully and said, "Here's to becoming king of Israel." David touched his cup to hers.

THE NEXT DAY DAVID ARRANGED A MEETING WITH HIS brothers, Josh, and Abiathar. He also requested his wife attend. They waited for the men in their newly refurbished rooftop meeting room.

David heard the scraping of the ladder and soon Rad and Nate appeared climbing onto the rooftop. Abiathar and Josh followed close behind. David stood and greeted them and Abigail directed them to sit on the reed mats. She handed around a bowl of fresh fruit.

Nate and Rad continued a conversation they were having as they entered David's house. "You say we have fifty matching swords? How did we get so many?" Nate asked Rad.

"They were provided by King Akish. He sent them over last week," Rad replied. "To help us prepare for our next campaign."

David cleared his throat, getting everyone's attention. Abigail and the men sat in a crescent, facing him. "I'm glad you are all here. I called this meeting because there is something important I have to tell you. Something I should have said a while back, but never really felt it was the right time." David gazed around the group, focusing on each person. "My brothers already know this. But it has come to my attention my secret may be out. Someone has been talking."

Rad's eyes got big. He glanced around at the others quickly. They were all still looking at David.

David continued. "Our main purpose here isn't just to keep out of King Saul's way. My true mission, actually since I was a young boy, is to become the next king of Israel. I was anointed by the prophet Samuel at my father's tents."

Josh beamed and clapped David on the shoulder. Abiathar blinked a few times. He fingered the fringe of his shawl, twisting a few strands. Nate gave a firm nod.

"I hope my wife will forgive me for not being forthright with her from the beginning." He looked at Abigail, eyebrows raised, lips curved into a crooked smile.

She smiled back at him, then glanced down and toyed with her sandal strap. "I just hope I'm up to the task of being queen."

"There isn't anyone who would fill the role better," he said.

Josh split a fig and gnawed at the seedy interior. "Why the secret? I mean, I admit I thought so all along. Knew better than to say anything to anyone. *Your* business."

"We were afraid the clan would want to start an uprising if they knew," Nate said, his chin raised. He glanced at David. "And that's not how Dave wants to gain the throne."

David nodded. "I will not harm the presently anointed King. It has to happen in God's time. In God's way."

"Who…who told?" Abiathar said.

"What?" David asked.

"Who told?"

"Good question. Nate? Rad?" David said. "Any idea how this came out?"

Nate gazed around the circle of companions. Rad squirmed. He took a sudden interest in the hem of his tunic. Unable to help himself, he looked up at Abigail. She already had her eyes fixed on him.

David noticed this exchange between his wife and Rad. "Rad?" he said again.

Rad shut his eyes tight. He sighed. "It was me. I told someone…. It was *Timnah*. She promised not to tell anyone. But it looks like she did."

All were quiet. David felt their anticipation acutely. What should he say? Keeping this secret all these years was fatiguing. Maybe it's good they knew. He looked into their expectant faces. "Women!" he said, laughing. "They can't keep a secret!"

Rad let out a relieved sigh. Abigail raised an eyebrow.

He continued, "I hope all of you do promise not to let this go further. I'm still not ready to go on the offensive. I don't…I don't think the whole clan should know yet. I'm waiting on the right timing. Abiathar prays every morning for guidance and protection. He will let me know when he hears from God." The priest smiled appreciatively.

"Can I have your word that you will keep this to yourselves?" David looked at each of his companions in turn, waiting for their nods of agreement.

He handed the empty fruit bowl to Abigail. "Please take this down and have Timnah fill it up again."

Abigail rose from the reed mat and stepped down the ladder carrying the bowl. Soon, Timnah came up with it

Rad got up quickly to help Timnah as she went to step back down the ladder. She jerked her arm from his grasp and parried with a look. He swallowed, and whispered, "When can we meet?"

Timnah glanced behind her. The group was all talking and eating. She turned back to Rad, her eyes steely. "Tomorrow morning. At the market," she said, and made her way down the ladder. Rad returned to the reed mats

"Abiathar, you may go back to your morning routine," said David. "Thank you for joining us here." He then addressed the three remaining men, "I would like you to stay so we can discuss our upcoming campaign with King Akish. He means for us to join him in a battle against King Saul in one month." His face was creased with worry. "This may mean we will be fighting against our own countrymen."

42

The Medium at Endor

King Saul was in a bad mood. King Akish and the other rulers of the five Philistine cities once again declared war on Israel.

The Israeli army was encamped at the foot of Mount Gilboa, north of Gibeah. King Saul rode out secretly with a small group of soldiers to survey the extent of the enemy army, across the valley, in Shunem. He was discouraged by the size and strength of the Philistine military—the many chariots, new, flashy weaponry, and mighty cavalry. He watched them at drills from afar. The thunderous sound of hoofbeats reverberated to the hillside where King Saul sat on his horse. The whirring of hundreds of chariot wheels sounded like a swarm of locusts. He tightened his grip on his spear and turned his horse abruptly.

King Saul returned to camp incensed and annoyed. He was getting too old for this. With his son Jonathan and General Abner at his side, the great Israeli army still had a good chance to beat the Philistines, but at what cost?

He wished he was back in Gibeah, back at the palace, eating honey cakes and drinking wine. Listening to David play his lyre once again and—well…never mind. That David was a traitor, anyway. He had treated him as his own son. Taken him in and gave him every opportunity to succeed. Given him his daughter for a wife! And what did he do? That son of Jesse stabbed him in the back. Formed his own army hiding out there, in the wilderness. Gaining supporters. And why? To usurp his kingdom. King Saul was sure it's what he wanted to do all along.

For awhile there he had a suspicion, but when Mical talked to him, he knew it was true. She was tired of waiting for her husband to return, and who could blame her? He was glad to wed her to the trader, Palti, and move her back into the palace. And, out of gratitude, Mical enlightened him of David's true intentions, to become king of Israel. He knew as long as David was alive his dynasty was at an end. There would be no future for his sons or ancestors. He couldn't let that happen.

He wished he had taken the opportunity back there, on Hakilah Hill. He could have easily overcome David and his sorry band of followers. But that was his biggest weakness, he was just too forgiving, too soft. He thought the next time he had the chance he would make sure to defeat his biggest foe. Just after conquering the Philistines. It would be his next mission.

But for now, he had to concentrate on this war. It was times like these that he wished Samuel the prophet was still with him, still advising him, still getting word from God about how best to proceed.

General Abner was summoned to the King's tent. As he entered, King Saul said, "Oh, why can't Samuel be here at a time like this, eh? He always knew what God wanted me to do. God won't talk to me anymore. Not like He used to speak through Samuel. Who else can I depend on? Did any of my other prophets show up?"

General Abner sat on a bench across from the King, leaning forward, his elbows propped on his knees. "Look, I know you banned all psychics and fortune tellers from Israel, but I know of someone—" He looked behind himself toward the tent opening, and then back at King Saul. Lowering his voice, he said, "I heard of someone who can tell the future. A woman from Endor. A medium. They say she's pretty reliable."

King Saul raised his eyebrows. "Can she speak to the departed? Could she speak to Samuel for me?"

"I hear she's quite skilled. You should go see her. Perhaps she can help you."

"Find her for me," the King hissed through clenched teeth.

The following night King Saul, disguised in peasant clothes, rode out with a guide—a soldier who was likewise dressed. General Abner gave them the directions to Endor, and to the medium's residence. They left their horses tethered near the edge of the village and walked the remainder of the way.

The woman who answered the knock on the door was dressed in the ordinary clothing of the local women. The coarse brown headscarf hid most of her hair. A few strands of dull gray hung loose, down to her waist. She clutched at the front of her tunic and raised the hem a little to make room for her bare feet as she answered the door.

King Saul could see the hardened eyes peering at him through the few inches of doorway she allowed. He could smell the strong breath, laced with garlic and onions. As she spoke a lone tooth wiggled in her lower jaw. "What? What do you want?"

Recklessly, King Saul said, "I need you to perform a séance and call up someone from the dead. You can call up a spirit for me, can't you?"

The only thing keeping the woman from slamming the door in the King's face was his sandal-shod foot on the threshold.

"Shh! Do you want to get me killed? If word got out about what I do—"

"Well, sister, as you can see, word has gotten out," King Saul said. "Or else how would I know, eh?"

"How do I know you aren't setting a trap for me?"

"I promise you, by the name of the living God of Israel, that no harm will come to you if you help me. Let me come in and I will tell you what I want." King Saul thought a moment. "Look," he jingled a bag at his waist, "you shall be richly paid."

Finally, the woman agreed to allow the disguised King and his companion into her house. The three took their places on a woven rug in the center of the small front room. The rug was encrusted with years of dirt, soot, and lamp fat. A water jug and a few baskets containing herbs and eating utensils were arranged against a wall. A lone window let in the moonlight.

"Before we begin," the medium said in a hushed voice, "You must swear by the spirit you wish me to call up that you will speak to no one of this meeting." She reached across the rug and clawed at King Saul's forearm. She held his sleeve tight in her grip and said, her voice cracking, "Swear it!"

King Saul yanked his sleeve out of her grasp. "I promise, sister. I promise."

The medium set a burning oil lamp on the center of the rug. "Whose spirit do you wish me to call up?"

"Samuel, the prophet."

The medium performed the rituals for calling up the dead. She reached into a basket behind her and pulled out a bunch of dried herbs. "Mint," she explained, "to cleanse the room." She touched the mint to the lamp flame and placed it on a round clay platter beneath the window.

The pleasing scent filled the room as it smoldered. King Saul was beginning to enjoy this. She filled a bowl with water and placed it next to the burning lamp on the rug.

She closed her eyes and said, "Samuel…Samuel… Samuel…We call you up from your place of rest. Speak to us, oh Samuel."

King Saul gazed at her intently. After a moment, she opened her eyes and said, "Now we wait till the water is disturbed. Sit very still."

Now he had to wait? This was taking too long. He glanced at his companion beside him, who was staring at the bowl of water with unblinking eyes.

King Saul opened his mouth to say something, when he glanced down and noticed a ripple across the surface of the water. It undulated rhythmically, as if disturbed by heavy footsteps coming toward it.

The medium reached down and lifted the lamp. The glare of the single flame blinded King Saul, and he shielded his eyes from it. He then heard the voice of Samuel's spirit say, in greeting, "Your Highness, King Saul."

She dropped the lamp and jumped up, leaving the room in sudden darkness. Hiding her face in her hands, she backed away from the King. "Why? Why have you done this to me? I knew it was you. I felt it even as you came in the door. I should never have let you in."

King Saul stood up and reached for her shoulder, "Relax. I assure you, nothing will happen to you." He sat down again and patted the rug in the place where the she had been sitting. "I *did* promise. You should know you can trust me, eh?"

The medium sat down again across from the King and re-lit the lamp on the still-glowing bunch of mint. She watched him through narrowed eyes.

King Saul's expression was penetrating. He said earnestly, "I told you, you will not be punished. I really need your help. I need to hear from Samuel. Now, please, why don't you tell me what you see?"

She fixed her eyes on the money bag lying in plain view and struggled to compose herself. Swiping a strand of hair from her eyes, she peered into the lamp flame and said, "I see an old man, bent, leaning on a walking stick. He is dressed in a brown robe, and his white beard reaches below his belt. Around his neck hangs a little vial on a string."

"Samuel!" King Saul said. He sat upright in excitement.

A voice sounded. It came from nowhere, and everywhere. It filled the room. "Why are you bothering me, calling me back from Heaven?"

King Saul, amazed he was actually having a conversation with the dead, was temporarily speechless. Finally, looked up to where he thought the voice was coming from, he said, "Because, because I need guidance. God has left me and won't answer my prayers. He won't speak to me by dreams or by any of the other worthless prophets I have."

"Why should I answer you if God will not?"

"Please." He got on his knees and clasped his hands. "I have no one to counsel me. We are at war with the Philistines and I need to know what to do—how to ensure our success. I need you to advise me."

"I will advise you. But you won't like what I have to say. God has taken the Kingdom from you and given it to your rival, David. Tomorrow you will be defeated in battle by the Philistines, and then you and your son, Jonathan, will be here, in paradise, with me."

King Saul fainted. Many moments passes until he was conscious of his companion and the medium speaking to him in low, slurred voices. He said, "Jonathan?"

The voices were getting clearer. King Saul sat up and eyed the medium. "Where am I? Is this still Endor?"

"Yes, you are still at my house. See? I have made a meal for you. It will sustain you on your trip back. Please eat it." She offered flatbread with cheese and a cup of sour wine.

Thus nourished, King Saul and his guide retrieved their horses and rode side by side, headed back to camp. The King thought back to Samuel's words. Did he hear him right? "Did you hear what Samuel said back there?" he asked the guide.

The soldier hesitated. "I don't really know. It was frightening, hearing the dead speak to us. I…I don't remember what he said."

"Fool! Of course you know, don't you? You just don't want to say."

The soldier kept silent.

King Saul turned to him, facing him with eyes that flashed in the moonlight. "He said I would be *dead* tomorrow. My time is *up*."

With that, the King spurred his horse and sped through the darkness until returning to the smoldering fires of his army camp.

43

In League with the Enemy

As planned, King Akish and the Philistines mobilized against the army of King Saul. Regiments from the Five Cities traveled north, to Shunem to engage in combat in the valley by Mount Gilboa. David and his army of six hundred were to march behind the Philistines. Still in character as an Israeli expatriate, he made preparations to accompany them with feigned enthusiasm. They were to leave the next morning.

As dawn broke, David lay sleeping with Abigail, his arms wrapped around her, his face nuzzled into her hair. They woke to the mournful call of the turtledove nesting in the fig tree. It's song mimicked their mood, and soon they began talking about what was most on their minds—the upcoming campaign.

"What if you have to actually fight the Israelites?" Abigail said, turning onto her other side to face David. "What if *you kill* one of them?"

He didn't know what to say. He kept remembering the last thing he heard King Akish say when he, Nate, and Josh had their meeting with him a year ago: "After going to war with us, all Israel will despise their former hero. David will be locked in service to us forever." When he decided to hide out in the country of his enemy, he didn't imagine he would be trapped there, obligated to King Akish. In addition, how would his own countrymen—the nation of Israel—view him, knowing he went to war against them? They wouldn't want him to be their king. He should have thought this through better. Escaping King Saul was foremost on his mind, back there in Maon, after the encounter at Hakilah Hill. But now moving here seems like a bad idea.

Abigail rubbed her hands. She reached for the little pot of lanolin next to the bed and worked it into her dry knuckles. She lay still for a moment, then said, "What if *you* get killed?"

"Me?"

"Yes, *you*." She sat up in bed. "You might get killed. You don't have power against a sword thrust. Or an arrow." Her throat tightened. "Then…then what about becoming king?"

A long moment of silence stretched between them, David thinking up a response that would ease her worry, and Abigail fighting anxious tears.

He sat up next to her. "God will protect me, my dove. He's brought me this far, and has saved me from harm again and again" He tried to sound positive. He had grown used to her being the emotionally strong one—reassuring him, encouraging him when self-doubt threatened. Today he would have to find the words to help her through this concerning time, despite feeling unsure himself. "I have always trusted in God's direction, and Abiathar said we should agree to march out with the Philistines against King Saul."

Abigail sniffled. "He would. Of course. He has his own reasons."

"I know…Yet he has always reported to me honestly. If God told the priest we shouldn't go, he would have told me."

She rubbed her hands.

"I know it's hard to believe, but this must also be part of God's plan," he said, his voice earnest. "He anointed me the next king of Israel, and I know, someday, *I will be*." Saying it aloud helped him feel a little more confident, and he could hear the prophet Samuel's voice in these words, giving him the resolve to move ahead, despite the absurdity of what he was about to do—go to war against his own people, allied with the enemy.

Abigail looked at him, her eyes moist. He leaned in and kissed her forehead. "I *will* come back to you," he said.

"I'll be waiting," she said quietly.

He got up and prepared to meet his army.

As David trudged through town he realized it was getting harder to keep up this charade, and harder yet to keep his soldiers consistent. Many didn't even know who they were fighting. They were used to following he and Nate's direction without question and were enthusiastic about their next military action. They were told they would be joining the Philistines in battle, but weren't informed against whom. Rumors circulated in the city that they would be fighting the Canaanites, in the north, who had been resisting Philistine occupation for many years. David did not try to quell this rumor.

He knew some of his men still had family in Israel, and Abigail's concern that they may end up fighting people they knew wasn't groundless. As far as he knew, his eldest brother, Eliab, was still serving in King Saul's army. What if he encountered his brother in the battlefield? Or what if it was Jonathan? His heart tore within him thinking he may have to take his deception so far as to actually attack one of them.

He shook his head. He had to stop this unproductive line of thinking. Perhaps since they were taking up the rear guard of the army, they wouldn't be involved directly in battle. Maybe they would be recovering fallen soldiers and caring for the injured.

David passed the guards at the city gate and gave them a friendly nod. With Josh's help, he had organized about a hundred armed men to rotate shifts, standing watch at the city gates at all times.

The volunteer army stood in formation outside the walls of Ziklag. David inspected the troops before they set out for the march to the royal city of Gath. Thanks to King Akish, they were well equipped with the latest in weapons, well-fitting armor, and swift, strong horses. They looked and felt like warriors.

This was really going to happen.

Nate, Josh, and David led companies of two hundred each, half of which were mounted soldiers. They planned to meet King Akish and his regiments in Gath, and then, together, they would travel northward two more days, until reaching the rest of the Philistine army divisions in Shunem, near Mount Gilboa. Several supply wagons and camels loaded with provisions were part of the assembly. Rad had been busy all that week gathering enough food, animal feed, and supplies to equip the army.

After a day's travel the volunteer army camped outside of Gath. Nate and Josh met with David in his tent that evening. He offered around the dried venison Abigail sent with him as they took their places on the tent floor.

Nate shook his head. "Deborah is so nervous about me going to war. Since little Leah was born last week, everything worries her. Obed proclaimed he would be man of the house in my absence."

"He's a good son," David said.

"He is. I take him riding with me during training exercises. He's becoming a good shot with a bow."

"What do they think about their little sister?"

"Caleb sings to her. It calms her crying. Obed is a little afraid—"

Josh cleared his throat. "King Akish. He's to meet us here come morning?"

"I sent a message to him as we approached Gath," David said. "We will be awaiting his arrival in full military formation at daybreak. Our journey to Mount Gilboa will take two days, so we must set out as soon as possible." He looked down at the rug and sighed. "This is the biggest thing we have done, and to be honest, I am a little worried."

"Me too," said Josh. He was quiet for a moment. "My brother is in the Israeli army. And some of my cousins."

"Well, I'm ready to take on King Saul," said Nate, tossing back his head. "I'm tired of his running us all over the wilderness. Time he got what was coming to him."

David shook his head. "That's not it, Nate. Don't you understand? Remember this war is against *our own people*. And it will also strengthen our alliance with our enemies. How much longer can we play this game?"

He got up and strode to the tent opening. He could see most of the cooking fires in the encampment were smoldering. Camels and horses were calm in their tethers. The few soldiers that remained seated at campsites were talking quietly to each other, or were silent, drinking a last cup of tea before settling in.

Turning back, he paced the length of the tent. He reached down and grasped the sword of the giant, drawing it out of the scabbard and examining it, remembering when he first held it, when he first used it. He envisioned himself a youth again, hurling the stone from the sling, vanquishing the giant, Goliath, and killing him with his own sword.

At that moment, David felt his rapid heartbeat slow down and his anxious, choppy breaths relax. Warmth washed over his body. He looked at his hands—they were trembling.

He turned to Nate and Josh, excitement in his eyes. He held up the sword. "I got this sword when I was young and foolish," he said. "I naively trusted God to help me win a fight against a foe four times my size. And I was right to believe—God *did* help me. We must trust Him in this situation, too. He has a plan for my life, for *all* our lives. And we must trust Him to accomplish it. God said to march with the Philistines, and that is what we will do. As I said when I challenged Goliath many years ago—this is God's battle, not ours."

Early the next morning David, Nate, and Josh stood with their regiments, fully packed and mounted, awaiting the arrival of the army from Gath, ready to travel with them to Mount Gilboa.

Before long, King Akish appeared silhouetted against the dawn sky, mounted on a huge beast of a horse, accompanied by four guards.

The King dismounted and left his horse with the guards. He joined David, and the two stepped away from the army for a private conversation. It was times like these that made David glad he worked hard to become proficient in the language of the Philistines. Having a conversation with King Akish was much less awkward in his own tongue.

"I'll come right to the point," King Akish began, "My commanders disagree with letting you join us in fighting the Israelites."

David stopped walking and raised his eyebrows at the King.

King Akish held up his hands, palms out. "I'm sorry. I told them, 'David has been loyal to me since he defected from King Saul. I have never found any fault in him, and his men are well skilled in all kinds of warfare. You should be glad to have them on our side.'"

"I appreciate your faith in me—"

"—My general said, 'David may be on our side now, but don't you think he may be tempted to change sides once again, and reconcile himself with his former master, King Saul? He's defected once, he may do it again.'"

David stood silent, waiting for the King to continue.

A breeze kicked up and blew wispy strands from the fringe of hair around the King's large bald spot. He brushed the hair away from his eyes and focused on something in the distance. He cleared his throat and said, "The other thing is…We get reports about anything that affects our military. I know, for example, that when you were on the run from King Saul in the wilderness those years ago, that you had a chance to kill him," he looked directly at David "but you *didn't*.

"Now, I'm not worried about that. You have been faithful to me for almost three years. But," he shrugged his shoulders, "what's to say if called upon, you wouldn't be able to finish him off this time?"

David didn't have an answer. It was a situation he hoped he wouldn't be confronted with. He held his peace, not sure where this conversation was headed. This King, his enemy, was treating him with fairness and understanding, and all he was saying was true. On his end, King Akish had to be certain of each of his warriors' loyalty to the campaign, and he found David wanting. Evidently, he was willing to overlook this defect, but at what price? Would David be called upon to prove his faithfulness in some other way?

The war with Israel was just getting started, with the two great armies facing off—the grand, well-trained Israelites against the sweeping resources of the Philistines. Who would be the victor? Would David be forced to remain loyal to King Akish if he conquered Israel, trapped in an alien country? The thought "he will be locked in service to us forever" darted through his mind, prodding him. This was not the position he wanted to be in. He would have to actively search for ways to release himself, and the clan, from this obligation as soon as he could.

Abigail entered his thoughts. This was not fair to her, the uncertainty of where they stood among the region's powers. She deserved a life undisturbed by calamity, a life where she can raise her sheep—and hopefully their children—in harmony with others in the area. She ought to have a permanent home in Judah, a place where…*What was King Akish saying?*

"…What I'm saying is," King Akish continued, "I hope you understand when we ask you to sit this one out and return to your city."

David's heart leapt. This was the deliverance he was hoping for. Without even considering this as an option, he was being completely let off. Within, he was already rejoicing, but, as he didn't want to give himself away, he looked at the ground, kicked a stone, and glanced back up at the King. "I do understand. I don't want you to have any conflict with your commanding officers. We'll go back to Ziklag. Perhaps next time…"

"Right. Next time." King Akish clapped David on the shoulder. "Thank you for your cooperation." He returned to his horse and headed back to Gath.

What a close call. David looked back at his soldiers, waiting, in formation, at the ready to march out. He thought how far he had come with this group of outlaws and runaways, how far they all had come. His heart surged with gratitude to his brothers and followers. For their loyalty to him. And to God who protected and sustained them during the time they spent hiding in the wilderness, and who, today, sent deliverance to them in the eleventh hour.

David gave the order for retreat, and he and his army began journeying back to Ziklag.

44

Making Up

Rad meant to meet Timnah at the town market the day after the big meeting with David, when he revealed his secret to Abiathar and Josh. That whole month kept him busy, however, preparing for the upcoming campaign with the Philistines. He amassed enough armor and weapons to equip the entire army. Extra food, fuel, and animal feed had to be collected and loaded on supply carts. As a result of all the additional work, he was unable to make time to see Timnah, collapsing in bed, each night. He hoped working this hard would prove to David that he could be trusted, despite betraying the family secret.

Now that the volunteer army was on the way to Gath, Rad had time to deal with a personal matter. He made plans to go to David's house in the late morning. He had already ascertained that Abigail would be away from her house for a while, having observed her strolling with Deborah and the new baby in the town market, stopping at stalls, admiring pottery and linens. He knew the combination of the women talking and shopping would ensure they would be away for at least an hour, maybe more.

Walking through the market, Rad's heart swelled at the sense of personal fulfillment he experienced. The marketplace, well-stocked granaries, and herds of their own sheep and goats that grazed on the hillsides outside of the city were all products of his doing, with help from Deborah and other select townspeople.

The Egyptian, Sayed, was indispensable in assisting Rad with his work—scheduling shepherds around the clock to keep watch over their flocks on the hillsides, and managing shearing times. The wool not needed by Ziklag was used to trade for other goods in surrounding villages. Abigail, also, showed a keen interest in working with the sheep. She was developing a breeding program to improve the quality of fleece.

Despite his sense of pride in his work, he felt the dark cloud of discontent in his heart over how his relationship with Timnah had deteriorated. He had to make it right.

Rad made his way to David's house and paused in the courtyard entrance. The door was open and he could see Timnah inside, sweeping the packed dirt floor with a straw broom. She looked up as he stood in the doorway, her face steeled against another disappointing encounter.

He felt a weight on his heart when he saw her. Her slender frame and that expression on her face, eyebrows drawn together and lips in a pout, accentuated her fragility, both in body and spirit. This girl was hurting.

"Hey," he said in greeting.

"Hey, yourself." She continued sweeping absently, going over the same place again and again.

He knew he had to confront her. But he also knew she could shut down with a word, so he would have to proceed cautiously. He tread through the courtyard and sat down in a chair in the far corner.

Timnah wandered over. "What do you want?"

"Nothing. Just wanted to talk."

She leaned the broom against the wall and sat down."Okay then. Talk."

He sighed heavily. "I understand you spoke to Abigail." He let that hang in the air for a moment. "You gave away the secret I told you."

She turned her head and gazed out the window. "So? She had a right to know."

He squeezed his eyes shut for a second. "That's not the point. I *trusted* you. I thought I could confide in you. Don't you understand? You betrayed me."

She twirled a strand of hair into a tight twist. "You just don't—"

"*And*—David doesn't feel he can rely on me anymore." His voice became strident. "You know how hard it is to regain someone's trust? I've been working at it day and night all month."

Timnah's eyes were moist and a lone tear shone on her cheek. She stood up and reached for her broom. "Hm. I don't know why you're so afraid of your younger brother anyway."

"I'm not afraid of him. I *respect* him. And *support* him. Just…just like Nate does." He stood up. It annoyed him that she was now back at her work, sweeping, instead of taking him seriously. Instead of really listening to him.

She stopped sweeping and glared at him. "It's just as well we didn't get married yet. Why would I want to marry an *errand boy*?"

He advanced upon Timnah and grasped the broom handle. "You don't know anything. You need to remember your place."

Her eyes flashed and her knuckles went pale as she gripped the broom. "It's time you left."

Rad knew nothing could redeem him from the awful thing he had just said. Why did he say it? He didn't mean it. It just came out. A quick response to her hurtful words.

He left Timnah in the courtyard and wandered down his own street purposelessly, dragging his feet in the dust, sidestepping someone trying to call out a greeting, not wanting to talk to anyone. Sayed met him at the door.

Rad walked through to his sleeping room and sat on a bench near a washing stand where Sayed had fresh water ready for him. He dipped a cloth into the water and wiped his face, relishing the coolness it brought. He removed his sandals and wiped the dust of the day off his feet. He wished he could remove the residue of hurt and resentment from Timnah's heart so easily.

Despite being skilled in negotiations with leaders in neighboring villages, despite having a gift for communication, he failed in his interaction with the girl. What he had wanted to do was get at the bottom of why she betrayed him. What was really going on? And the second thing he wanted to talk with her about, the second thing was the relics she held onto. Did they mean anything? Was she worshipping false gods?

That evening, Rad and Sayed were seated outside the front door finishing dinner. The house they shared with Abiathar was newly built along the main thoroughfare. They didn't have an enclosed courtyard so they usually ate at a cooking fire outside. Abiathar was still meeting with builders in the city center, completing plans for the Synagogue.

Sayed rose from his seat before the fire to begin cleaning up. He topped off their cups with the remaining tea and rinsed the vessel in a basin of water by the door.

Rad glanced up to see Sayed gazing over his shoulder. He looked back at Rad and raised an eyebrow. Curious as to what he had seen, Rad turned around and noticed Timnah walking toward him. The setting sun shone through strands of her hair drifting loose in the breeze. He rose from before the fire and stepped onto the street to meet her. She looked small and frail in her brown tunic, fingers interlaced in front of her. She looked up at him through moist, red-rimmed eyes.

Rad took her hand wordlessly and guided her along the streets to the city wall in the waning twilight, to their favorite place to talk.

"Why were you—"

"I wanted to say—" The two started talking together.

He smiled gently. "You first."

She leaned back against the wall and rubbed her foot in the dirt. "I wanted to say I'm sorry for telling. I know you trusted me."

"Okay…I'm trying to figure out why you would do that. Are you mad at me?"

She looked up at him and took a deep breath. "Well, truth is, Yes! I'm mad at you. It's because you wouldn't help me find my sister. She's my only sister, and she means a lot to me. When we escaped from our master in Egypt, she risked her life for me. If it wasn't for her, I might still be there. I wouldn't have ever met Abigail." She became quiet. "Or you."

Rad's heart swelled. He wrapped her in his arms. The sun was hanging near the horizon, bathing the buildings in golden hues. Holding her now, absorbing the warmth of her body and inhaling the scent of sweet herbs in her hair, he felt his love for her like an uncontrolled fire. Like the year of the famine back home, when a spark lit the dry grass of the pasture on fire. The wind spread the flames until they totally engulfed the hillside. The fire roared and reached heights taller than the pines. Rad and his brothers barely got the sheep to safety in time.

This was the strength of love he felt. Nothing else mattered.

"I'm sorry," he said, his voice full of emotion. "You mean everything to me, and I'm…I'm sorry about what I said when I left today. I didn't mean it. I know it hurt you. When I'm angry, I say things…."

"Hmm. I know. It's okay. I do too."

He kissed the top of her head. "And I hope you will always be honest with me from now on if I make you mad. I don't want anything to come between us."

Her mention of Egypt a moment ago brought something to his mind. He was loathe to bring it up now. Now that they were in good with each other. Now that there was forgiveness, and togetherness. Why risk it?

But he knew he would just be prolonging a conversation they should be having now, or perhaps should have had already. He could do this.

Gently, he approached the subject. "And since we're being honest. There's a second thing I have to talk about with you." He took a step back and looked at her, his mouth fixed in a meek smile. "When you were in Egypt. Is that when you got that cat figurine? Isn't that an…an Egyptian goddess?"

She placed a hand on her hip and tilted her head to the side. "So?…So what? So I have a figurine. I'm allowed to have a few personal things. Just because I'm a servant doesn't mean I can't own anything. Abigail doesn't care. Or she wouldn't care if she knew. She's not like that. I have some of my own money, too. And a few pieces of jewelry, and—"

He held out a hand. "Shh…It's okay. Just tell me it's only a keepsake. Not something you…you worship. Not the goddess Bastet. I could never agree to that."

She looked into his eyes and reached for a lock of hair. "No—I gave that up when I began working for Abigail." She paused. "Truth is…I *did* take that figure from my former master in Egypt. I prayed to her. I prayed my master would be kinder to me and my sister. But it didn't help me any. He still came to us in the goat house several nights a week. And he kept food from us for days if we displeased him. We used to chew on the goats' grain…." She was silent for a moment, remembering.

He reached out and drew her in close again. This new information about what she suffered in Egypt was disquieting. Could he be a source of comfort and strength to her, showing her the love of *his* God?

She lay her head on his chest. "When I moved in with Abigail, she told me about the one true God who created the heavens and the earth. She said He cares for all people. She said He cares for *me*. That He helped me get to Carmel, and helped me find my way to her. I then decided to serve only Abigail's God. I observe all the feast days and try to obey His commandments. Abigail was so good to me, it was an easy choice to make."

Something about her statement bothered him. Was that the only reason she believed in God? Because Abigail said she should? He hoped she had real faith in God, and not the kind that shifts and wanes with the present circumstances.

"And if it makes you feel better," she continued, "although I took on your religion mainly to please Abigail, when I pray to Him, I feel that he really hears me. I feel it in my heart. So I don't pray to those other gods anymore."

Rad tightened his hold on her. It felt good—the warmth of her body as she relaxed against him. The past two months lasted forever. He missed what they once had and it was a relief to be in harmony again. He gazed up at the night sky and sent a word of thanks to God.

Breaking from their embrace, he held her shoulders at arm's length. "I promise you, as soon as David and the army return from their campaign, we will get married. And then we will go to the land of the Amalekites to look for your sister."

Timnah lowered her eyes and whispered "Thank you."

45

King Saul Succombs

―――――――

Several evenings after David and the army returned from Gath, David found himself outside a strange city. The air was misty and there were curious noises—of weeping and of celebration. He was alone, walking, reins in hand, his horse trailing behind. They were trudging across stony ground covered in thorn bushes. The thorns pulled at his clothing and razed his skin, leaving traces of fresh blood on his legs. He approached a high wall of stone and masonry, damp, and dotted here and there with growths of emerald moss.

He looked up. The persistent fog made it hard to see clearly. In the shadows, he stretched out a hand and felt along the wall, as high as he could reach. He touched the bottom of a sandal. *What's this?*

David mounted his horse and worked his way up onto his feet, balancing carefully on the saddle, supporting himself against the wall with both hands. At eye level now, he made out the shape of the foot, the leg, the body. Peering above, he could see the lifeless head, suspended by a rope. He could make out the black wavy hair and thick growth of beard. He saw the streak of white hair falling over the forehead.

Saul!

He awoke in a sweat, Abigail stirring beside him. "What's wrong, love?" She said. "You were breathing hard. And you said 'Saul.'"

David sat up in bed. He had been scratching his legs, and when he looked at his hands he could see blood under his fingernails. Still disoriented, he gaped around and finally noticed his wife next to him. Relieved, he put his head in his hands and said, "I was dreaming. I had a dream about King Saul. He was dead. Hanging on the city wall."

Abigail sat up and reached her arm around his back. "It was a *dream*. Not *real*." She rubbed his back for a few moments. "Yet, who knows? Perhaps it's a sign, or prophecy."

Earlier that week, the volunteer army took their time returning to Ziklag once they knew they wouldn't be fighting alongside the Philistines. It was a relief to David, Nate, and Josh. The soldiers still weren't sure what it was all about, and grumbled a little on their return trip.

David thought, maybe he should come clean. Maybe this was a good chance to inform his army of his true mission. And yet…. It was a little tricky, with the country in which they resided at war with Israel. He didn't want any of his men to think this was a good opportunity to go on the offensive, or defect to the Philistines.

He would continue to wait on God.

He turned and kissed his wife, reaching around her, drawing his fingers through her hair, so full and loose after sleeping. The two clung to each other in the early morning light, unsure what the dream might mean.

Two days later, David and Abigail were in the courtyard having a cup of wine after supper. Their peaceful evening was interrupted as a man in a tattered military uniform stumbled through the doorway of the courtyard, pursued by David's two bodyguards.

Automatically, David jumped out of his chair and stepped in front of his wife.

The bodyguards seized the man and began dragging him back toward the street. "I'm sorry!" said one. "He broke through as we changed guards."

The man, clutching an army issue leather sack in his arms, protested loudly. "Please! Let me go. I have to talk to David." The bodyguards looked back at David, who made a conciliatory gesture, waving them back.

The man kneeled before him and said, "Forgive me for intruding on you like this. You see, I am a Philistine soldier. I lived in Ziklag before you came to this country. I…I was hoping to return—"

David nodded. "Perhaps."

"I'm a prisoner of war, and escaped from the Israelites two days ago. They were marching us to prison. I broke away as we approached Gibeah."

Noting the shorn hair, typical of the Philistines, and the torn clothes and weakened condition of the soldier, David found his story plausible.

Over the past week, he had been getting regular reports of the fighting between the Philistines and Israelites. Because of the distance to Mount Gilboa, however, most news was two or three days old. It was touch and go, with both sides sustaining many losses. He still didn't know if it was over.

Abigail gave the young man a cup water. He drank it down in large gulps.

"Well? What do you have to report?" David said, waving a hand.

The Philistine soldier finished his water and wiped his mouth on his arm. He focused on David as he delivered the news. "King Saul and his son are dead."

The words came like the powerful backwards kick of a war horse, knocking the wind out of David's lungs. He clutched at his chest. "How…? How do you know?"

The soldier looked around at the others. Abigail glanced at David, and then back to the soldier, giving him a nod. He began to give an account of the battle. He concluded with, "—so then, the Israelite army retreated. Many lie on the battlefield, dead or wounded. I lost my weapon, but escaped being hurt. I was wandering among those injured and dead lying there on the ridge. I thought maybe I could pick up a sword.

"Then suddenly I heard a rumbling sound, and there, at the bottom of the hill, I could see *my army,* in the distance, coming back." In his excitement, the Philistine solider leapt up, and began pacing back and forth.

"I was so scared! I had to get out of there before the chariots ran me over. So I started running down the other side of the ridge. That's when I came upon King Saul. He was injured, bleeding, and next to him was Jonathan." The soldier stopped pacing in front of David. *"He was dead."*

"No."

David sat down on the stone bench and Abigail hastened to his side. She faced the young Philistine. "Please, continue. What else happened?"

He looked askance at David.

Abigail glanced at her husband, who was gazing with unseeing eyes. She turned to the soldier. "It's okay," she said, "It's just, well…they used to be friends."

The soldier picked up his narrative. David closed his eyes and listened to him.

"When I got near King Saul—I could see that white hair on his forehead, so I knew it was the King of the Israelites—he was kneeling down, bleeding, and leaning on his sword. He was having trouble talking. I leaned closer, and he said to me, 'Come here and thrust me through. Please don't let me fall into the hands of the Philistines.'"

The young soldier let that sink in. He was looking very pleased with himself. "So I did."

"Did what?" David asked, his eyes suddenly sharp and accusing.

He faltered, momentarily put off by David's stern look. He glanced around at the others listening to him, Abigail and the two bodyguards.

"Well, I ran his sword through him. I killed him. I killed King Saul." He reached into the leather bag and dug through the other items to the bottom. "And look," he held up two items "his dagger and gold bracelet. For you, my lord." The soldier bowed, and proudly placed the trophies at David's feet.

David rose to his full imposing height. "You dare kill the Lord's anointed?" He no longer cared if his scam of loyalty to the Philistines was foiled. This Philistine soldier took the life of King Saul, and he would pay.

"What? Hey!"

"You shall be severely punished," David said, and ordered his guards to take him away.

They grasped the Philistine by the arms and dragged him away. The young soldier kicked and grappled with his captors. "I knew it!" he shouted. "I knew you were a traitor. King Akish should never have trusted you!"

Finally alone, Abigail led David back to their private room. There, he let out the pent-up emotions he held deep within. Shaking with silent sobbing, his grief overwhelmed him. Abigail waited with him in the waning evening light until he was spent, until there were no more tears, and her husband was finally at peace.

Later that night, David returned to the courtyard and sat on the stone bench, drinking tea and watching the dying embers of the cooking fire. He was aware of Abigail, stepping up the ladder to the rooftop. She usually went up before him on these hot nights, to lay out the bed and take down her hair. He would join her later.

A fluttering sound caught his attention and he looked down to see the turtledove at his feet. She pecked at his sandal. He broke up a bit of flatbread, sprinkled it on the ground, and watched her snatch up the crumbs. When finished, she flew back to her favorite perch on the fig tree to roost for the night.

He reached for his olive-wood lyre—the instrument he made when this all started, hiding from King Saul in the caves of Adullam. It had replaced the one he played in his youth, making music for the King to soothe his anxious spirit. Those were promising times, times of favor with the King, at the very beginning of his quest.

He tuned the instrument and plucked out a familiar melody—a sad, slow tune. As he strummed, he sang:

Your pride and joy, O Israel, lies dead on the hills.
How the mighty heroes have fallen.

How beloved and gracious were Saul and Jonathan.
They were swifter than eagles, they were stronger

than lions.
How the mighty heroes have fallen.

Jonathan's body lies upon the hills.
I weep for you, my brother Jonathan.
How the mighty heroes have fallen.

Stripped of their weapons, they lie finally at peace.

2 Samuel 1

46

"Long Live King David!"

Abiathar was invited to have a private supper with David and Abigail the next evening. Timnah prepared a simple meal of flatbread baked with cheese and seasoned with garlic and dried herbs.

Abiathar pushed his chair away from the table. He blinked his eyes in Abigail's direction. "That was a…a delicious meal. Thank you for having me."

She smiled gently. "We are happy you could join us."

David reached across the table for his wife's hand, and addressed the priest. "Now that Saul and Jonathan are dead…" He closed his eyes and swallowed hard, silent for a moment. "Now that they're dead, I need you to seek direction from God. What am I to do? How should I proceed?"

Abiathar nodded. He took a last sip of wine and left the table. He climbed the ladder to the rooftop as they waited below.

Abigail nibbled the last bit of cheesy flatbread. She giggled.

"What?" David said.

Her whole face lit up. "It's just…I'm excited. This whole time, you hiding and running for your life, waiting for your time to come. It's finally *here*. I can *feel* it." She took his hand in hers. "Don't you?"

He looked at her and smiled. "Yes. Yes I do."

A moment later Abiathar strode across the courtyard. He was fingering the fringe of his shawl. "I…I have your answer."

"By the way you're smiling, I think I know what it is," David said, standing up next to the table.

He reached out to David and grasped his forearm. "Go to Hebron, in Judah. God says, 'It's time to claim your throne.'"

Late that night, the news of King Saul's death and what it meant to David began to grip him. There was really no love lost between David and King Saul. The animosity that built between them over the years, and the distrust, cooled much of the admiration he used to feel for the former King. The emotion he felt was more respect for a formidable adversary, a worthy predecessor.

His true sorrow was for his beloved friend, Jonathan, a man who loved him like a brother and treated him as an equal. He felt the loss in his heart like a dry well.

As David lay in bed next to his wife, her breaths coming soft and regular, he thought of the journey he had endured. He was once again the young shepherd boy, watching over his flock in the monotonous sunshine of his hometown, Bethlehem. He remembered the uncertainty he felt after the prophet Samuel's visit. Wondering if it all was real, wondering if he was up being king of Israel.

He had similar feelings of apprehension now that it was actually happening, and forced himself to believe in himself, remembering Samuel's encouraging words to him as a young boy: *Man looks on the outward appearance, but God looks on the heart.*

David thought about the triumph of his victory over Goliath. It was the beginning of his success as a warrior, which also brought about King Saul's distrust of him. And his unceasing efforts to control him.

He remembered Mical. And, to his satisfaction, he was able to think of her without feeling that familiar pang in his heart. He turned his head to look at his wife. He had Abigail now.

Abigail. She came to him in the wilderness. In all his wanderings she was the best thing that happened. In addition to becoming King of Israel, she made everything he endured over the past six years worth it.

He closed his eyes and let his thoughts drift back to those days in the wilderness. He recalled Jonathan's visit, and his promise to him, when he and the hundreds of volunteers encamped in Ziph. His eyes misted as he realized that Jonathan wouldn't be his right hand man now.

These were the sacrifices that were made. His brother, Ozzy, too. He was loyal to the end. Fighting to free the city of Keilah.

They were among the ones who truly believed in him. *I wish they were here now…*

Unable to sleep, he got up from the fleece mattress and walked to the edge of the rooftop. Sleeping on the flat roof of their house during the hot dry months had become routine for them, and the knee-high wall enclosing the space offered privacy. He noticed a patch of moonlight in the corner of the rooftop. It shone on his sword—the sword he took from Goliath—discarded for now along with his armor. He strode over to the sword and picked it up. *A shame how tarnished it's become.* Maybe that was a good sign, maybe it meant an end to warfare. He placed the sword into the sheath and lay it down among the armor.

Despite the deaths of Saul and Jonathan, General Abner and the Israeli army had actually been victorious in the war with the Philistines. Josh reported that King Akish led his army in a hasty retreat, with battalions beginning to arrive back in Philistine country just last evening. It was a good time to re-join his native land. He hoped there wouldn't be any trouble with King Akish, and resolved to leave the Philistines alone as long as they respected the Israeli and Judean borders.

Abigail stirred in bed. He watched as she reached a hand over to where he usually lie. Not finding him, she sat up, saw him standing at the wall, and joined him there. She took his hand and they stood, thus, looking at the stars shining against the midnight sky like the diamond dust of sand on a brilliantly sunny day. He thought of them shining down on Judah, on Israel. On *his* kingdom. The kingdom entrusted to him by God. His ambition was to unite the clans and tribes into a single great country of Israel, hopefully bringing peace to the land at last.

Abigail broke into his reverie. "Love," She said, a sparkle of mischief in her eye. "Now that you are going to be King, do I have to call you 'Your Highness' and make an appointment when I wish to be with you?"

He reached his arm around her waist. "Hmm. Only before my subjects. Okay? In private you can continue to treat me as the weakling lamb I become when I'm with you." He kissed her gently. "You know I owe much of my success to you. You have always had faith in me, and always gave me good advice. Plus, the soldiers are afraid of you."

She laughed gently. "No they're not!"

"Ha ha! It's true. And the priest is, too. Don't you notice how nervous he gets when you are around?"

"Mm. I'm sorry. I hope he feels vindicated at last."

"Yes. Yes. Josh, as well. Remember I told you about his baby daughter? I will never use terror or coercion to rule my people. That's not God's way."

"*Your people*," she said with a grin.

"So many things are happening," he continued. "Rad's finally settling down and getting married, Nate and Deborah's boys are almost ready for Bar Mitzvah…"

"*You're becoming King*…."

He looked into her eyes, glowing with anticipation. "Yes. There's that."

She brought his hand to her lips and kissed the rough tanned skin. She held it against her cheek.

Presently, David spied something on the floor. He stepped back and reached down, picking up a stray branch that had fallen onto the roof from the fig tree. He bent it into an "O" shape and twisted the ends together. He placed the leafy branch onto Abigail's head. "I crown you Queen of Judah, and queen of my heart."

———————

A WEEK LATER, MANY OF THE RESIDENTS OF ZIKLAG packed their belongings and traveled to Hebron with David and Abigail. There, leaders from all over the region gathered and watched David, at age twenty-eight, crowned King of Judah.

A week of feasting was enjoyed in honor of the new King. Abigail, Nate, Rad, Josh, and Abiathar sat at the head table with him. Speeches were made. King David gave awards to those who proved themselves in battle or with other feats of bravery.

He praised a group from Jabesh-Gilead, east of the Jordan River, in the tribal lands of Gad. They had always been loyal supporters of Saul, who, when he first became king, had mobilized his newly formed army against invaders into Gad and their city. They told of how, just last week, they crossed the Jordan and traveled to Mount Gilboa at great peril to claim the bodies of Jonathan and Saul. They wanted to give them a decent burial.

He gave them a few moments to tell their story: "We found their bodies in the city of Beth-shan. The ruler of the city didn't care that we took their remains. He said, 'They're hanging on the city wall—go ahead and take them.'"

Abigail, seated next to her husband, whispered, "Your dream." He smiled sadly, and squeezed her hand.

"So we took them down, cremated their bodies, and buried the remains beneath the Tamarisk tree, in Jabesh."

"You will be greatly rewarded for your devotion," he said, "and for your kindness to him even after death. I hope all of my subjects are as faithful and loyal to me as you have been to your former king."

Nate, seated to his right, stood and lifted a cup. "Long live King David!"

He was joined by a great shout that rose to the heavens, to the Living God who saw David through the past seventeen years of his quest, to the prophet, Samuel, David's spiritual father, to Ozzy, his brother, and to Jonathan, his greatest friend.

All present raised a cup and joined in proclaiming, "Long live King David! Long live King David!"

AFTERWORD

Rad and Timnah were the first couple to marry in Hebron, under the reign of the King David. Abiathar officiated in the wedding. And, yes, they had *doves*. Shortly after, they set out to look for Jadah, Timnah's sister, in the land of the Amalekites.

King Saul's son, Ishbosheth, ruled the region of Israel, north of Judah, during this time. So the nation was divided for seven years, David ruling Judah and Ishbosheth claiming his right as heir to the throne in Israel.

Eventually Ishbosheth was assassinated and David united the nation, ruling both regions as the Kingdom of Israel. He then moved to Jerusalem, which became the royal city, the City of David. It remains the symbol of the glory days of Israel to this day.

LIST OF BIBLE REFERENCES

Bible passages are quoted from either the New Living Translation or the New International Version. Some paraphrasing has been done by myself to improve readability. Not all Psalms are included in their entirety. I encourage the reader to look up these passages and view them in the context in which they were originally written.

Chapter 2: Psalm 23 NLT

Chapter 16: Psalm 59 NIV

Chapter 17: Psalm 139 NIV

Chapter 18: Psalm 18 NLT

Chapter 21: Psalm 33 NLT

Chapter 24: Psalm 52 NLT

Chapter 28: Psalm 102 NIV, 13 & 54 NIV

Chapter 29: Psalm 142 NLT

Chapter 34: Psalm 121 NIV

Chapter 39: Psalm 47 NIV, 103 NIV

Chapter 45: 2 Samuel chapter 1 NLT

Story of Judah and Tamar: Genesis chapter 38

David conquers Goliath: 1 Samuel chapter 17

Acknowledgements

David's passion for his quest, and his dependance on God, learning to be patient and *wait*, taught me how to better follow God's path for my own life. Proverbs 16:9 says, "In their hearts people plan their course, but the Lord establishes their steps." In other words, "Make all your plans in pencil...."

Helping me to complete my first novel was my editor, Youngstown State University graduate, McKayla Rockwell. She showed much kindness and patience regarding my feeble first attempts, and helped me to write a book twice the size of the original draft by her gentle admonishment, "This has to be a *scene*." I am also grateful to the wonderful people at Luminare Press for helping develop this book into one I am truly proud of.

MEET THE AUTHOR

A voracious reader all her life, Silke Chambers' childhood favorites were *all* the Oz books by L. Frank Baum, and *The Little Prince* by Antoine de Saint-Exupéry. Her love for reading grew into a love of writing, and she has won awards and published short stories related to her work as a nurse through Writers' Digest and local journals. She lives in northeast Ohio, where nothing happens, with her family, and writing buddy, a cockatiel named Jesse. View her website at www.stories-that-inspire.com

Permissions

Made in the USA
Columbia, SC
25 July 2022

63878930R00243